The
Caribbean
Connection

The Caribbean Connection

ROBERT CHODOS

A Last Post Book

James Lorimer & Company, Publishers
Toronto   1977

433400
C

ISBN   0-88862-116-7 cloth
       0-88862-117-5 paper

Design: Don Fernley

Printed and bound in Canada

A Last Post Book

James Lorimer & Company, Publishers
35 Britain Street
Toronto, Ontario

This book was made possible by grants from the Ontario Arts Council and the Explorations Division of the Canada Council.

Canadian Cataloguing in Publication Data

Chodos, Robert, 1947-
  The Caribbean connection

"A Last Post book."
Includes bibliographical references and index.

ISBN 0-88862-117-5 bd.   ISBN 0-88862-116-7 pa.

1. Canada — Relations (general) with the Caribbean area.
2. Car-ibbean area — Relations (general) with Canada.   I. Title.

FC251.C37C56   301.29'71'0729   C77-001037-7
F1029.5.C37C56

**for Frank Kennedy
in memoriam**

Also by Robert Chodos

The CPR: A Century of Corporate Welfare
Right-Of-Way: Passenger Trains for Canada's Future
Winners, Losers: The 1976 Tory Leadership Convention (with Patrick Brown and Rae Murphy)
Let Us Prey (with Rae Murphy)
Quebec: A Chronicle 1968-1972 (with Nick Auf der Maur)

Contents

Preface

This book is principally about Canada. Canadians have often, especially in recent years, tended to be inward-looking, and to focus exclusively on their internal problems. While self-examination can be a good thing, it is also wise to try to retain some sense of the larger picture. This book is based on the proposition that one cannot understand one's own country except by seeing it in the context of its relationships with other countries.

Most of the information in the book was collected during three visits to the Caribbean, and through interviews in Canada and the United States, in late 1974 and early 1975. Already, some things have changed, and it has not always proved possible to update the information; therefore the profile of the Canada–West Indies relationship presented here is of that time.

Researching this book brought with it, to my great pleasure, the opportunity to become acquainted with the Caribbean and to meet a wide variety of people there, many of whom shared some ideas with me and often some rum as well. Caribbean hospitality is famous, and from Havana, Cuba, to Skeldon, Guyana, I was privileged to enjoy a full measure of it. The number of people who contributed in some way to this project is large, and I would like to express my gratitude to all of those who helped me — to officials of the government of Canada, both in Ottawa and in the Caribbean, of Caribbean governments, of international organizations; to representatives of corporations and other institutions active in the region; and to trade unionists, university lecturers, politicians, librarians and all the others who extended their assistance and co-operation.

Finally I would like to acknowledge my debt to Kari Levitt, who in her work and her ability to bridge the gulf between the two regions represents the best of the Canada–West Indies relationship. **R.C.**

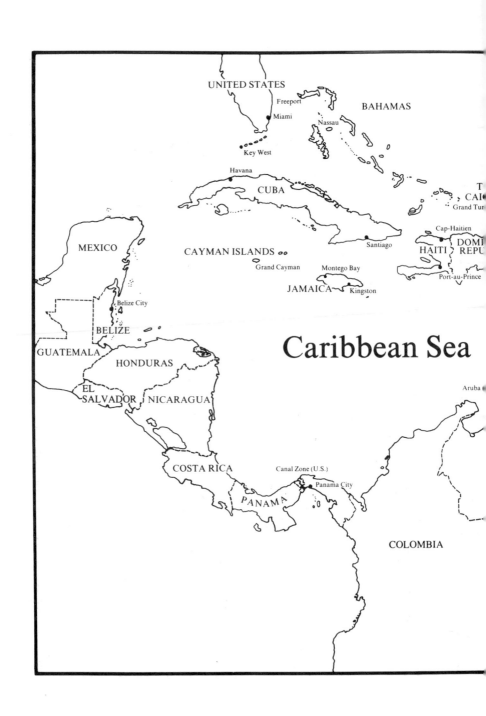

Atlantic Ocean

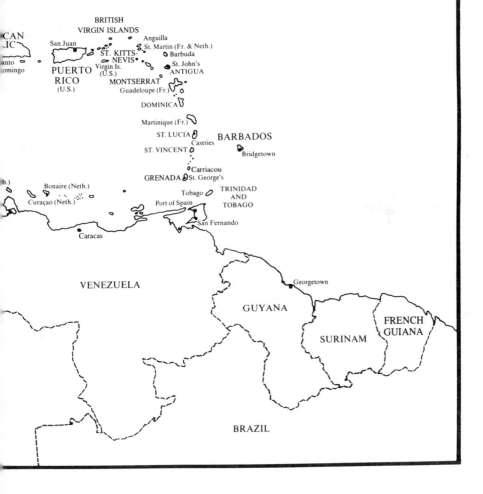

KS AND
S ISLANDS

BRITISH
VIRGIN ISLANDS

CAN
IC

San Juan   Anguilla
                            St. Martin (Fr. & Neth.)
ST. KITTS-   Barbuda
nto   NEVIS
omingo   PUERTO   Virgin Is.   St. John's
         RICO   (U.S.)   ANTIGUA
         (U.S.)   MONTSERRAT
                  Guadeloupe (Fr.)

DOMINICA

Martinique (Fr.)

ST. LUCIA   BARBADOS
        Castries
ST. VINCENT   Bridgetown

                 Carriacou
GRENADA   St. George's

h.)
     Bonaire (Neth.)   Tobago   TRINIDAD
                                        AND
     Curaçao (Neth.)   Port of Spain TOBAGO

                              San Fernando

     Caracas

VENEZUELA   Georgetown

            GUYANA
                                  FRENCH
                                  GUIANA
                        SURINAM

                 BRAZIL

1/Southern Canuck

No, there weren't a lot of Canadian reporters down here. What there was, was a lot of phone calls.

Sterling Garland,
Development Officer,
Turks and Caicos Islands

Port-au-Prince, Haiti,
December 1974

In the Caribbean region, fragmented by geography and history, it is necessary to travel only a short distance to experience startling social, cultural, political and economic changes. The flight from this squalid city to Grand Turk, Turks and Caicos Islands, British West Indies, is such a journey.

You are leaving the capital of the poorest country in the Western Hemisphere, and although the island you will be landing on is also poor, it is a different sort of poverty. No women in torn dresses and carrying ragged babies beg for coins in the streets of Grand Turk, and when you go out at night you will not have to step over people huddled on the sidewalk for want of anywhere else to sleep. But then there is no sidewalk in Grand Turk, and you will see almost as many donkey-carts as cars.

The flight in a nine-seat Islander takes barely two hours, with a stop at Cap-Haitien, the old capital at the northern tip of Haiti. Here King Henri Christophe built his enormous Citadel, back in the proud days of the early nineteenth century, when Haiti had just accomplished one of history's great revolutions and become the second independent state in the new world.[1] Then the plane flies over a stretch of ocean so limpid that you can easily see the bottom from the air. After some time you see a small barren-looking island to your left; it is Salt Cay, the southernmost of a widely scattered group of islands at the end of the Bahamian chain which are grouped administratively as the Turks and Caicos. Minutes

13

later you land at the airstrip on a U.S. Air Force base in Grand Turk.

Few Canadians had ever heard of the Turks and Caicos Islands until early 1974, when the tiny British colony was brought to their attention by Max Saltsman, the irrepressible New Democratic member of parliament for Waterloo-Cambridge. The State Council of the Turks and Caicos had passed a resolution favouring association of the islands with Canada, and Saltsman announced that he supported the idea and would crusade for it. Choosing one of the coldest days of the Canadian winter to launch his campaign, he submitted a private member's bill, Bill C–249, "an Act respecting a proposed association between Canada and the Caribbean Turks and Caicos Islands."

Max Saltsman, always a maverick in the NDP caucus, was not elected the people's representative for Waterloo-Cambridge to preside over the dissolution of the Canadian empire. "We have to be prepared to dominate the Caribbean politically," Saltsman said later. "We have to cease to be nice people. The Canadian government can't do it without being tough and aggressive." He undertook the Turks and Caicos venture as a small first step in an effort to set the world right. "Since 1919 the world has been coming apart. Now we have to put the world back together, but on a voluntary basis. These people were volunteering. For the first time since the Wilsonian doctrine of a world made up of independent states began to come into effect after World War I, someone said 'Independence isn't worth a goddamn.' The Wilsonian doctrine has brought nothing but misery."

On one level, Saltsman's campaign was a roaring success. He had correctly surmised that many Canadians would find the prospect of having their own islands in the sun agreeable, especially in the middle of a January cold spell, and the proposed union of the Turks and Caicos with Canada quickly became an "event" in the press. Some of the more intrepid newspapers even sent reporters down to look around and report back on what these islands, which the press had already informally adopted as "ours", looked like.

At the official level, however, the response was much more sub-

14

dued. The Department of External Affairs soon nixed the idea, saying that union would raise complicated questions of tariff, taxation, defence and immigration policies and would create "a new relationship which could be represented as neo-colonial."[2] Canada just doesn't *do* that sort of thing.

In the Islands, the idea of association with Canada met with an enthusiastic response. Almost every car carried a maple-leaf bumper sticker. One overzealous supporter of the "Canadian Connection", as it came to be known, even lowered the Union Jack on South Caicos and hoisted the Canadian flag in its place.

A year later, with the Canadian Connection still not connected and the prospect of its ever becoming so increasingly remote, disillusionment and cynicism had set in. H. E. (Bertie) Sadler, local storekeeper and author of a seven-volume history of the Islands, was saying, "There's not much you can do with the Canadian Connection. Why would the Canadians want the Islands? If Britain pulled out it would be more logial for the Americans to take over."

And yet, as Sadler said, the two principal promoters of the scheme were well served by it. Liam Maguire, the South Caicos hotelier, developer and member of the State Council, who was the main spokesman for the Canadian Connection in the Islands, wanted to bring down Canadian tourists and development money. Saltsman wanted to get his name into the Canadian papers. They both succeeded.[3]

Just east of Sadler's store, as the inhabited part of the island fades into open field, an obvious stranger is greeted by two young boys, bold and friendly. "You from the Navy Base?" one of them asks. "No." "You a Canadian?" "Yes." "Do you want me to show you around the island?" "I think I can find my own way around the island." "Then give me a quarter." "Okay, but you have to share it with your friend." "We're going to join your country." "Do you think that's a good idea?" "Yes." "Why?" "Because." "Do *you* think it's a good idea?" the Canadian asks the other boy. "Yes."

Back on the main street, the United Nations poster on the door of Government House says, "Population is a *world* problem." The population of the Turks and Caicos Islands is generously estimated at six thousand.

To the south of Government House, toward the Air Force base, is the Turks Head Inn. In its open-air bar and restaurant, a visitor is likely to meet Hubert James, the owner of the Turks Head; John Houseman, the expatriate Englishman who edits the *Conch News,* the Turks and Caicos Islands weekly newspaper ("It comes out every week but some weeks are longer than others"); and others knowledgeable about local affairs. Both James and Houseman are somewhat at a loss to explain the basis of Grand Turk's economy. "Sometimes I wonder myself how some of the people get along," says James, who was born in the Turks and Caicos and has lived there most of his life. Houseman divides the Grand Turk work force into four categories: roughly one-quarter work for the government in some capacity, one-quarter work for the two American military bases, one-quarter are self-employed in service industries and one-quarter simply can't be classified. And yet no one is visibly starving. In the Caicos Islands fishing is an important industry. The salt industry, once the mainstay of the islands, is now confined to Salt Cay, and dwindling even there.

Houseman notes that as a result of the publicity surrounding the Canadian Connection, there has been a thirty-six per cent increase in visitor arrivals. The visitors are of two kinds: "One is miscellaneous travellers, and . . . " "And the other," James interrupts him, "is ten-cent developers."

Although the population of the Turks and Caicos is small, it is surprisingly diverse in origin. John Houseman travelled the world before settling in Grand Turk in 1966, and has been off the islands for a total of nine days since then. Liam Maguire is an Irishman, described by Max Saltsman as "a cross between Cecil Rhodes and Errol Flynn." A large and gentle man named Jesse who runs the local bakery has the courtliness and drawl of his native Louisiana. Bertie Sadler is a white Jamaican who came to Grand Turk as a food commissioner in the 1940s when the islands were under Jamaican jurisdiction, and stayed to devote himself to minding his store, building a fortress in the fields west of the town, and proving that the San Salvador where Columbus first landed in 1492 was not Watling's Island in the Bahamas, as most historians believe, but Grand Turk.[4]

Whether the recorded history of the Islands began in 1492 or somewhat later, it has included the phenomena — piracy, colonialism, slavery, and latterly, tourism — that have made the Caribbean, while not the poorest part of the world, arguably the most dependent. Because of the extreme smallness of the Turks and Caicos, their economy has been even more fragile than most. The salt industry, begun by Bermudians in the seventeenth century, was long the only stable activity. Wrecking — the plundering of ships that ran aground on the reefs — was less certain but more spectacular.

The Islands were at various times under Bermudian, Bahamian and Jamaican tutelage, interspersed with periods of direct British rule. Along with their Jamaican parent the Turks and Caicos entered the West Indies Federation in 1958, but when the Federation collapsed in 1962 and Jamaica became independent, they reverted once again to colonial status. Despite their proximity to the Bahamas, they have little interest in becoming part of that newly independent country. The Bahamas' only significant population centre, Nassau, is far away and, says Turks and Caicos development officer Sterling Garland, "We're not Bahamians. They're a new nation and have problems of their own. They have 700 islands — we would be number 701."

For the moment the Islanders are reasonably content to remain a British colony and continue to receive a British subsidy that amounts to about $3 million* a year. But Britain has long since given up bearing the white man's burden and is divesting itself of its remaining colonies as fast as it can. What will happen to struggling, isolated places like the Turks and Caicos when the day of reckoning comes? There are some, like John Houseman, who advocate independence. Liam Maguire and Max Saltsman had other ideas.

In recent years the most visible economic activity on Grand

* Dollar figures refer to Canadian dollars, except where otherwise specified.

17

Turk has surrounded the two American military bases, the Navy base at the north end of the island and the Air Force base at the south end. South Base, as it's known, is a missile tracking station and is run for the Air Force on contract by Pan American Airways and RCA. The commanding officer, Major Priebel, is the only military man on the base. The recreational facilities on the base are open to the local people to a limited degree and are used mostly by the expatriate community; Hubert James calls the base "an entertainment centre for the expats." He complains that beer is sold for twenty-five cents in the club on the base while the Turks Head and the other hotels have to sell it for seventy-five cents.

Nineteen Turks Islanders are employed at the Navy base at the north end of the island. Lt. T. C. Browne, executive officer of the base, is young and personable and explains that the purpose of the facility is oceanographic research. When asked if he could expand on that he smiles and shakes his head. Is the base directly connected with any other bases or does it operate by itself? "For the purposes of your book it's by itself." Other base personnel are equally reluctant to talk about what they do.

Max Saltsman suspected that the secrecy was designed to cover up, not some activity of vast strategic importance, but rather the fact that the base doesn't do anything very important at all. In any event, he didn't figure that the presence of the U.S. military facilities would be any obstacle to the Islands' becoming part of Canada; we could sit down with the Americans and work it out.

One Canadian who was particularly interested in Saltsman's proposal was a civil engineer and developer named Andrew Zsolt, who has built up his own $25-million-a-year company, Inducon Holdings Ltd., based in Don Mills, Ontario. Inducon has bought and taken options on a total of 150 acres of South Caicos, with the intention of turning the site into a self-contained tourist development on the model of the highly successful Clubs Méditerranées, with which the French have dotted the world. Zsolt believes that tourism is the best — in fact the only — possible mode of development for the Turks and Caicos. "There's nothing else for these

Islands," he says. "There's not enough population base for industry. They're too far off. Communication is too clumsy. Fishing? They're already overfished."

So Zsolt plans to create an enclave of North-American-style luxury in the midst of these poor but until now not unhappy Islands. He would offer direct weekly charter flights from Toronto direct to South Caicos — which he chose because it is the only one of the islands that has an airstrip that can handle jets — and upon arrival the visitor would have at his disposal sailing, scuba diving, fishing, tennis, excursions to the nearby cays and a one-day trip to the coast of Haiti. He estimates that when the development has reached its full extent of two hundred rooms (he hopes to open it with thirty-six) it would provide employment directly for 150 people at the site and indirectly for another 150 as suppliers. Sensitive to criticism that foreign-owned tourist developments in the Caribbean tend to shun local products, he plans to base the restaurant on Caicos Islands seafood. Ironically, however, the main impact of the development on the economy of the Islands could be from increased imports, since import duties are virtually the only source of government revenues in the tax-free Turks and Caicos.

In his more visionary moments, Zsolt talks about using the sewage from the development to fertilize the soil of South Caicos and make agriculture possible there again. There used to be trees on the Caicos Islands, but when the salt industry was introduced the trees were cut down to drive the rains away and make the already dry Islands even drier. Now the salt industry is gone, but the dryness remains.

In any case, all of Zsolt's plans are still in the uncertain future. As of October 1975, he had not lost his enthusiasm for the project, but its timing depended on "the economy of the Western Hemisphere."

A more precipitous Canadian is Jim Johnstone, late of Oakville, Ontario, who by December 1974 had established a company, Southern Canuck Ltd.; bought an old two-storey house with a balcony overlooking the ocean, on the main street of Grand Turk, turned it into a guest house, The Windjammer, and taken up residence in it; gone into partnership in the local bakery with the bear-like Jesse; and firmly set his mind on taking the Turks and Caicos by storm.

Most of his considerable energy had so far been expended on getting the Windjammer into shape, equipping it with furniture flown in from Miami and even designing uniforms for the staff. ("I don't want to call them uniforms . . . . Windjammer attire — how does that sound?") Grand Turk was for him the fulfilment of a dream. He had first gone to Grand Cayman, largest of the Cayman Islands group to the west of Jamaica, but found it wanting; like the Bahamas, it had succeeded in using its tax-haven status to attract international bankers and fly-by-night financiers, and had begun to turn itself into a grotesque extension of North America. But the Turks and Caicos had just made the papers in Canada, so Johnstone decided to look at them as well, and this time he discovered the tropical island he had been searching for. By the autumn of 1974 he was ready to pull up stakes in Oakville and head for Grand Turk.

And beyond this dream there was another: a development in North Caicos that so far existed only as a faraway look in Johnstone's eyes: "Turks Islanders are nice but *Caicos* Islanders — it's hard to believe there still *are* people like that." He talks of the magnificent white beaches of North Caicos, where you can walk for miles and not meet a soul. You say that you have become fond of the Turks and Caicos but are enchanted by Jamaica and Trinidad as well, and he says, "Those are *populated* places. I don't like populated places."

But it is not in Jim Johnstone's nature to lie in the sun and to live life at a tropical pace. Rarely dressed in anything but an open shirt and shorts, he is everywhere in the course of a day: at the post office, at Government House, at the customs shed seeing what has happened to some furniture he was expecting (Christmas is approaching and it *has* to arrive on time), visiting Lars Ibsen, the United Nations planner from Denmark whose imminent departure for Montserrat in the Leeward Islands he regrets because "he could have helped us make something of this island", at the airport picking up or delivering a guest. He has decided that what he has to sell at the Windjammer is personal attention, and he is solicitous, perhaps a bit too solicitous, of his guests, wanting to know if he can help and trying a little too hard to make them feel comfortable. As evening approaches he serves drinks, puts the Johnny Mathis record of 'Silent Night' on the stereo, and invites the guests out onto the balcony of the Windjammer. He looks up at the sky where the faint white trails of American B-52s flying their regular patterns can be seen, and down to the orange sun setting into the ocean, and says, "It's going to be a good Christmas."

"He'll accommodate himself to the island," said one Canadian with more experience of the Caribbean, "or else he'll leave."

Saltsman, Zsolt and Johnstone are dreamers, and not in any bad sense of that word. Each man is also, in his own way, concerned with the welfare of the Turks and Caicos Islands. But all three see the future of the Caribbean lying in continued dependence on the metropolitan powers. They are far from alone in that. That assumption underlies the Caribbean policy of the metropolitan countries, including Canada. It is a major ingredient of the philosophy of Canadian aid toward the region, which the Canadian International Development Agency itself is now re-examining. It is the basis of the Caribbean's traditional role as a sugar producer and its more recent status as a tourist destination. It has never occurred to most Canadians — or Americans or Europeans — that it could be any different. "Who else are they going to turn to?" asked Max Saltsman. "Each other? They have nothing to offer each other except misery."

Even in the West Indies, many people see dependency as an inevitable fact of life. V.S. Naipaul, perhaps the most distinguished of West Indian writers, has written:

The island blacks will continue to be dependent on the books, films and goods of others; in this important way they will continue to be the half-made societies of a dependent people, the Third World's third world. They will forever consume; they will never create. They are without material resources; they will never develop the higher skills.

Identity depends in the end on achievement; and achievement here cannot but be small.[5]

While this remains a widespread view, it is no longer a universal one. There is a growing feeling that the Caribbean not only can make it on its own, but has to. Although dependency is the main current of Caribbean history, this counter-proposition has deep roots in that history too. It was present when Toussaint L'Ouverture and Jean-Jacques Dessalines led the slaves of Haiti to freedom and independence in the 1790s, and when the people of Cuba gained their liberty in 1959, after ninety-one years of struggle. In the English-speaking Caribbean it has been reflected in the increasingly militant stances of recent West Indian prime ministers such as Michael Manley of Jamaica and Forbes Burnham of Guyana; in the formation, since the attainment of formal independence, of new political groups, some of them socialist, many of them not, but all preaching self-reliance; in the music and poetry of Jamaican reggae singers such as Jimmy Cliff and Bob Marley and Trinidad calypsonians such as the Mighty Chalkdust and Valentino; in the work of younger West Indian writers such as Roger McTair, who imagines Dessalines saying to Toussaint L'Ouverture:

.... Food, we
will grow. Homes

we will build. Our women and
children we will protect with

blood. With blood
we made them free. We

are all we need. We are all we have. We
will sustain us [6]

Canadians have long harboured a touchingly romantic and often dangerously naive view of their own role in the Caribbean. We have generally seen it as being both larger and more benevolent than it really was. Max Saltsman's grand scheme was his attempt to introduce some "realism" into the relationship; there are still people in the Caribbean who go for schemes like that, but it is unlikely that their number is increasing. For once, the trends in the larger world have not passed the West Indies by. West Indians have not only been part of the movement toward what is being called a new economic order, they have been among the leaders of it. As these changes take place Canada can only respond, but how it responds is of some importance to the West Indies and of more importance to ourselves. And if present indications are borne out, Canada will find itself, needlessly but typically, on the wrong side.

2/Dis Place Nice

Business expandin,
More banks dey buildin,
So it's de capitalists
An dem who should sing —
   Trinidad is nice,
   Trinidad is a paradise.
But I hear me sister talkin
About revolution day:
Fire on de way.

Lord Valentino,
Dis Place Nice (1975)

The Caribbean most Canadians know best is the tourist Caribbean. It bears about as much relationship to the real Caribbean as a visit to Walt Disney World does to the real United States. The tourist is presented with a made-up world, a façade behind which the poverty and squalor in which many islanders live and the vitality and creative force of the region are alike concealed. For Canadians seeking to examine their country's role in the Caribbean, the first step is to examine what the Caribbean is.

The pre-independence West Indies were perhaps the most thoroughly colonial societies in the world, and the islands will be living with the effects of that colonial history for many years to come. The Caribbean colonies fit neither of the two classic models; they were not colonies peopled by settlers from the old country, as was Canada, nor were they colonies where an idigenous population was ruled by a government imposed from abroad, as was, say, Kenya. Rather they were societies to which people were brought against their will. "These Caribbean territories," wrote V. S. Naipaul, "are not like those in Africa or Asia, with their own internal reverences, that have been returned to themselves after a period of colonial rule. They are manufactured societies, labour camps, creations of empire."[1]

The very term "West Indies" is colonial and derivative, originating with Columbus's mistaken belief that he had discovered India.

25

Historically it meant the Caribbean region as a whole, but now it more commonly refers to the countless islands and two mainland enclaves that either are or have been under British rule. It is in these territories, more accurately but more clumsily known as the Commonwealth Caribbean, that Canadian involvement has been most significant, and they will be the focus of this book.

The Commonwealth Caribbean stretches from Belize in Central America, just south of Yucatan, northeast to the Bahamas off the coast of Florida, then southeast to Trinidad, tucked into a bay off Venezuela, and further south and east to Guyana on the South American mainland. The islands are tiny specks of land scattered over more than a thousand miles of ocean; the mainland territories are larger but, except for a few pockets, virtually uninhabited.

Although the population of the whole is barely five million, smaller than that of Ontario or Quebec, it is divided among six independent countries, five self-governing associate states, and five Crown Colonies. The largest territory, Jamaica, has just over two million people; the smallest, the Turks and Caicos, has six thousand.

Two hundred years ago the West Indies were the jewel of the British Empire. The "triangular trade", in which British ships carried Negroes from Africa to the Caribbean to work as slaves on the plantations and then took the sugar and other crops they produced to the mother country, made England rich. Its importance has been eloquently described by the distinguished Trinidadian historian, Dr. Eric Williams:

> By 1750 there was hardly a trading or a manufacturing town in England which was not in some way connected with the triangular or direct colonial trade. The profits obtained provided one of the main streams of that accumulation of capital which financed the Industrial Revolution. The West Indian islands became the hub of the British Empire, of immense importance to the grandeur and prosperity of England. It was the Negro slaves who made these sugar colonies the most precious colonies ever recorded in the whole annals of imperialism.[2]

The foundations of the present-day West Indies were laid then.

From the beginning the society was organized to fulfil, not its own needs, but the needs of an alien and faraway country. The islands existed only to produce sugar, and everything else, including the population, was imported. They sold all their produce in the mother country and bought all their goods there. England was the only point of reference; the islands could not form their own ties. They were divided not only from their Caribbean neighbours but from each other.

They were also from the beginning multiracial societies, based on extreme racial inequality, first in the form of slavery, and later in other forms. Dr. Williams argued that slavery was established in response to economic imperatives, and was abolished when those imperatives changed. Humanitarian considerations were secondary.[3] For all its advantages slavery was an inefficient mode of production, which could thrive only in conditions of monopoly. In the late eighteenth century the sugar monopoly was challenged by the spectacular growth of the French sugar colony of San Domingo. That growth was arrested by the epochal slave revolt and the transformation of San Domingo into the independent kingdom of Haiti, but other challenges followed. Sugar was being grown in Cuba, in Brazil, in India. The industrial revolution came, free trade followed, and the day of the old monopolies was gone forever. The British sugar islands went into decline, and even the abolition of slavery in 1834 could not halt the slide.

"By the end of the nineteenth century," wrote historian Gordon K. Lewis:

> the Caribbean had become, in place of its once splendid tradition, a forgotten derelict corner of the world, a condition that remained, indeed, until the strategic imperatives of the Second World War brought the area back into the limelight. The occasional literature produced upon it was by the occasional traveller who almost stumbled upon it, as had done Columbus in the beginning, by accident. It became a precarious "windfall economy", dependent upon intermittent bursts of activity like the construction of the Panama Canal. As the metropolitan mercantile houses withdrew their capital from the islands the latter declined into a state of somnolent stagnation.[4]

In some places, and particularly in the newer southern colonies of Trinidad and British Guiana, where unclaimed land was plentiful, the black sugar workers left the plantations almost as soon as they were freed and became small independent farmers, or went into the towns to do manual labour or open small shops. The planters, faced with a shortage of labour and unwilling to rationalize the industry through technological changes, turned to a new source of manpower: indentured workers from Madeira, China and especially India. Hundreds of thousands of Indians, enticed by the prospect of guaranteed employment, were brought over in ships from Calcutta and Madras between 1845 and 1917. Indenture differed from slavery in that it was initially voluntary on the part of the worker and lasted for a fixed period of time, but while he was on the plantation the indentured worker was as tightly bound to his employer as any slave. "Slave, where is your free paper?" was the taunt that blacks, who had so recently emerged from that state, hurled at the Indians in the streets of Port of Spain.[5] The Indians, in turn, looked down on the blacks. Although return passage to India after ten years' labour in the Caribbean was offered free or at partial fare, most of the Indians chose to stay, their ancient and complex culture largely intact, adding a new element to the delicate racial mix of the West Indies.

In the twentieth century new industries were developed which reduced the dependence of the West Indies on sugar but not their dependence on outside powers. Oil was discovered in Trinidad early in the century and developed by Texaco; other American and European oil companies followed later. The Aluminum Company of America began to exploit British Guiana's rich bauxite reserves in 1919; these later passed into the hands of Alcoa's offshoot, the Aluminum Company of Canada. Alcan, Alcoa and a number of other American aluminum companies later extracted Jamaican bauxite as well. But the industry that seemed to hold out the greatest promise for the islands was tourism. It was based on resources — sun, sea and sand — that were possessed by all the islands and, better still, that were never depleted. The Bahamas and the north coast of Jamaica were playgrounds for wealthy Americans from the early years of the century. After World War II tourism as a major industry spread to Barbados, Antigua, Trinidad's sister island of Tobago, and to a lesser extent, to St. Kitts-Nevis, St. Lucia, Grenada and the other islands of the Leewards and Windwards. In the 1960s, with the original tourist paradise, Cuba, closed off, tourism came to account for more than half the Gross National Product of several of the more popular islands.

The gross inequalities and degradation that marked West Indian life throughout the colonial period did not go unopposed by their victims. Slave revolts were common in the latter days of slavery, and planters and colonial officials in all the British islands lived in fear of another Haiti. In the post-emancipation period, the conflicting interests of Jamaican planters and ex-slaves led to increasing militancy on the part of the latter; in George William Gordon, they even had a spokesman in the planter-controlled Jamaican House of Assembly. Encouraged by Gordon and led by Paul Bogle, a rebellion broke out at Morant Bay in 1865. It was brutally suppressed, the House of Assembly was abolished, and Gordon and Bogle were hanged. Today, both are recognized as Jamaican National Heroes.[6]

The poor of Kingston, Jamaica, rioted in 1918 and 1919. The "barefoot man" of Trinidad found a champion in the years after World War I in Captain A. A.Cipriani, labour leader and mayor of Port of Spain, whose monument now stands in the centre of the Trinidad capital. Finally, in 1937 and 1938, a series of uprisings spread throughout the West Indies, setting in motion a process of political change that would bring the old colonial system to an end.

In Trinidad, the revolt centred in the oilfields, where a messianic and spellbinding leader, Tubal Uriah Buzz Butler, led the oil workers against the companies and the colonial system. In Jamaica, strikes broke out among both the agricultural labourers in the country and the urban workers and unemployed of Kingston. A charismatic figure came forth there too. William Alexander Clarke, light-skinned and from the *déclassé* petty plantocracy, had left Jamaica as a youth in 1905 to spend twenty-nine years wandering through the United States and Latin America; he returned as a man of fifty with a new name, Bustamante, and a new perspective

29

on his homeland. He focussed attention on the country's problems in a series of incisive letters to the Jamaica *Daily Gleaner*. By 1937 he had emerged as a trade-union organizer and by 1938 he was recognized as the leader of the discontented masses of the island. When Bustamante's activities caused him to be jailed, he was joined in his movement by Norman Manley, his cousin and one of Jamaica's most prominent lawyers. Later Bustamante and Manley became bitter political rivals, and the two-party system they founded is still the basis of Jamaican politics.

Even Barbados, the most conservative of West Indian societies, was touched by the movement of 1937–38. Out of the Barbados uprising came a significant labour organization, the Barbados Workers Union; a political instrument, the Barbados Labour Party; a leader, Grantley Adams, like Manley a lawyer and Oxford graduate; and a challenge, if not an end, to the untrammeled control of the island by white Bajan planters.

The strikes and riots succeeded in impressing upon London the need for change. A Royal Commission was appointed and came back with a detailed and damning report on West Indian life, describing the inequities of the islands' political and economic systems and their gross deficiencies in health, education, housing and other areas. In its recommendations, however, the Commission limited itself to suggesting an improved welfare system, which was duly introduced. Despite the Commission's reticence, the necessity for political changes had also become evident, and institutions of self-government were gradually brought into being in the 1940s and 1950s.

The last act of the direct British colonial presence in the larger islands of the Caribbean was the foredoomed attempt to set up a West Indies Federation. In the long series of meetings and conferences that began after World War II and led to the establishment of the Federation of ten island territories in 1958, no serious effort was made to deal with the historic inter-island divisions that British colonial policy had fostered. Problem after problem was either delayed or swept under the rug. As a result, the new federal government was weak from the start. The two most important West Indian political leaders, Premier Norman Manley of Jamaica and Dr. Eric Williams, the historian who had become Chief Minister of Trinidad, stayed out of federal politics and stuck to their own islands. Sir Grantley Adams of Barbados assumed the high-flown title of Prime Minister of the West Indies but it meant little. There was no agreement on a common market or on freedom of movement from island to island, and the federal government was given no income-taxing powers. Even the postal service was a joint federal-territorial responsibility.

The Federation did not last long. Trinidad, which was worried about an influx of people from the smaller and poorer islands, was intransigent on the question of freedom of movement, and Jamaica, which wanted to protect its own fragile industries, was intransigent on the question of the customs union. Alexander Bustamante became the chief opponent of the Federation and campaigned for Jamaican withdrawal; in a 1961 referendum, a majority of the Jamaican people agreed with him. The choice was now between a reduced Eastern Caribbean Federation and total disintegration and it lay largely in the hands of Trinidad. "Ten minus one," said Dr. Williams, "leaves nought," and the Federation collapsed.

Instead of the Federation becoming independent as a unit, as had been planned, the individual islands now proceeded to independence on their own. Jamaica was first, under the seventy-eight-year-old Bustamante as Prime Minister, running up its new flag on August 6, 1962, followed by Trinidad and Tobago on August 31 of the same year, Barbados in 1966, and Grenada in 1974. Guyana (formerly British Guiana) and the Bahamas, which had not been part of the Federation, also became independent states. The other islands of the Leewards and Windwards became associated states and talked about becoming independent in a few years.

Some regional institutions, notably the University of the West Indies, with campuses in Jamaica, Trinidad and Barbados, survived the collapse of the Federation. Others, such as the Caribbean Free Trade Association (CARIFTA) and the Caribbean Development Bank, were set up in the late 1960s. In 1973 CARIFTA was transformed into CARICOM, the Caribbean Community and Common Market. There were endless schemes for renewed political union, but all of them collapsed before they were realized. More than a decade after the Federation went under, West Indian union remained on the agenda but not near the top of it, and Trinidad's opposition Tapia group described it as a dream deferred.

This was despite the espousal of the idea by virtually everyone in the region from radical political groups to representatives of multinational corporations; however, it is one thing to espouse union, and another to come to terms with the formidable economic, political and psychological problems it involves. One of these problems is the justifiable suspicion, dating back to the days before the Federation, that integration is simply a tool to organize the region more effectively for outside exploitation. In recent years this suspicion has taken concrete form in the widespread charge, vigorously denied by CARICOM Secretary-General Alister McIntyre, that the main beneficiaries of the common market have been the multinational corporations with manufacturing interests in the region, which now have a wider market for their goods. Thus the goals of union and the form that it takes are crucial questions.

Another obstacle is the increased power now in the hands of the local governments of the region; entrenched politicians see union not as increasing the scope of their activity but as limiting it. Nor does the physical basis for union exist in the form of a proper inter-island transportation and communication system; the communications of each island are directed more toward metropolitan countries than toward its neighbours.

But if the tendency of the Caribbean countries to orient themselves primarily toward external powers remained, the pattern of relations with those powers changed considerably.

That the United States would become the dominant power in the Caribbean was apparent to at least one observer as early as 1895. In his last letter, unfinished at his death in his country's war of independence, the great Cuban revolutionary José Marti wrote, "At last I am daily risking my life for my country and — since I understand it so and have the spirit to carry it out — for my duty of preventing in time, by securing the independence of Cuba, the spread of the United States across the Antilles, and of stopping it from pouncing with this added impetus upon our American lands."[7]

Marti's warning was not heeded, and the United States burst dramatically onto the Caribbean scene in 1898. President William McKinley, egged on by newspaper publisher William Randolph Hearst, intervened in the Cuban war against Spain, the better to get a handle on events in the newly independent island; in 1902 Congress passed the infamous Platt Amendment, establishing the "right" of American intervention in internal Cuban affairs. The former Spanish colony of Puerto Rico was annexed outright, along with the Philippines and Guam in the Pacific. A little more than a decade later the United States occupied Haiti and the Dominican Republic, and while the Dominican occupation was terminated in 1924, the marines stayed in Haiti right up to the proclamation of the "Good Neighbour" policy by Franklin D. Roosevelt in 1934. Even this was not the end of American willingness to intervene militarily in the Caribbean when events there were displeasing to Washington. Since 1960 the United States has invaded Cuba and the Dominican Republic, been involved through the Central Intelligence Agency in the assassination of Dominican dictator Rafael Trujillo and in repeated attempts to kill Cuban Premier Fidel Castro, and carried out the blockade of Cuba beginning in 1962.

Because it was under firm British control, the Commonwealth Caribbean did not become a major focus of American activity in the region. But U.S. economic interests in the West Indies grew steadily, as such corporations as United Fruit, Texaco, Alcoa, Kaiser Aluminum, Reynolds Metals, Standard Oil of Indiana, Anaconda, W. R. Grace and the Chase Manhattan and First National City Banks established operations there. From 1941 there was an American military presence as well. In the return for some fifty obsolete destroyers, London gave the United States the right to establish bases in British colonies from Newfoundland to Trinidad. Chaguaramas, in the northwest corner of Trinidad, became a large U.S. Navy base. The presence of the sailors had a deep psychological effect on the island, which was best captured by its unofficial historians, the calypsonians, as in this calypso by Lord Invader:

> So she told me plainly,
> She love Yankee money,
> And she said, Lord Invader,
> Money for to find rum and Coca-Cola,
> Don't bother, if you know you ain't
> Got the Yankee dollar.[8]

In the late 1950s, Dr. Eric Williams, who had swept into office in Trinidad on a nationalist platform in 1956, fully committed his administration to getting rid of the American base, with the slogan "The road to independence leads through Chaguaramas." Although they were eventually successful, the victory was long in coming — the Americans did not leave until 1967 — and only partial when it did come, for even after the sailors cleared out, a "tracking station" of indeterminate nature remained. This was later revealed to be part of the Navy's worldwide Omega navigation system, useful primarily to nuclear submarines, and when that revelation reached Trinidad in 1974, it caused a flurry of press speculation that the station might make Trinidad a potential target for nuclear attack. Opposition political groups demanded that it be removed.[9] The U.S. military had also been a major customer for Trinidad oil, and thirteen per cent of all U.S. military spending in the Western Hemisphere outside Canada and the United States between 1960 and 1970 was in this small country of a million people.[10] As of 1975, the United States also maintained naval bases in Grand Turk, Antigua and Barbados, missile tracking stations in the Bahamas, Grand Turk and Antigua, and a Coast Guard installation, again in the Bahamas.

One U.S. policymaker described the American presence in the region as only a "residual strategic interest," and said that "technology has grown to the point where actual installations so close to the U.S. aren't that important." Most of the bases in the Commonwealth Caribbean are small and many are civilian-manned; the only full-scale American bases in the Caribbean are at Guantanamo in southeastern Cuba, maintained despite repeated protests from the Cuban government, and at Roosevelt Roads in Puerto Rico. Still, this same official reacted strongly to suggestions that the United States really isn't very interested in the Caribbean: "We demonstrated enough concern for the region to occupy Haiti from 1915 to 1934, and the Dominican Republic for a somewhat shorter period, and more recently to send a considerable force to the Dominican Republic to stabilize the situation there."

Another aspect of the American presence in the West Indies is the influence exercised on the official West Indian trade union movement by the American labour movement, and through it by the U.S. government and the CIA. In a 1971 essay on U.S.–West Indies relations Frank McDonald wrote:

> American corporations and AID [Agency for International Development] programs . . . represent only two sides of a triangular penetration of the Commonwealth Caribbean economy. The third side, without which the ease of this process would be severely threatened, is the organized "Americanization" of the Caribbean trade union movement's role in Caribbean politics. With the sole exception of Trinidad, most major political parties are rooted in a labour union and the vast majority of premiers, prime ministers, and even leaders of the opposition are themselves trade unionists. Thus, the axiom holds that the politics or ideology of the trade union movement will affect the policies of the regional governments and that the more receptive Caribbean labour is to the presence of American investment and management patterns, the more so will be the regional politicians.[11]

The chief instrument of this labour penetration is the American Institute for Free Labour Development (AIFLD). Established by the AFL-CIO in the early sixties, it is run by a tripartite board made up of business, labour and government representatives; its chairman as of 1975 was J. Peter Grace, president of W. R. Grace and Co., a company whose far-flung interests include the Federation Chemicals fertilizer factory that the Williams government lured to Trinidad with lucrative concessions. One of the AIFLD's main activities is the courses it conducts in such subjects as "democracy and totalitarianism" at its Front Royal, Virginia, headquarters,[12] and many West Indian trade union leaders are graduates of these courses.

The AIFLD has also co-operated in many countries with the CIA and is referred to by former CIA agent Philip Agee as a "CIA-controlled labour centre."[13] This aspect of the Institute's activities provoked Dr. Williams into expelling it from Trinidad in 1972 with an angry denunciation; Trinidad and Tobago Labour Congress President Nathaniel Critchlow, in turn, attacked Dr. Williams' move on the grounds that it interfered with trade union independence. In British Guiana the AIFLD, along with the London-based Public Service International Labour Secretariat, was involved in the CIA-sponsored campaign to bring down Marxist Premier Dr. Cheddi Jagan in the early sixties.[14]

With its corporations, its aid program, its sometimes undiplomatic diplomacy (Ambassador Vincent de Roulet had to leave Jamaica after his intervention in the 1972 elections there[15]), its military presence and its labour activity, the United States has clear title to the position of dominant power in the Commonwealth Caribbean. Canada's position, achieved largely on American coattails, is substantial but secondary, as is Britain's. But in the 1970s a whole new group of powers has arisen with the resources to exercise considerable influence in the region and, increasingly, with the will to use those resources for that purpose.

In January of 1975, Venezuelan President Carlos Andres Perez delivered the opening address to a major conference on Caribbean tourism in the lavish Hotel Tamanaco in Caracas. Perez's presence was only one indication of the importance the Venezuelan government attached to the event; delegates were treated to an exhausting round of official receptions, including one at the presidential palace, and bombarded with Venezuelan tourist-promotion material.

In his speech, Perez forthrightly set out his country's intention to play a more active role in the Caribbean. In the past, he said, Venezuela had lived

> with the cold shoulder to its responsibility in the Caribbean. Today, we realize how distant we are, and to be honest, we are aware of the mis-

givings existing among us on account of this lack of communication and of active friendship. And the essential and efficient cause of this reality is that we have not been our own masters. . . . And those peoples which, during the last century, have not had the luck to separate from their metropolis by obtaining their independence, have likewise been made to live with the cold shoulder toward their Latin America.

Now, however, all that was going to change, and Perez spelled out what change would mean:

We will endeavour to demonstrate the need for lifting all barriers that have been created among our peoples by the manipulation of our interests. We will take the flag, clutching it together with the other Spanish-speaking peoples of the Caribbean, for accepting the responsibility of making the Spanish language a permanent study language among all English, Dutch- and French-speaking peoples, in order that, some day, together with the languages they have as a legacy from colonial times, Spanish may be incorporated as an official language, because we cannot allow the old Biblical curse to serve anew in the '70s to divide our Latin American peoples.[16]

The West Indian delegates, few if any of whom had ever thought of themselves as Latin Americans, were wary but not hostile toward the Venezuelan initiative. "Many of the states in the region," said one, "are simply not in a position to refuse the kind of financial help Venezuela is prepared to provide." Newly rich from oil, with a long Caribbean coastline, and with twice the population of the whole Commonwealth Caribbean, Venezuela is uniquely well placed to be a major power in the region. But as Perez indicated, there is a long way to go, and it is not only historic divisions and cultural differences that make the West Indians cautious. The double-edged nature of Venezuela's initiative was illustrated by an emergency loan it extended in 1974 to Leeward Islands Air Transport (LIAT), the island-hopping airline of the smaller West Indian states. The loan bailed LIAT out when it was in serious financial trouble, but it was also to be repaid at fourteen per cent interest. In addition, Venezuela has never renounced its territorial claim to Guyana's Essequibo County, which constitutes roughly two thirds of the area of that country.

Venezuela has been the most prominent new protagonist in the

37

Caribbean, but there have been others as well. Brazil has indicated an interest in the region, although there have been few concrete signs of it yet. Mexico's peripatetic President Luis Echeverria visited Jamaica in 1974 and Trinidad in 1975, and his country has signed scientific and technical agreements with both Caribbean states and a bauxite deal with Jamaica. And Cuba, a Caribbean nation in its own right but isolated from its neighbours for more than a decade, has begun to take a greater interest in regional affairs. Premier Castro visited Trinidad and Guyana in 1971, and the following year those two countries along with Barbados and Jamaica established diplomatic relations with Cuba, making an early break with the American-led boycott of Havana. In 1975 Prime Ministers Forbes Burnham of Guyana, Eric Williams of Trinidad and Michael Manley of Jamaica all made pilgrimages to Cuba and expressions of Cuban–West Indian friendship abounded. There has been a limited revival of trade and technical co-operation, and the first Jamaican tourists since the 1950s visited Cuba in early 1975.

In West Indian political circles, relations with the Latin countries, and particularly with Venezuela, have become a matter of heated controversy. Michael Manley of Jamaica has been an enthusiastic supporter of closer ties, but Trinidad's prickly Dr. Williams sees in them the spectre of recolonization by a new master.

Dr. Williams first developed the recolonization theme in a speech in San Fernando, Trinidad's second city, on April 13, 1975, while his country was preoccupied with strikes in the oil and sugar industries.[17] A month later, at a meeting of the United Nations Economic Commission for Latin America (ECLA) in Chaguaramas, he succeeded in having the Caribbean rim countries — Venezuela, Colombia and Mexico — excluded from a new committee of Caribbean ministers within ECLA.[18] And in June, he launched a searing attack on the bauxite deal Jamaica had signed with Venezuela three months earlier. He claimed that the agreement would seriously harm plans for a CARICOM smelter to be built in Trinidad, taking advantage of its natural gas supplies, and fed by bauxite from Jamaica and Guyana.

Having called together his People's National Movement in special session to discuss the recolonization threat, he told the crowd, "My friends, one man can only take so much, and I have had enough. To smelt or not to smelt, no big thing as there is no shortage of claims on our gas. I have decided to take no further part in the matter." He added that it was simply not possible to view Venezuela's projected expansion of aluminum production from 55,000 to 330,000 tons a year as anything but a calculated attack on the Caribbean smelter project. And "if Trinidad and Tobago's CARICOM colleagues . . . were ever to decide on a policy to erode CARICOM as a first step toward its destruction, their policy would not differ materially from the agreements already entered into."[19]

Manley replied that the proposed Venezuelan expansion had been public knowledge when plans for the CARICOM smelter were first made. He defended the sale of Jamaican bauxite to Venezuela on the grounds of diversification of markets, and said that "so far from being an example of colonialism, this is an example of classic strategy in the search for economic independence."[20]

But while the debate focussed on specifics, much deeper issues were at stake. Were closer relations with their Latin neighbours a threat to the embryonic unity of the West Indian countries, or were they a logical extension of that unity? Was the influence of countries that were nearby and historically exploited likely to be any more benign than the influence of countries that were far away and historically dominant? Were West Indians simply Latin Americans who through an accident of history happened to speak English? And if not, what were they?

3/Doctors and Mimics

Above all, we lack power, and we do not understand that we lack power.
We mistake words and the acclamation of words for power; as soon as
our bluff is called we are lost.

V.S. Naipaul, The Mimic Men

The independence now enjoyed by the Commonwealth Caribbean states was achieved with a minimum of struggle, in fact with Britain's blessing. Mother turned her children out, but gently. There is no longer any direct colonial presence but neither has there been a clean break with the colonial past. The politics of the West Indies are post-colonial but not anti-colonial. West Indian regimes are characterized by almost absolute power within a limited sphere, and almost absolute powerlessness in the larger context. Lloyd Best of the Tapia group in Trinidad, in referring to the "Doctor Politics" of the Williams regime, emphasizes the first of those aspects; V.S. Naipaul, in writing of West Indian politicians as "Mimic Men", emphasizes the second.[1]

No complete picture of West Indian politics is possible without taking into account both of these characteristics. This particular combination of circumstances is largely foreign to North America, although less so to places such as Quebec and Newfoundland that are somewhat removed from the North American mainstream. Maurice Duplessis, Jean Drapeau or Joey Smallwood could be fitted into a West Indian context without too much difficulty, but Bill Davis or Ed Broadbent could not.

The most striking example of the impossibility of applying North American categories to West Indian politicians is Guyana's all-things-to-all-people Prime Minister, Forbes Burnham. Burnham has been the toughest of West Indian leaders in dealing with foreign companies, and has nationalized the Alcan and Reynolds bauxite interests and the Bookers and Jessels sugar estates. He has

41

turned Guyana into a "co-operative republic" and more recently proclaimed his commitment to a Marxist-Leninist brand of socialism. He has emphasized Guyana's Third World identity and assisted African liberation movements. But he came to power supported by the Americans and the British as an alternative to the Marxist regime of Premier Cheddi Jagan, and has stayed there through flagrantly rigged elections designed to keep Jagan out.

Much of this has to do with the particular political background of Guyana. The British left a legacy of racial division between the East Indian majority and the substantial black minority unique in degree, if not in kind, in the Caribbean. Nevertheless, when the first election under universal suffrage was held in 1953, the Guyanese gave their overwhelming support to a biracial group, the People's Progressive Party, under the leadership of the East Indian Dr. Jagan and his black lieutenant, Burnham. But the PPP was Marxist and anti-colonial, and British Prime Minister Winston Churchill was not prepared to brook that. Troops were sent in, the constitution suspended and direct colonial rule restored. The PPP, always more a coalition than a genuinely united party, broke apart under the strain. When suffrage was restored Dr. Jagan became Premier again and Burnham went into opposition. The early sixties were marked by strikes against the Jagan government, in which CIA involvement has since been documented, and widespread racial violence. In the 1964 elections Burnham's People's National Congress, in alliance with the right-wing, business-oriented United Force, came to power, and the country was granted its independence two years later.

Since then Burnham has played his hand to its limit; one observer has described him as "the original skater on thin ice." He has had supreme success in keeping himself in power and by no means inconsiderable success in making advances for his country. But all he has really done has been to carry out the original program of the PPP, and that slowly. The Booker-McConnell sugar interests, so powerful that the country was once nicknamed "Bookers' Guiana", were finally taken over in 1976. In the meantime, most of Burnham's energy was absorbed by the sterile feud with the PPP.

By 1975, with the government taking an increasingly independent stance and with the country beset by threats from its much
larger neighbours and by the possibility — which many Guyanese,
not without reason, considered to be serious — of American action
against it, any political content there had ever been in the
PPP–PNC split had disappeared. In August of that year, Dr. Jagan
made the first move toward breaking the stalemate by declaring
his "critical support" for Burnham. A year later, the PPP returned
to the National Assembly, which it had boycotted for three years
on the grounds that the irregularities that had surrounded the 1973
elections had made a mockery of the whole process.

These were encouraging signs, but much more would be needed
from both sides before the long history of division and hatred
could be overcome.

Michael Manley of Jamaica is another West Indian politician who
can vary his attitudes according to the occasion. He has since his
election in 1972 consistently spoken of his commitment to socialism, and as host and chairman of the 1975 Commonwealth Heads
of Government Conference emerged as a leader of the Third
World countries, calling for a new international economic order.
During his visit to Cuba in July 1975 he told a mass rally that
"every step that you take, you do not take alone, because the feet
of the Jamaican people are marching beside you."[2]

On his return to Kingston, he was asked at a press conference
whether there was any difference between his vision of socialism
and the Cuban system. He said there were two major differences.
One was that "we believe in Jamaica in a political system that rests
on the right of groups or individuals to form political organizations
which can compete with equal access for the votes of people in
elections," and the other was that "in the long future of economic
development, there is a permanent and valid role for the private
sector . . . . And we feel that as a method of producing goods and
services, that private enterprise has a role that can be made harmonious with the national interest."[3]

For Michael Manley's socialism bears more resemblance to that of James Callaghan than that of Fidel Castro. The son of Norman Manley, Michael succeeded to the leadership of the People's National Party when the elder Manley died in 1969. The Prime Minister at that time was Hugh Shearer, Alexander Bustamante's cousin and political heir, and he was openly pro-capitalist and had developed a reputation for laziness. It was a fatal combination, and the next election resulted in a convincing PNP victory. Since then Manley has run a more dynamic government than his predecessor, requiring the bauxite companies to pay substantially increased taxes, and bringing in repressive legislation in an attempt to deal with Kingston's terrible street violence.

In 1976 that violence had reached the point where a State of Emergency was needed to deal with it. The government was able to stave off a financial crisis only by borrowing $70 million of Trinidad's oil money and smaller amounts from other Caribbean countries. Like Burnham's government in Guyana, the PNP believed itself the victim of covert American activity to "destabilize" it, and, as in Guyana, the belief had a certain amount of plausibility if not evidence to support it. The opposition Jamaica Labour Party, meanwhile, suspected Manley of plotting to turn the country over to the Cubans. But amidst all this, Jamaica retained elements of the historic political stability that has always seemed uncanny in a society with so many anarchic tendencies.

This political stability derives from the remarkable two-party system that Bustamante and Norman Manley left as their legacy to the country. The JLP is rural-based and eclectic, while the PNP has an industrial and middle-class base and took its inspiration from the British Labour Party. In policy terms, however, there is about as much difference between them as between the Liberals and Conservatives in Canada, although Jamaicans hold to their JLP or PNP affiliation with a passion that has largely gone out of mainstream Canadian politics. In addition, each of the two major trade unions is tied to one of the parties. Even the warring Kingston street gangs claim a PNP or JLP affiliation. Jamaica's wealthy white families, who still have considerable power, are represented in both parties; Eli Matalon, a member of one of the oldest and wealthiest of Jamaica's elite Jewish families, is a senior cabinet minister, and his brothers Moses and Myer hold other government posts. "The presence of Matalon in the government," said one deeply conservative small businessman in Kingston, concerned about some of Manley's stronger statements, "gives me confidence to keep building this business up."

Another observer, a Trinidadian, visiting Jamaica after hearing some of those same statements, said, "If this is socialism then Trinidad has been socialist for ten years."

There is an air of unreality about Trinidad's politics, as there is about so many other aspects of Trinidadian life. It is widely believed in the country that Prime Minister Dr. Eric Williams practises *obeah*, the characteristic West Indian form of witchcraft comparable to the voodoo of Haiti, and has stayed in power for two decades by hexing his opponents. And indeed there is something of the supernatural about Dr. Williams' capacity for survival.

Since 1970 he has survived massive Black Power street marches, a mutiny in the army, two elections, in one of which he obtained the support of only twenty-eight per cent of the electorate, a guerrilla movement, a virtual general strike, and even his own resignation, which he submitted in a fit of pique in 1973 and then withdrew when neither of the two candidates for the succession who emerged from his People's National Movement met his high standards. Calypsonian The Mighty Chalkdust suggested to Richard Nixon that a study of Dr. Williams' methods might have helped him stay in power:

You shed a tear
For now you resign you cannot come back,
But the Big Boy here,
He resign last year and then he backtrack.[4]

Dr. Williams was not always an object of anger and derision. The PNM in the 1950s was the most broadly based mass movement Trinidad has ever had, and its motive forces were nationalism, anti-colonialism and hope for the future. Well after it led the country to its independence in 1962 the PNM retained broad support among Trinidad's black majority. But by 1970, with the promise held out by independence fading, much of that support had eroded.

The Black Power uprising that broke out in February 1970 marked a watershed: before it, Dr. Williams had been widely regarded as a force for progressive change and after it, he was regarded as an obstacle to that change. The Black Power movement had a more profound political and cultural effect than anything else since Dr. Williams' movement fifteen years earlier, but unlike the PNM it never turned itself into a political party. It was one of the few groups of Trinidadians that was so reticent. The PNM has been able to stay in power with its declining support not because there has been no party ready to take its place, but because there have been too many such parties.

The Democratic Labour Party, the traditional opposition, consigned to a permanent minority position because its appeal was only to the thirty-five per cent of Trinidadians who are East Indian, split apart, and each of the repeated attempts to heal the split resulted in a worse row than the last. The PNM itself spawned several split-offs. The intellectual New World movement of the 1960s gave rise to the moderate Tapia and the pro-Soviet Moko group. There were the West Indian National Party, the United Freedom Party, and others.

But the most serious challenge to the PNM came from a group of trade unions, which in 1975 banded together as the United Labour Front. The PNM is the only ruling party in the West Indies that is not trade union based, and although the official Trinidad and Tobago Labour Congress is conservative and generally pro-government, powerful independent trade unions have grown up in the key industries of oil and sugar. Joined together as the ULF, these unions closed down both industries in early 1975 and virtually brought the island to a halt. This alliance had particular significance because it united the two major racial groups, blacks and East Indians. Although these groups, unlike their counterparts in Guyana, had never been at each other's throats, they had traditionally gone their separate ways. The ULF proclaimed that its struggle was political, formed itself into a party for the 1976 elections, and won ten of the thirty-six seats to become the Official Opposition. With its broad base of support, the ULF may be the instrument that will finally bring Dr. Williams' long reign to an end.

Most of the political currents that sweep the Caribbean seem to bypass Barbados. Notorious in the region for its continuing attachment to things English, it struck Gordon K. Lewis as "an English market town, Cheltenham, as it were, with tropical overtones,"[5] while a Canadian visiting the island a few years later, after the tourist industry had had a chance to become further entrenched, saw it as a "tropical Blackpool."

It is summed up in the nickname "little England", which many Barbadians use without irony, but which has a derisive implication when used by other West Indians. "Little Canada" might be just as appropriate, for Barbados has assimilated many of the same cultural values that the people who founded English Canada brought with them across the water: the work ethic, functionality, conservatism and a certain stodginess. Not surprisingly, Canadians favour Barbados as a tourist spot, and have a rapport with Bajans that is often lacking with other West Indians.

The politics of the island tend to be stable and placid, and governments under Sir Grantley Adams and, after 1961, under Errol Barrow, managed to stay in office for long periods of time without resorting either to *obeah* or to electoral hanky-panky. Barbados and Jamaica are the only West Indian countries where something of the substance, instead of just the form, of two-party, elections-every-four-years, Her-Majesty's-Loyal-Opposition democracy has been transmitted from London. As in Jamaica, there is little difference between the two major Barbadian parties. But the violence, both overt and latent, that is the other side of Jamaican life is lacking in Barbados. Although Barrow was initially elected as part of a "Young Turk" movement, he proved, like his predecessor, to be no radical while in office. Nor were any fundamental changes expected from Tom Adams, son of Sir Grantley, who displaced Barrow in the elections of 1976. Adams's victory, like Barrow's fifteen years earlier, was based primarily on his relative youth and freshness and the feeling that it was time for a new face.

The enforcement mechanism for this tendency toward conservatism is the tourist industry, which dominates the Barbadian economy and which has the dual effect of heightening social problems and discouraging people from trying to do anything about them: rapid or indecorous change might scare away the tourists. So far, there have been few people in Barbados ready to run that risk.

"When we get together at regional conferences," said a researcher in the Central Bank of the Bahamas, "I find that the three B's — Bermuda, Barbados and the Bahamas — have a lot in common." If the transition of Barbados to an independent state was quiet, that of the Bahamas was virtually undetectable. In fact, when the Bahamas became independent in 1973, most of the efforts of the government of Prime Minister Lynden Pindling were devoted to persuading people that nothing was really going to change.

And in the event not much did. For in the Bahamas there was more than just tourists to worry about, although tourism makes up some seventy per cent of the Gross National Product and the independence celebrations themselves were turned into a tourist event. There were the international bankers, promoters, real-estate speculators and other investors who had come to the Bahamas to take advantage of its inviting climate and even more inviting tax laws, and they became nervous at even the suggestion of change.

The tourists and the investors had all been lured to the island by the previous United Bahamian Party government, led by Sir Roland Symonette as Premier, but dominated by the Minister of Finance and Tourism, Sir Stafford Sands. The UBP, however, spoke only for the twenty per cent of Bahamians who are white, and it was only a matter of time before Pindling's Progressive Liberal Party, representing the black majority, would displace it. Even at that it was a hard go: it was 1967 by the time Pindling finally won a narrow victory. Pindling has effectively let black Bahamians in on a larger share of the action, but he has neither the inclination, nor, ultimately, the power to tamper seriously with the Bahamas historically parasitic economy.

There is an air of prosperity in downtown Nassau, although little of it extends "over the hill" where most ordinary Nassauvians live. There is even more of an air of prosperity at Lyford Cay, at the other end of New Providence Island, where Canadian financier E. P. Taylor has turned what was once a mosquito-infested swamp into an exclusive retreat for the rich of the western world. Despite Pindling's constant assurances, there has been a limited flight of capital from the Bahamas to other tax havens such as the Cayman Islands, where the Union Jack still flies. So far, however, this has been kept more or less under control, and Pindling has managed to maintain the difficult balance between the demands of the poor and black Bahamians who put him into office and those of the rich and white foreigners whom he cannot afford to offend.

Grenada, by contrast, joined the roster of independent states with an impact that belied its miniscule size and long-standing tranquillity. Known to most people, if at all, as an attractive, lush and rather exotic tourist spot, and as the producer of a large proportion of the world's nutmeg, Grenada had serious social problems that had escaped the notice of North American tourists passing through.

But as early as 1971, they began to read headlines that suggested that all was not well in Grenada: "Island is called 'terror-stalked Little Haiti'," "A dictatorship amidst the nutmeg?" "Grenada: Rape, murder, looting," "Grenada's bleak thanksgiving," "Dictatorial leader grinds Grenada."[6] The erstwhile Garden of Eden was now a fear-ridden hellhole. But the new image was as incomplete and inaccurate as the old one, for while the tensions that caused the eruption of late 1973 and early 1974 are serious and real, the island of 100,000 people has responded to these tensions in a different manner than people accustomed to larger societies might expect.

And so, a year after twenty thousand people marched in the streets of St. George's, the capital, denouncing Prime Minister Eric

49

Gairy as a dictator and chanting "Gairy must go!", Gairy could still appear in the capital unguarded, in contrast to the heavy, and still inadequate, security apparatus that surrounded such "democratic" leaders as Gerald Ford. Violence as a means of effecting social change is still foreign to Grenadians, and no one understands that better than Eric Gairy. This was the reason that his own use of violence, in the form of police beatings and the fatal shooting of Rupert Bishop, the father of one of the leaders of the opposition New Jewel Movement, had such a stunning impact in the country.

New Jewel and the other opposition groups, motivated as much by outraged decency as by political radicalism, remain unclear about just how they are going to remove Gairy from power. Mass demonstrations and a general strike have been tried and have failed to budge him; no one trusts Gairy to run a free election, any more than anyone in Guyana trusts Burnham to run one; and violence — no one talks about that. So Gairy remains, and his highly personal and semi-mystical rule ("I feel that my assignment is a Divine one and I feel that the Master himself is keeping me here and will remove me when he wants me to be removed"[7]) has led Grenada not only into dictatorship but to the verge of bankruptcy. There are periodic crises brought on by the approach of payday in the public service and they are generally resolved by Gairy's flying to the United States and getting a new infusion of money from his mysterious "sources" there. As the first of the Windwards and Leewards to become independent, Grenada is regarded as something of a model for the others, which one by one have been announcing plans to follow in its path. While Grenada has demonstrated to its sister islands that political independence is possible, it has also shown them that the benefits it can bring, if unaccompanied by more basic changes, are highly limited.

Some of the islands began to borrow aspects of the Grenadian model even before their independence. In Dominica, Premier Patrick John took it upon himself to declare war on the "pseudo-intellectuals" and "agents of international communism" who were "eating through the region's organizations and institutions like cancer"[8] and he had a law passed giving citizens the legal right to shoot dead on sight members of a banned organization, the Dreads. In Antigua, Premier George Walter cracked down on opposition newspapers by requiring them to buy libel insurance before they could publish, a tactic later picked up by Gairy himself.

Meanwhile, the 1974 election in St. Vincent featured two rival groups, both claiming to be the same party, and when the election was over two members of the new house, one of them the wife of a Cabinet Minister, were both claiming to be Leader of the Opposition. There were people in the small dependency of Carriacou who wanted to separate from Grenada, people in Nevis who wanted to separate from St. Kitts (an attempt some years earlier by Anguilla to secede from the original three-island state had culminated in a comic-opera British invasion), people in Barbuda who wanted to separate from Antigua. Never had doubts about the political system bequeathed by Britain been so pervasive.

Two other responses to colonialism have been seen in the Caribbean, and each of them, in its own way, is more logically consistent than the catch-as-catch-can politics of the West Indies. The first of these is to attempt to beat the colonial system, an option represented by Cuba. The opposite strategy is to join it: the French islands of Guadeloupe and Martinique and the American island of Puerto Rico have gone this route. Not entirely by their own choice, the Commonwealth Caribbean countries have taken neither path, and as a result they tend to appear from Havana, San Juan or Fort-de-France as something of a backwater, even in Caribbean terms.

In some circles, the Cuban revolution of 1959 is regarded as having accomplished merely the exchange of one colonial master for another: the United States moved out, and the Soviet Union moved in. Events such as Premier Castro's declaration of support for the Soviet invasion of Czechoslovakia in 1968 are regarded as proof of this. But while there is no question that the Soviet Union exercises a great deal of influence in Cuba, particularly in the area of foreign policy, there is also evidence that the relationship between Havana and Moscow is fundamentally different from the traditional relationship between the islands of the Caribbean and the colonial centre, and that the Cubans have achieved a kind of independence never before attained by any Caribbean country.

This is so for profound historical reasons. Cuba's fight for independence from Spain lasted thirty years, and the struggle to get rid of the American neo-colonial presence that immediately supplanted the Spaniards continued for another sixty. The successful revolutionary war of the 1950s took twenty thousand Cuban lives. Even in the 1960s Cuba had to beat back an American-supported invasion and survive an American blockade. All this left the Cubans with a fierce pride in what they had accomplished and a determination not to give it up.

To an extent, independence was forced on the Cubans. The traditional market for their sugar, the supply of consumer goods, the tourists, all were gone at one stroke. While the Soviet Union was the first country to step into the breach it was by no means the only one. By 1975, forty per cent of Cuban trade was with western countries, including Canada, and Japan. Technical assistance also came from western countries, again including Canada, as well as Soviet-bloc ones. The economy is entirely in Cuban hands, and geared to Cuban priorities. Cuba's problem is not that it must answer to outside interests, but that there are no precedents for what it is trying to do. As a result, the procedure has had to be trial and error — sometimes massive error. What, for instance, is the role of the sugar industry in a sensibly planned Caribbean economy? In the early sixties, a precipitous industrialization program was undertaken under the leadership of Che Guevara and sugar was de-emphasized. In the second half of the decade, the emphasis swung back to sugar and heroic, although not always successful, efforts went into fulfilling the high production goals set by the government. It is only in the seventies that some sort of balance has begun to be achieved.

While Cuba is trying to cope with the problems of independence, Martinique remains firmly tied to Mother France. "Independence?" responded a taxi driver in Fort-de-France, the capital, when asked by a visitor whether there are any moves in that direction on the island. "*Independence?* But we're a department of the Republic, just like any other department." The tone was one of disbelief at the slightest suggestion that any group of people who had achieved that exalted status could possibly want anything else. Even socialists in Martinique generally favour autonomy rather than independence.

The contrast between Martinique and its neighbouring Commonwealth islands in the Windwards and Leewards is economic as well as psychological. "You can certainly argue dependency in the French islands," said one Caribbean economist, "but it's hard to argue exploitation in the classic sense. There's no doubt that France runs a substantial deficit on those islands." The effects of the money France has poured in are evident in the presence of industry on a scale unknown in the smaller Commonwealth islands; the relatively advanced infrastructure; and the air of bustle and modest prosperity in Fort-de-France, an atmosphere of economic activity that, in the Commonwealth Caribbean, can only be matched by Trinidad, which is much larger and better endowed.

In Puerto Rico, a similar trade-off of Caribbean identity for economic advance has been made. After World War II, "Operation Bootstrap" attracted large and small corporations to the island with the prospect of tax concessions and cheap labour, combined with free access to the American market. A tourist industry was built up, and the San Juan beachfront turned into a replica of Miami. Meanwhile unrestricted emigration to the mainland reduced the population burden. The result of all this was a somewhat diluted form of American material progress, and an unstoppable invasion of American culture. San Juan today is a thoroughly American city, and a bilingual one in the manner of Montreal; the visitor who speaks only English is no more likely to lose his way on the Avenida Ponce de Leon than he is on the Rue Ste-Catherine. The Puerto Rican independence movement, although vocal and active, is small, and most of the population is divided between a majority that wants to continue the current "commonwealth" status and a minority that wants Puerto Rico to become the fifty-first state.

Since the end of World War II, the Puerto Rican model of industrialization by invitation has been followed by other underdeveloped areas, from Nova Scotia to South Korea, which are seeking to deal with their persistent economic problems. Among these have been the countries of the Commonwealth Caribbean, but without the key Puerto Rican advantage of a customs union with the United States the success of their programs has been at best mixed. Examining the case of Trinidad, economist Edwin Carrington found in 1968 that the industrialization program had resulted in a much smaller growth in employment than expected because the new industries tended to be capital-intensive; little saving in foreign exchange; greater dependency; and a worsening of the island's fiscal problems, because of the ruinous concessions needed to attract foreign companies.[9]

By the early seventies, West Indian governments were beginning to see new merit in the sector they had for so long maligned: agriculture. Enthusiasm for sugar ebbs and flows with each fluctuation of the London Daily Price, and with the high prices of 1974–75 it was at a flood-tide. Prime Minister Barrow, who ten years earlier had looked forward with hope to the day when no more sugar would be grown in Barbados, now was out symbolically cutting cane to demonstrate the importance of sugar to the Barbadian economy. Dr. Williams was conferring with American multinational corporations with the intention of inviting them in to revitalize agriculture in Trinidad.

This was all agriculture in the classic West Indian mould: foreign-controlled and export-oriented. But proposals were also being made that the West Indies should improve their lagging domestic agriculture. For although the islands have grown large quantities of sugar, bananas, cocoa and other crops for consumption abroad, they have never satisfied their own food needs, and imported meat, fish, fruits and vegetables have long been part of the West Indian diet. Furthermore, a large proportion of the tourist dollar brought into the Caribbean (estimates range up to ninety per cent) goes right out again to pay for the North American food the tourists eat. If there is going to be a tourist industry, some West Indians argue, it could at least provide a market for West Indian agriculture. And yet, the obstacles to agricultural development in the West Indies are severe, and as of 1975 reform remained mostly at the level of talk.

Not the least important of these obstacles is the policy of the commercial banks, almost all of them foreign owned and many of them Canadian, which make consumer loans much more eagerly than they do loans to small farmers. But there are more than strictly economic reasons for the undeveloped state of West Indian agriculture. Farming is still regarded as slave-work, and few West Indians will engage in it by choice. Moreover the region, and particularly its middle and upper classes, have over the decades developed a taste for imported goods that is strengthened by tourism and other manifestations of North American cultural penetration. It is a common joke in Trinidad that the national drink of the island's white elite is Scotch whiskey, and its national fruit is the Canadian apple.

This tendency reinforces the judgment of which V.S. Naipaul is so fond: that the West Indies are a cultural we well as an economic colony of the metropolitan countries, a region that can produce nothing of its own. It is noteworthy that although many West Indian states have undertaken programs of import substitution in which the importing of certain commodities has been banned in order to encourage their production locally, the only one that has really been able to make it stick is Guyana, which has no tourist industry and a cultural orientation that has not been quite as heavily influenced by North America as that of the island states.

In the end, however, Naipaul's judgment is only part of the truth, and indeed there is no better example of the creative potential of the region than Naipaul himself, who has for some time occupied a position in the first rank of English-language novelists. It is a twist that Naipaul, the master of irony, would appreciate. Other West Indian writers, notably the St. Lucia-born poet and playwright

55

Derek Walcott and the Barbadian novelist George Lamming, have justly gained international recognition as well. In fact, it might fairly be said that the West Indies have manifested an astonishing cultural vitality despite the apparent handicaps of a small population and material poverty.

Several of the most important intellectual leaders in the international fight for decolonization have been West Indians. Marcus Garvey built a mass movement of black people in both Jamaica and the United States and, in the words of C. L. R. James, "managed to convey to Negroes everywhere (and to the rest of the world) his passionate belief that Africa was the home of a civilization that once was great and would be great again."[10] George Padmore, a Trinidadian, founded the African Bureau in London, and there came into contact with and influenced such African leaders as Jomo Kenyatta and Kwame Nkrumah. C. L. R. James, novelist and historian, used his art to advocate the liberation of both Africa and the West Indies, and eventually entered active politics in his native Trinidad. So of course did Dr. Eric Williams, one of the foremost of the anti-colonial historians. Jamaican economist Norman Girvan's studies of the bauxite industry have been of international importance in uncovering the methods of operation of the multinational corporations and their implications for Third World countries. Walter Rodney, a Guyanese, stands out among the new generation of black historians.

These people are, no doubt, exceptions. The phenomenon of the sterile, denationalized intellectual, with little relation to his society, is all too familiar in the West Indies. But the very fact that there are so many exceptions indicates that the soil for a more positive intellectual and cultural tradition exists too. The circumstances of the region's history have helped shape that tradition. West Indians have been among the most penetrating observers of colonialism precisely because the colonial experience has been most complete in the West Indies. And West Indian writers have often described that experience in particularly arresting language, because they are part of a culture that has a great, almost an exaggerated, respect for language and in which words are commonly used with colour and originality. On the whole, West Indian artists and intellectuals exist in the context of a rich folk and popular culture, and the best of them have recognized their debt to it.

Occasionally manifestations of that popular culture reach North America, but removed from the context of West Indian life they are stripped of most of their essence. The "calypso" that Harry Belafonte introduced into North America in the 1950s conveyed much of the sound but little of the spirit of Trinidadian calypso. Jamaican music is now going through a similar process, and in 1975 Edith Cherry of RCA, the label on which Belafonte records, was in Kingston looking for "marketable reggae."[11]

Fortunately these North American incursions have not destroyed the characteristic Caribbean forms of expression. In Trinidad during the calypso season, lasting from Christmas to Carnival, no Trinidadian content regulations are needed to get the radio stations to play calypso in proportions approaching a hundred per cent. Conversations turn to the question of which calypsonian will be Road March King as inevitably as November conversations in Canada turn to the question of who is going to win the Grey Cup. Calypso cuts across different levels of society and what are regarded in North America as different forms of art. High artist engaging in social commentary, popular artist whose compositions are played daily on the radio one month and forgotten the next, folk artist carrying on an old tradition of storytelling: the calypsonian is all three.

Jamaica, which had a longer period of British rule and assimilated more of the British cultural tradition, maintains more of these formal cultural distinctions, but there too they are beginning to break down in response to social pressures. The National Pantomime is a musical comedy form borrowed from Britain and performed annually in Kingston; in 1975 for the first time, it was done in Jamaican speech and took a Jamaican historical theme, the strike of Kingston dock workers in 1938:

Shillin' a hour, shillin' a hour,
Dem have de money but we have de power.
We askin' far a treepence more
Before anadder ship leave de shore.[12]

The exquisite rural folk music of Jamaica, as collected and performed by Olive Lewin and the Jamaican Folk Singers, has become an urban entertainment — an excellent one, and one handled with taste and respect, but nevertheless something removed from its roots. It is the urgent, pulsating reggae that comes out of the West Kingston slums that is the most significant cultural expression of urban Jamaica today. Reggae incorporates many of the same elements as North America popular music, especially black music, and it is not surprising that American groups now borrow reggae rhythms and even cut albums in Kingston. But true reggae is thoroughly Jamaican, and grows out of the Jamaica's unique cultural, political and religious life.

Reggae has a close affinity with Jamaica's Rastafarian movement, a link personified by the immensely popular Bob Marley. Rastafarianism is only one in a series of messianic movements that have taken root in Jamaica. Alexander Bedward, the Revivialist Prophet and Shepherd of August Town, attracted a wide following before 1920. Hordes of his followers flocked to August Town on December 31, 1920, to watch him ascend to Heaven as he had announced he would; when nothing happened, Bedwardism went into decline.[13] Marcus Garvey's movement had a greater political element in it but it captured much of the same spirit, with its vision of the Promised Land awaiting in Africa. The Rastafarians preach peace, godliness and black pride, use marijuana ritually, wear their hair in "dreadlocks" and believe in the divinity of the late Emperor Haile Selassie of Ethopia. When Selassie's death was announced in August 1975 the "Rastas" refused to believe it: "We Rastafarians," Brother Historian, secretary of the Rastafarian Movement Association, told the Jamaica *Daily Gleaner,* "stand firm and know that God remains one mighty, one forever that can never die and never dies. It is the colonial philosophy that told us that one can die."[14]

All through the West Indies, both mainstream religion and indigenous sects such as the Rastafarians have an importance that has been lost in most of North America. The religiosity of Jamaican life extends even to the passenger train that runs between Kingston and Montego Bay, onto which preachers come at each stop to preach for a small tithe. The Dreads of Dominica take their inspiration and borrow their hairstyle from the Rastafarians. The evangelical Pilgrim Holiness Church has followers throughout the Eastern Caribbean. In Trinidad, the Spiritual Baptists bear little resemblance to North American Baptists, while *shango* and *obeah* are mixtures of Christianity and African magic. This all suggests the existence of a distinctive West Indian way of looking at reality, with manifestations in all aspects of religious and secular life, and subject to wide variation from island to island. Its apotheosis, the all-consuming two-day Carnival, is unique to Trinidad. No description of Trinidad Carnival can begin to convey the single-minded fervour with which Trinidadians prepare for it and engage in it; the electric charge which sweeps through Port of Spain and the other cities and towns of the island as the panmen begin to play and move through the streets before dawn on *j'ouvert* morning, and which is sustained undiminished until the Last Lap the following midnight; the colour of the bands and the sound of the steel and brass, and the overall mesmerizing assault on the senses that makes it impossible for even the most spiritless to remain mere observers.

It is argued that Carnival helps divert attention from less innocent pursuits, such as politics; the ancient formula for keeping people content is, after all, bread and circuses, and Trinidad, where many people have only a little bread, relies heavily on the circus side of things. That is true, but is not the whole truth. The history of Carnival is largely the history of attempts by rulers of Trinidad to suppress it and successful resistance to these attempts by the masses of people. The steelband, which grew out of the poverty-ridden John John hills of East Port of Spain during World War II, won a difficult battle for social acceptance after the war. Today it is the principal organized activity of young Trinidadians and thousands of them, none of them professional musicians, spend every night in the two months before Carnival practising in panyards across the island. One young Trinidadian, wont to criticize his countrymen for their lack of discipline, could only shake his head at the spectacle of a steelband painstakingly perfecting its interpretation of a calypso. If Trinidadians have no discipline, he was asked, then what was this? "One one time," he said.

Perhaps it is precisely because West Indians have been forcibly excluded from the economic race that consumes North Americans that they have turned their attention so successfully to other pursuits. West Indian culture has survived slavery, colonialism and the multinational corporation, but could it survive prosperity? Eric St. Cyr, chairman of the Department of Management Studies at the University of the West Indies, St. Augustine, Trinidad and a West Indian intellectual in the best tradition, was asked whether his countrymen, if given the choice, would give up their way of life for material benefits. If the average Trinidadian were offered a North American standard of living, but in exchange he actually had to work for eight hours a day, obey the traffic laws, and give up Carnival and calypso, would he accept it?

"Yes," was St. Cyr's answer, "because he would never believe that he would really have to pay the price."

4/All in the Empire

Forbes Burnham, Prime Minister of Guyana, didn't twitch a muscle when
Mayor William Dennison referred to him as Prime Minister of Ghana yes-
terday.
  Nor did his composure break when Mr. Dennison repeated the mistake
a second, third and fourth time. But his smile grew slightly more benign.
  ''I understand you've got economic problems in Ghana. . . .'' Mr. Den-
nison began after greeting Mr. Burnham and his party of 14 in Mr.
Dennison's City Hall office, Mr. Burnham agreed.

Cameron Smith,
Toronto Globe and Mail,
July 14, 1967

The stories of Canada and the West Indies have been intertwined
for a long time, since the era when the two regions were pawns in
the same colonial wars. The same treaties that shifted different
parts of Canada back and forth between England and France
shifted the West Indian islands from one European power to
another; of the territories that currently make up the Commonwealth Caribbean, only Barbados was under British rule
throughout the colonial period.

  In 1760, with negotiations in progress in Paris to end what
became the Seven Years' War, a lively controversy arose in London. Britain had captured both Canada and the Caribbean island
of Guadeloupe from the French, and one or the other would probably have to be given back. The question was which one, and the
anonymous pamphleteers of London had much to say on the
matter. One pamphlet in favour of Canada was well received and
was acknowledged by its author, Benjamin Franklin. But it was
soon answered by another, entitled *Reasons for keeping Guadaloupe at a Peace, preferable to Canada, explained in Five Letters
from a Gentleman in Guadaloupe to his Friend in London.* The
author of the *Five Letters* argued:

  The having all North-America to ourselves by acquiring Canada,

61

dazzles the eyes, and blinds the understandings of the giddy and unthinking people, as it is natural for the human mind to grasp at every appearance of wealth and grandeur, yet it is easy to discover that such a peace might soon ruin Britain. I say the acquisition of Canada might be destructive, because such a country as North-America, ten times larger in extent than Britain, richer soil in most places, all the different climates you can fancy, all the lakes and rivers for navigation one could wish, plenty of wood for shipping, and as much iron, hemp, and naval stores, as any part of the world; such a country at such a distance could never remain long subject to Britain; you have taught them the art of war, and put arms in their hands, and they can furnish themselves with everything in a few years, without the assistance of Britain, they are always grumbling and complaining against Britain, even while they have the French to dread, what may they not be supposed to do if the French is no longer a check upon them; you must keep a numerous standing army to over-awe them; these troops will soon get wives and possessions, and become Americans; thus from these measures you lay the surest foundation of unpeopling Britain, and strengthening America to revolt; a people who must become more licentious from their liberty, and more factious and turbulent from the distance of the power that rules them; one must be very little conversant in history, and totally unacquainted with the passions and operations of the human mind, who cannot foresee those events as clearly as anything that can be discovered, that lies concealed in the whole womb of time; it is no gift of prophecy, it is only the natural and unavoidable consequences of such and such measures.

By contrast, he said that the West Indies "must always be dependent upon her, or some other such power . . . as they produce nothing that the mother country does."[1] Even though he disclaims the gift of prophecy, one can only marvel at the prescience of this particular pamphleteer. But more immediate considerations were to prevail, as another pamphleteer of the time, Israel Mauduit, feared they would:

> During the whole of Mr. Pitt's administration, no one had so much of his confidence as Mr. Beckford [a member of one of the most important Jamaican sugar families]. He was made to believe that he held the City by Beckford's means, and gave free admission to him, while he kept himself inaccessible to everyone else. The revealer of his will in

the House of Commons was Mr. Beckford, for Mr. Pitt himself seldom went thither. I heard him making most fulsome panegyric on Mr. Beckford's abilities; and three times following insult the whole House for presuming to laugh at Mr. Beckford's professing disinteredness. Beckford dreaded the increase of our sugar islands, lest that might lessen the value of his lands in Jamaica, and hence proceeded Mr. Pitt's invincible aversion to any attempts on the French Islands; and the speech he made on the first day of the Sessions 1760 . . . . in which he expressly declared against making any further conquests in the West Indies.[2]

Historian William L. Grant commented, "Let us hope that no such motives really influenced the Great Commoner."[3] Be that as it may, William Pitt, like Joey Smallwood two centuries later, chose Canada.

From then on, with Canada and the West Indies (minus Guadeloupe) securely in the British fold, the relationship between the two areas was an intra-imperial one, and largely took the form of trade. Although metropolitan Britain was the sole market for West Indian products, the American colonies had become the islands' chief suppliers, and as early as 1774, with trouble brewing in the Thirteen Colonies, Britain began to think seriouly about having Canada take over that role.

For forty years after the American Revolution, abiding by the old principles of mercantilism, which decreed that all trade should remain within the Empire, Britain tried to prevent any commerce between the West Indies and the new Republic. According to economist Peter K. Newman of the University of the West Indies, "it was clear to [the West Indies] that their whole economy was built on American provisions, and that the Canadian colonies would not prove an adequate source of supply."[4] In 1822 the prohibition on American goods entering the West Indies, which had proved unenforceable in any case, was relaxed, and free ports were established to which American provisions could be brought.

Thus, from early times, relations between Canada and the West Indies existed under the long shadow that the United States cast over both areas. "The fluctuating course of Candian–West Indian economic relations," wrote Newman, "can only really be understood in the light of this dominant role of the United States, which affected relationships between the two areas to an even greater degree than did British Imperial trade policy. West Indians, especially toward the end of the nineteenth century, were afraid to enter into trade ageements with Canada for fear of antagonizing America."[5]

Nevertheless, a trade relationship did begin to grow up, particularly between the Caribbean and the Atlantic colonies. It was an exchange of the staples of one region for those of the other; ships carried salt cod from Nova Scotia and Newfoundland and brought back sugar, molasses and rum from the West Indies. Newfoundland saltfish, cooked with ackees and served with rice, became the national dish of Jamaica, while Jamaica rum, imported in barrels and renamed "screech," became the national drink of Newfoundland. Screech was, and still is, among the harshest of West Indian rums, while the least desirable fish was known as "West Indie" in Newfoundland because of its destination:

Oh now comes the merchant to see your supply:
"The fine side of fishing we'll have bye and bye,
Seven dollars for large and six-fifty for small."
Pick out your West Indie, you got nothing at all,
And it's hard, hard times.[6]

The flourishing trade being conducted out of Halifax around the time of Confederation led to the growth of that city as a banking centre. Branches of the Halifax banks followed the trade routes, and since some of the more heavily travelled routes led to the Caribbean it was not long before branches were being set up there. The Merchants' Bank of Halifax, later the Royal Bank of Canada, established its first branch outside Canada at Hamilton, Bermuda, in 1882 — before it had one in Montreal — and by the end of the century it had branches in Cuba and Puerto Rico as well. The Bank of Nova Scotia had a branch in Kingston, Jamaica, by 1889 — before it had one in Toronto — and had soon spread to other parts of that island. In 1900, the Union Bank of Halifax set up shop in Port of Spain; the Union Bank was later absorbed into the

Royal and provided the foundation for that bank's penetration of Trinidad.

The earliest human contacts between the West Indies and British North America also involved the Maritime colonies. In 1795 a rebellion broke out among the Maroons of Jamaica, a proud community of free Negroes who had refused either to follow their old masters or submit to the new ones when the British had driven the Spaniards from the island 140 years earlier. After a series of hard-fought battles the rebels were defeated, and it was decided to deport some 600 of them. The place of exile chosen for them was Nova Scotia, where they were put to work building the Citadel at Halifax.

But the Northern winter was harsh and the white inhabitants were less than friendly — the same problems that future generations of West Indian immigrants were to encounter. According to a 1935 article in *Canada-West Indies Magazine,* "When the following Spring came round, it was soon noticed that the Maroons showed no desire to work. The cause of their conduct was soon explained. If they refused to work they would be sure to be removed to a warmer climate, they thought."[7] In 1800 the Maroons were shipped to Sierra Leone.

Among the first Canadians to live in the West Indies were Nova Scotian missionaries. Rev. John Morton, minister of the Presbyterian church in Bridgewater, Nova Scotia, went to Trinidad for his health in 1864 and found in the heathen, unlettered East Indians a ripe opportunity for missionary work. "I at once determined," he later wrote, "to secure a missionary for them or to go myself."[8] He approached the Church of Scotland and the Presbyterian Church in the United States but neither would agree to support his proposal for a mission. His own church was more sympathetic, and so in December 1867 Morton again sailed for Trinidad, appointed there by the Foreign Mission Board of the Presbyterian Church of the Lower Provinces in British North America, and arrived a month later, having survived a severe storm at sea.

Since Morton was not only the first person to undertake the religious conversion of the Indians but also the first to pay attention to their education, there was much to be done, and he soon asked for a second missionary. This request led to the appointment of Kenneth J. Grant in 1870. Both Morton and Grant remained in Trinidad for many years, and a photograph published in 1911 shows Morton and his wife, a stern and dignified elderly couple against a background of palm trees.[9] The Canadian Mission grew rapidly and had a great impact on Trinidad and to a lesser extent British Guiana, to which it spread toward the end of the century. The missionaries turned their attention to more wordly pursuits as well. Morton took an active interest in agriculture and acted as an advisor to the Cadbury cocoa estates. T. Geddes Grant, Kenneth's son, went into business, and the trading company he founded in 1901 became one of the largest in the West Indies. His sons and grandsons maintained their ties with the Presbyterian Church and continued to run T. Geddes Grant Ltd. The company began by importing almost exclusively from Canada and although its business has diversified considerably, trade with Canada remains an important part of it.

Although the commercial relationship between Canada and the West Indies didn't fulfil the promise some had seen in it, ties between the two regions, within the British Empire and shaped by the influence of the United States, were deepening steadily. By the 1880s a discernible West Indian interest had emerged in Canada, just as there had always been one in Britain. The Canadian capitalist class was just embarking on the most expansive and optimistic period of its history, and was eager to extend its operations beyond the constricting boundaries of the Dominion. To a considerable degree it succeeded particularly in those fields — banking, insurance, utilities — that had become its principal interests at home, the ones left to it by the burgeoning American economic power in Canada.

The Caribbean, both Commonwealth and otherwise, and the mainland of Latin America became the main objects of Canadian attention. As we have seen, Canadian banks flourished in the Caribbean by 1900. The Sun Life Assurance Company established an office in Barbados as early as 1879. After retiring from the active direction of the Canadian Pacific Railway, Sir William Van Horne built a railway from Santa Clara to San Luis in Cuba, then turned his attention to Guatemala. A young Halifax-based financier, Max Aitken, amused himself by buying tramway companies and electric utilities in the Caribbean while preparing himself to take on the larger challenges of Montreal and eventually London, where he soon acquired a peerage and became Lord Beaverbrook.[10]

"Between 1885 and 1910," wrote historian Robin W. Winks of Yale University, "the British West Indies became to Canada what China was to the United States: a source for constant visions of 'unrivaled trade opportunities.' Americans wanted to sell matches to every Chinaman ('Just think,' one allegedly said, 'if every one of those Chinese were to buy just one box of matches a week! ') and Canadians wanted to sell unpalatable cod to every West Indian."[11]

The growth of the Canadian economic interest led to pressure for Canada to take the West Indies, or parts of it, into some form of political association. The Canada First movement of the 1870s favoured "closer trade relations with the British West India Islands, with a view to a closer political connection."[12] In 1882 a Sun Life-related Planter's Bank of Canada was incorporated, and a group of its shareholders, acting through a publicist named A. Spencer Jones, advocated a Canada–West Indies union through letters to the press.[13] In 1911, there was a brief flurry of interest in annexing the Bahamas to Canada, which had something of the same spirit as the Turks and Caicos affair sixty-three years later. The Max Saltsman of the 1911 effort was T. B. Macaulay, then managing director and later president of Sun Life. Sir Etienne Dupuch, in 1975 still actively associated with the Nassau *Tribune* as editor emeritus, remembers meeting Macaulay and other members of a Canadian delegation who came to Nassau to sell the idea of union.

None of these attempts got very far. The chief obstacles were the continuing opposition of the Colonial Office and the West Indian interest in London and the race question in Canada. The idea of their country's taking on a new contingent of black citizens was unpalatable to many Canadians. At the time of the Canada–Bahamas affair Sir William Grey-Wilson, governor of the Bahamas and an advocate of union, faced the race issue squarely. In a speech made in Toronto during a private visit to Canada and reported in the Toronto *Globe*, Sir William said, "I believe we could get over the suffrage difficulty by putting the qualification of an elector in the Bahamas so high that we should automatically shut out the ignorant blacks of the colony. This would also shut out some of the whites, but I do not think that would be a grievance."[14]

On the West Indian side, political union with Canada, like closer economic ties, was always looked upon as a distant second choice to some sort of association with the United States. In 1884 the Jamaica *Daily Gleaner* dismissed a proposal then in the air for Jamaican union with Canada as a British trick to get rid of the colony; if Britain did want to ditch Jamaica, the *Gleaner* said, it would be better to annex the island to the United States then to "tack us on as a sort of hospital for Canadian Government rheumatics."[15]

Trade ties followed the ups and downs of American tariff policies. The first major Canadian tariff concession to the West Indies came in 1898, when W. S. Fielding, Finance Minister in the Laurier government, granted a twenty-five per cent preference to raw and refined sugar from the West Indies and the United Kingdom. The Caribbean sugar colonies were in distress at the time because of the obstacles placed in the way of their entering the American market. A British Royal Commission had investigated that distress in 1897, but had come to the conclusion that "the United States affords the best and the natural market for the West Indies, and if that market should be closed or lost to West Indian sugar the Colonies must suffer severely."[16] Closed the market was, and with Britain of little help, Canada was next in line to assume its Imperial responsibilities; besides, granting a preference might help stimulate exports to the region. As a result of the preference, Canada became the main market for West Indian sugar after the turn of the century.

A British Royal Commission on trade relations between Canada and the West Indies reported in 1910, suggesting a general agreement between the two areas on grounds of Imperial co-operation. The West Indies, still shut out of the American market, were favourable to the idea, and Canada, having rejected reciprocity with the United States in the 1911 election, was looking for alternative trade outlets. The first Canada–West Indies reciprocal trade agreement was signed in 1912 and, with modifications in 1920 and 1925, governed Canada–West Indies trade for the next half-century. As Peter K. Newman pointed out, however, it did not notably increase that trade,[17] and Canada's proportion of West Indian trade remained roughly constant over a long period of time, then declined in the fifties and sixties. One of the more lasting results of the trade agreement was the establishment of a regular shipping service, both freight and passenger; Canadian National Steamships' "Lady" passenger boats became something of a symbol of the more sentimental aspects of the Canada–West Indies relationship. In 1958, however, the Diefenbaker government used a Seafarers International Union strike on the Great Lakes as the occasion to let CN drop many of its unprofitable shipping services, the West Indies run among them.

In the area of investment, Canadian involvement in the Caribbean increased steadily. The Royal Bank of Canada and the Bank of Nova Scotia, which had both been in the region before the turn of the century, continued to spread until the late 1920s and then, after a pause for the Depression and the War, again in the 1950s and 1960s. They were joined after World War I by the Canadian Bank of Commerce and in the late 1950s by the Bank of Montreal, the latter through its participation with British interests in a joint venture called the Bank of London and Montreal. The insurance companies also continued to expand. Alcan's presence in British Guiana and later in Jamaica represented a significant new interest. These remain the largest Canadian investments, but Canadian firms have also been involved in tourism, forest industries, utilities and light manufacturing.

For many years the chief lobbyist for closer Canada–West Indies relations remained the Sun Life head, T. B. Macaulay.

Along with Lord Shaughnessy, who succeeded Van Horne as president of the CPR, Macaulay in 1911 founded the Canadian–West Indian League, whose self-proclaimed goal was "to promote friendship and commerce within the Empire."[18] Macaulay was president of the League until 1934, when he was succeeded by S. R. Noble, Inspector of Foreign Branches for the Royal Bank of Canada. One of the League's principal activities was the publication of the *Canada–West Indies Magazine,* which every month contained articles promoting trade and tourism and chatty items about the islands; although the League disbanded in 1950 the Magazine continued to come out under private auspices for another decade.

By 1960 only vestiges remained of the traditional Canada–West Indies relationship, based on declining trade, existing in the context of a fading British Empire and characterized by a dewy-eyed sense of general goodwill on both sides. The new relationship that had been developing was based on investment rather than trade, was part of an American- rather than a British-dominated network of ties, and had a much harder edge to it, leading eventually to conflict and to Canada's reputation among many West Indians as, not a benefactor and partner, but an exploiter.

Despite the rougher sailing, the relationship continued to have its proponents, and one of them was every bit as energetic, and as influential, as T. B. Macaulay had been in an earlier period. New Brunswick-born and American-raised, Ken Patrick was a senior engineer for RCA after World War II, then formed his own company, Canadian Aviation Electronics Ltd. But in 1958 he was bought out of CAE in a shareholders' dispute; wealthy, out of a job and still in his early forties, he spent some time sailing around the Caribbean. In his travels he made friends with many government officials in the region, and bought up some tempting pieces of real estate, which formed the basis for a company, Marigot Investments, named after the bay in St. Lucia on which some of its choice holdings lay.

As Patrick's properties grew, his influence grew even faster. A man with considerable powers of persuasion (a former associate described him as "the world's greatest salesman"), he began to devote that talent to promoting closer relations between Canada and the West Indies. He had the ear of most of the West Indian premiers and several Canadian cabinet ministers, and if one of the premiers wanted something from Canada he was less likely to get in touch with someone in Ottawa than to call Ken Patrick at his sumptuous home in Bedford, Quebec. Patrick recalls getting a phone call in the late sixties from the Premier of Antigua, who told him that the island's electronic power generator was about to run down and that if they didn't get emergency generators Antigua might have a rebellion on its hands. Patrick phoned the then-Minister of National Defence, Paul Hellyer, and "they got the generators. By ten o'clock the next morning the stuff was on the plane. Hellyer didn't even call External."

The staging of the Canada–Commonwealth Caribbean Conference, held in Ottawa in July 1966, was also partly due to Patrick's influence. One West Indian living in Canada recalls having to go through Patrick to gain access to the Eastern Caribbean premiers during the conference, and after it was over the premiers were whisked off to La Reserve, a hotel in the Laurentians then owned by Patrick, where they were joined by five Canadian cabinet ministers for two and a half days of informal discussions. The Conference itself focussed mostly on trade matters, and what appeared at the time to be important concessions were made by Canada. As things turned out, however, trade continued to decline, and a few years later Canada would no longer be a customer for West Indian sugar. The Conference made only minor adjustments in the areas of aid and immigration, which were about to assume a much larger role in the relationship.

The Conference also fell somewhat short of fulfilling the dreams of Ken Patrick. He had come to believe that the West Indies should remain politically independent but in close association with Canada. Specifically, he argued at every opportunity — and continues to argue — that Canada and the West Indies should be joined in a monetary and customs union. Such an arrangement would have directed to the Commonwealth Caribbean a larger proportion of the money spent on transporting Canadians to the tropical sun and on bringing the fruits grown in that sun to Canada — estimated by Patrick at between $1 and $2 billion a year. It also would have meant that this "sun-seeking dollar" would remain a Canadian dollar. Patrick said that this "wouldn't have implied any political arrangement." It would, however, have implied an economic arrangement similar to that between the United States and Puerto Rico or between France and Guadeloupe and Martinique. For Canada it would have meant assuming the responsibility for a dependent economy. For the West Indies it would have meant trading the opportunity to determine their economic future for more of the table scraps of metropolitan prosperity. For Ken Patrick it would have meant what he called "the little reward one gets for feeling you're doing the right thing" (and might also have guaranteed the success of Marigot Investments).

But whatever the merits of the argument, events soon made the possibility of its implementation more remote than ever, and in the process put an end to Patrick's nascent West Indian empire. Perhaps appropriately, these events began with one of the many pies that contained a Ken Patrick finger.

For some years, Patrick had been on the Board of Governors of Sir George Williams University, a plebeian, YMCA-affiliated institution in downtown Montreal. One of his particular interests was encouraging Sir George to accept more students from the West Indies.

In April of 1968, six black West Indian students went before the Dean of Students, Magnus Flynn, to accuse Perry Anderson, a biology professor at Sir George, of discriminating against black students in his grading, and demanded that a hearing committee be set up to investigate their charges. On the surface, there was little in that issue to cause a major crisis, and if that had been all that was involved it wouldn't have. The students' original charges were, in fact, never proved. But from the beginning all sides handled the Anderson matter as if aware that much larger questions were at stake. The Anderson affair and events arising out of it would, over the next two years, bury the pleasant but mindless platitudes about race relations in Canada, cast Canada in a more sombre light in the Caribbean and profoundly affect the politics of the Caribbean itself.

It took eight months and a student sit-in before the Sir George administration set up a committee to investigate the students' charges, and when the committee was finally established its composition was not acceptable to the students. It met anyway on January 26, 1969, before an audience of 1300, but with the black students refusing to participate. The next day all classes were cancelled to give the situation a chance to cool down — but it didn't. When the same committee attempted to meet again on January 29, students broke up the meeting and later occupied the ninth-floor computer centre in the massive Henry F. Hall Building.

The occupation dragged through one week and into a second. Finally on February 10 lawyers representing the students and the administration worked out a compromise. Acting Principal Douglass Burns Clarke, however, insisted on taking the agreement to the Sir George Williams Association of University Teachers, and the SGWAUT, in a bitchy mood over the affair and incensed at Clarke's suspension of Anderson a couple of days earlier, rejected it. That night the administration called the police into the computer centre where they examined the computer, exchanged banter with the students, and then withdrew. The tension that had been building up for a year was now at its highest point. Half an hour later the police, reinforced by Montreal's newly formed riot squad, returned, and in the melee that followed ninety-seven students were arrested, a fire started and the computer severely damaged.

Interest in the affair now spread from Canada to other countries, notably those of the Caribbean. In late February Roland Michener left on a state visit to the Commonwealth Caribbean, the first-ever official journey abroad by a Canadian Governor-General. When he reached the University of the West Indies campus at St. Augustine, Trinidad, his entry was blocked by a group of students led by UWI Student Guild President Geddes Granger, an advocate of Black Power and a master of the characteristic Trinidadian skill of oratory. The students were demonstrating their displeasure with the way the Sir George affair was being handled and specifically the discriminatory bail requirements placed on the arrested students — up to $14,000 for some of the thirty-eight black students, while none of the white students was required to post more than $5,000, and an impressive total of a quarter of a million dollars for the eighty-seven students charged.

All along the students felt the full weight of the law. Each of the eighty-seven was slapped with twelve serious charges, and the resolution of the 1044 charges took several years. But the most dramatic trial was the first one, which began January 19, 1970, and involved ten Trinidadian students who had been singled out as leaders of the occupation. The trial was watched in Trinidad with growing resentment, and Blair Humphrey, a Canadian University Service Overseas volunteer in Port of Spain, said later that "they think the trial was just a monkey trial."[19] On February 26, Geddes Granger, by now head of a Black Power organization called the National Joint Action Committee, led a march of 200 UWI students on the Canadian High Commission and the main branch of the Royal Bank of Canada in the heart of Port of Spain. Within a few days the hundreds had become thousands, and the object of their protest had widened from the Sir George trials to the continuing domination of Trinidad by outside powers despite political independence; Canada, and particularly the Canadian banks, remained a major focus. When the jury in Montreal found eight of the ten students guilty and imposed fines totalling $33,500 the Trinidad government undertook to pay the fines in an attempt to defuse what had become an explosive internal situation. But the demonstrations continued, culminating in April in a State of Emergency and a mutiny in the 700-man Trinidad Regiment.

Canadian reporters were sent scurrying down to Trinidad to write about the novelty of their country's being the target for anti-colonial demonstrations. Amid the marching, the jeering and the window-smashing, one reporter, C. Alexander Brown, a black Jamaican-born Canadian writing for *Maclean's* magazine, was able to find a bright note. In a dim, sleazy Port of Spain nightclub, a black girl sat down beside Brown and asked, "Care for some female company?"

"I bought her a drink," Brown wrote, "and she relaxed to chat. 'Do you meet a lot of Canadians?' Yes, she met many. A Canadian with whom she spent a night a few months ago had stayed up talking to her, sympathetically, saying she shouldn't be doing this and should study and make something of herself. He told her that he'd find a vocational school for her in Canada. He was married and they couldn't correspond, but he'd do what he could.

"That, of course, was salve his soul talk, the girl thought. But two months later she was contacted by a vocational school in Don Mills, Ontario. Now she was saving her money to go. 'Canadians,' she said, 'are very nice.' "[20]

5/Good Guy

.... No doubt, an easy tool,
Deferential, glad to be of use,
Politic, cautious, and meticulous;
Full of high sentence, but a bit obtuse;
At times, indeed, almost ridiculous —
Almost, at times, the Fool.

T.S. Eliot,
The Love Song of
J. Alfred Prufrock

Awareness of Canada's role abroad — indeed, that Canada even *has* a role abroad — has grown slowly. And it has never quite caught up to the growing consciousness of another, apparently contradictory aspect of the Canadian position: the continuing domination of Canada's own economy by foreign, and especially American, interests. How can Canada be an imperial power if it doesn't even run its own show?

In 1969, the same year that the Sir George affair forced Canadians to think, however briefly, about their race relations, both internal and international, the biennial convention of the New Democratic Party was enlivened by the emergence of a bushy-tailed, university-based group called the Waffle, which urged the party to launch a determined assault on American economic domination. In late 1970, a few months after the trial of the Trinidad Ten in Montreal had lit a fuse in the defendants' homeland, a group of liberal Canadians headed by former Finance Minister Walter Gordon was forming the Committee for an Independent Canada to act as a nationalist pressure group on the government.

Since then there have been attempts to resolve this contradiction. Some nationalists, such as Liberal cabinet minister Alastair Gillespie, take the position that Canada's involvement abroad is a good thing, and that the way for Canada to win its economic independence is to develop its own multinationals that can compete

77

with those based in the United States, Europe and Japan. Other, more left-inclined nationalists argue that Canadian interests abroad are insignificant in comparison with foreign interests in Canada and that to all intents Canada can be considered simply an exploited colony. Another group of leftists sees Canada's activities abroad as not essentially different from those of the United States and other major imperial powers and speaks of "Canadian imperialism". Still others, not fully satisfied with either side of the argument, introduce more finely tuned concepts such as "sub-imperialism", "secondary imperialism" and "transferred dependency".

Writing in the generally nationalist journal *This Magazine* in 1975, Toronto researchers Tim Draimin and Jamie Swift spoke of the need "to get away from static arguments which are predetermined to see this country *either* as a colony *or* as an imperialist power. We believe that it is important for Canadians to investigate in which ways Canada relates to imperialism. However, such an investigation necessitates a perspective which sees imperialism as a complex process rather than a 'hierarchical scale' upon which relations are neatly 'arranged'."[1]

There is much in the pattern of Canadian involvement in the West Indies to indicate that it is overly simplistic to view Canada strictly as a colony, but little to suggest that it is an imperial power on its own. We have seen that Canadian relations with the West Indies grew up within the British empire, and that both British and American policies were major determinants of the progress of those relations. We shall see in the modern era examples of a Canadian firm active in the West Indies that is itself a subsidiary of an American company, a Canadian firm that holds its West Indian interests as a franchise from an American firm, a Canadian aid program that propagates a distinctly American view of how society functions and a giant Canadian company that gets political support from the American government.

In fact, it is arguable that, far from being in contradiction, the domination of Canada by foreign interests and Canada's own activities abroad are the two sides of the same coin. For as Draimin and Swift suggested, imperialism is a complex system and

Canada's position in it is itself complex. To the extent that Canada is an imperial power, it is so only within this wider imperial system, in which certain activities are allocated to it. And to the extent that it is a colony it is a privileged one, which gets to share in the fruits of its colonizer's adventures in less fortunate countries.

Perhaps the most striking characteristic of Canadian involvement abroad is its overwhelmingly economic nature. Writers on imperialism from V.I. Lenin to Eric Williams have emphasized its economic base, but they have also noted its political, social, cultural and, perhaps most important of all, military ramifications. Canadian corporations abroad are supported by the power of the Canadian state far less than corporations based in the United States or other imperial centres are supported by the state apparatus of their home countries. And the state agencies in Canada that do offer assistance to Canadian business in its foreign dealings are themselves economic in nature — the Canadian International Development Agency, the Export Development Corporation, the Department of Industry, Trade and Commerce.

The Department of National Defence is something of a vestigial organ, so closely tied to the Pentagon as to be little more than a minor branch of it. As for the Department of External Affairs, even the bureaucrats within it aren't quite sure what it does. While most writing coming out of Ottawa gives the impression that it is concealing something, the particularly vacuous quality of almost all discussions of foreign policy suggests that there is nothing to read even between the lines. Recent Secretaries of State for External Affairs have generally been politicians nearing the end of their careers who deserved a reward after serving their government in more immediately useful portfolios. Allan MacEachen had to be removed from the position because he was too valuable elsewhere. After all, does Canada really need a foreign policy? And if it had a foreign policy, what would Canada do with it?

Initially, Draimin and Swift used the term "sub-imperialism" to describe Canada's situation; the term was coined by the Brazilian sociologist Ruy Mauro Marini to describe his own country and is defined as "the form which dependent capitalism assumes upon

79

reaching the stage of monopolies and finance capital."[2] But, while this definition applies to Canada, other aspects of Marini's scheme, notably an increase in military expenditures and militarization of society which he saw as an essential feature of sub-imperialism, do not. (Draimin and Swift later adopted the term 'transferred dependency' as a better handle for the Canadian case.) Canada's defence expenditures declined from 3.75 per cent of its Gross National Product in 1963 to 2.04 per cent in 1973. Among western countries, only four — Ireland, Luxembourg, Switzerland and Austria — had a lower defence budget as a proportion of GNP in 1973, while the rate of decline of Canada's budget was the most precipitous in the world, except for those of Luxembourg, Haiti, the Dominican Republic and Mauritania.[3]

In 1963, a statement by a leading American general that Canada was not fulfilling its military commitments launched a national crisis and brought down the Diefenbaker government. By 1975 such statements were so commonplace, and so obviously true, that they caused hardly a ripple. In September of that year James Schlesinger, then American Secretary of Defense, spoke to an Ottawa news conference, just as Gen. Lauris Norstad had twelve and a half years earlier. "Canada's effort does indeed rank low," said Schlesinger. "I hope there's no further diminution in the overall capacity and contribution." He reiterated his belief in the need for a strong NATO force in Europe, adding that "unless we are prepared to defend parts of the world other than North America, we'd soon have nothing left to defend except North America."[4]

Canadian officials denied that the Canadian military contribution to NATO was below par, but it was perhaps no concidence that the long-delayed decision to replace the Forces' fleet of 32 Argus reconnaissance aircraft was announced a couple of months after Schlesinger's statement. Its choice of the Lockheed P-3 corresponded to American wishes as expressed in the "shopping list" of grievances against Canada leaked by the Nixon adminstration to the Chicago *Tribune* in 1971, and it briefly succeeded in silencing Canada's NATO critics.

But the deal with Lockheed later came unstuck as a result of the company's own questionable financial standing and Ottawa's unwillingness to commit any additional resources to financing the purchase of the plane, and finally went through only in modified form. In May 1976 the American ambassador to Canada, Thomas Enders, while declaring himself heartened by the Lockheed deal, once again criticized the low level of Canadian military spending.[5]

The Canadian military presence in the Third World is even more tenuous. Canada maintains a military assistance program for Third World countries, with a total budget of $440,000 a year, which consists of providing training in Canada for officers from the recipient countries. There are also two Canadian military training advisers abroad, one in Ghana and one in Tanzania, which along with Jamaica are the only countries that really take a serious interest in the program. Two other Commonwealth Caribbean countries, Guyana and Trinidad and Tobago, participate on a smaller scale.

Canada got involved in the military assistance business because Ghana was looking for a country with a clean international image to help develop its armed forces in the early sixties. The program was geared to countries that had recently gained their independence from Britain and even now most of the participants are Commonwealth countries. Although only the most rudimentary questions about the political nature of the recipient regimes and what they use their armed forces for are asked, one civil servant concerned with the program said that "Canada doesn't want to upset anyone or create trouble between neighbours." He added that the military assistance scheme is "more akin to a public relations program than any lofty program of foreign policy," and called it "a nice, tidy little project. It just smells good and it's protected by its very size. We leave it to other big countries to get into political trouble and they sure do."

As part of the agreement with Jamaica, Canadian troops are allowed to train on Jamaican soil, and beginning in 1970 the Canadian Forces undertook three annual battalion-scale exercises in jungle warfare there. This sent visions of Canadian troops being prepared to protect Alcan and the Royal Bank dancing before the eyes of both Canadian and West Indian radicals, but when budgets at National Defence were cut in 1973 the Nimrod Caper exercise, for so it was called, was one of the casualties. The one area of military activity in which Canada is seriously involved on a world scale is the production and sale of arms. This constitutes a multimillion-dollar annual market for Canadian business (or at least Canadian-located business, since many defence contractors in Canada are American-owned) and is assisted by a variety of federal government programs. But, wrote Ernie Regehr in his book on the Canadian arms industry, "Canadian arms sales abroad reveal no over-all political design. With the exception of regular sales to traditional allies and restrictions on sales to certain 'sensitive' areas, Canadian military products are sold simply to the highest bidder. The motive is profit, purely and simply."[6]

Canadian foreign policy is often suspected of serving similar goals. When Mitchell Sharp was External Affairs Minister, links were drawn between Canada's friendliness toward the Brazilian military junta and the interests of Brascan Ltd., a Canadian-based multinational that has large holdings in Brazil and of which Sharp was once vice-president. In a 1973 article in the *Last Post*, a Toronto group called Project Brazil said that "it is clear that [Sharp] is responsible for the continuation and preservation of a foreign policy dictated by the interests of a specific commercial sector *vis à vis* one country. As long as Mitchell Sharp runs our foreign policy, and Alastair Gillespie encourages the interests of multinationals like Brascan in industry, trade and commerce, Ottawa's foreign policy towards Brazil will remain what it is today: Brascan's foreign policy."[7]

The government itself, in its 1970 White Paper, *Foreign Policy for Canadians,* included "fostering economic growth" among the basic aims of Canada's foreign policy. This, said the government, "embraces a wide range of economic, commercial and financial objectives in the foreign field," including "promotion of exports," "trade and tariff agreements" and "loans and investments."[8]

Canada's very lack of an easily definable position on the world stage and its consequent appearance of innocence in international affairs have their economic uses. Tim Draimin and Jamie Swift wrote that Canada

> acts through its extensive investments in both Latin America and the Caribbean, laundering American capital through Canadian-based multinational corporations. In a continent which has a long-standing anti-Yankee tradition, the "Canadian" front (Bras*can*, Al*can*) and low profile (has Canada ever landed Marines in Latin America?) help to mystify Latin American sentiment about the actual bonds of dependency and control which continue to exist. Nations, conscious of their overriding dependency upon the U.S., see the diversification towards foreign investment from other countries as a way of altering that deleterious primary relationship. By welcoming Canadian capital as if it is very different from American capital, they become victims of covert mechanisms which camouflage U.S. control of the major Canadian multinationals.[9]

Most of the large multinationals that are thought of as Canadian are, at best, ambiguously so. Canadian stock ownership in some of the larger ones has gone above fifty per cent in the last few years, but that figure does not have the magic properties that are sometimes attributed to it. In a company where ownership is widely dispersed, control can reside in a relatively small holding of stock. Marsh Cooper, president of Falconbridge Nickel, roughly eighty per cent of whose stock is owned in Canada, has been quoted as saying, "Howard Keck and I, in that order, run Falconbridge";[10] the reference is to the Texas millionaire who owns the controlling block of shares. Inco, whose chief officers and political connections are American rather than Canadian, did not stop being run from its New York head office when its Canadian ownership went above fifty per cent. Alcan, wherever its control lies, is part of a North American aluminum cartel that shows an impressive community of interest.

There is a significant exception to this general pattern. The five big Canadian banks — Royal Bank of Canada, Canadian Imperial Bank of Commerce, Bank of Montreal, Bank of Nova Scotia and Toronto-Dominion Bank — are large institutions: by any standard of measurement, they are all well within the world's top hundred

83

banks.[11] The scope of their operations is global. And they are also unquestionably Canadian.

Banking, and related activities such as insurance, have long been an area of specialization for the Canadian capitalist class. It was these mercantile capitalists who formed the vanguard of Canadian expansion abroad. The Canadian banks spread through the United States, Europe, Asia, and above all the Caribbean and Latin America. There are few more pervasive institutions in the Caribbean region than the Royal Bank of Canada, which has branches in Haiti, the Dominican Republic, Puerto Rico, Guadeloupe, Martinique, Venezuela and Colombia as well as almost all the Commonwealth territories. The Royal was also the largest bank in Cuba before the revolution, and when the Castro government expropriated the banks and other major foreign enterprises in 1960 the Royal and the Bank of Nova Scotia were exempted — another demonstration of the advantage of being Canadian when operating in a touchy foreign country. An agreement was subsequently reached between the banks and the government and they were purchased for their book value.[12]

One of the advantages Canadian banks have enjoyed is federal banking legislation that has permitted the growth of coast-to-coast banks (unlike American law which restricts banks to operating in a single state) while at the same time protecting them from foreign competition. Recently, however, the contradiction between the free operation of Canadian banks abroad and the restrictions on foreign banks in Canada has become difficult to sustain, and it is significant that, given the choice, Canadian bankers have by and large opted for free competition, all around. This choice was finally formalized into government policy with the White Paper on Banking Legislation of August 1976,[13] which proposed allowing foreign banks to set up shop in Canada and was greeted with a chorus of cheers from Canadian bankers, whose minds were not far from their own foreign interests.

It is not extraordinary that Canada's foreign policy is primarily economic in nature, especially in an era when the most important questions of international relations not only have economic roots but are, for the most part, *explicitly* economic. While in the 1950s a political columnist could be expected on a slow news day to speculate about the possibility of America's going to war with the Russians to wipe out Godless Communism, in the 1970s he would be more likely to write about the possibility of America's going to war with the Arabs to get its hands on their oil. Nations are ranked as friendly or unfriendly (by all sides) less on the basis of their votes at the United Nations or what alliances they do or don't belong to than by what resources they have and what they propose to do with them.

If Canada's profession of an economic element in its foreign policy is unremarkable, the same cannot be said for its particular reponse to the new power of resource-producing countries. Canada is, after all, itself one of the most important producers of raw materials in the world. It exports such crucial industrial materials as iron ore, nickel and copper, as well as oil and gas. Nevertheless, in the developing conflict between countries that export raw materials and countries that import them, Canada has identified completely with the importing nations. Ballad-singer John Allan Cameron expressed it well when he sang:

> Canada produces 2,000,000 barrels of oil a day
> And consumes 1,760,000:
> According to government arithmetic
> This is known as a shortage.[14]

A standard radical and humanitarian critique of Canadian foreign policy is that Canada never gives up a commercial opportunity for a principle, that whenever there is a conflict between the dictates of "fostering economic growth" and those of "promoting social justice" — another of the declared goals of Canadian foreign policy — economic growth comes out on top. But Canada's diffidence in taking advantage of its position as a raw-material producer suggests something else: that there are times when Canadian policy will correspond neither to principle nor to strict economic logic. The other stated policy goals — "safeguarding sovereignty and independence," "working for peace and security," "enhancing the quality of life" and "ensuring a harmonious natural environment"[15] — aren't much help either. To conclude that on

85

many important questions Canada simply doesn't have an independent foreign policy, and in fact is in no position to have an independent foreign policy, is to exaggerate the case only slightly.

Part of the difficulty is a confusion about what is meant by "Canada". The oil question has brought out more clearly than before the relation between government policy and the needs of large corporations that are more often than not foreign owned and whose interests in any case have at best a casual relationship to those of the population at large. While a petroleum policy that puts Canada's needs first is without much doubt a good thing for most Canadians, it is arguably not a good thing for Exxon or Gulf. Similarly, whatever the merits of Canadian membership in an iron ore producers' body, such a proposition is unlikely to be looked upon favourably by the American steel giants that own the Iron Ore Company of Canada and Quebec Cartier Mining. These same contradictions face countries such as Libya and Venezuela, Jamaica and Guyana, but these countries, all with much less inherent bargaining power *vis à vis* the multinationals than Canada, have nevertheless advanced further in dealing with them.

For another element of Canada's particular position is historical and psychological. Canadians prefer to identify with the gentle and civilized Americans, English, Germans and Dutch who people the industrialized countries, rather than with the uncouth blacks, Asians and Arabs of the Third World. Canada may be a raw material exporter, but it is also wealthy, relatively industrialized and white. There was at one point some hope that this combination of circumstances would allow Canada to bridge the gap between the two groups of increasingly hostile countries but this has not come to pass. When Prime Minister Pierre Trudeau was in Port of Spain on a brief tour of the Eastern Caribbean before going to the Commonwealth Conference in Jamaica in April 1975, he was greeted by a Trinidad *Express* headline that said "Trudeau — friend of the Third World."[16] During the Conference itself, however, little happened to justify the *Express's* enthusiasm. Although one External Affairs official described Canada as having played a "pretty balanced role," Bruce Garvey of the Toronto *Star* saw Trudeau as the Conference's "responsible and at times grouchy guru" who

86

emerged as "probably the most conservative head of state among the thirty-three who attended." Trudeau, wrote Garvey:

> bluntly told the Third World producers their plans to resort to commodity cartels similar to the Arabs' oil monopoly were probably impossible to maintain and a bit of a hollow threat anyway. Canada produces too, he warned, and we would probably reap more benefit than most of the poorer nations .... Trudeau also said he didn't see much point in a transfer of wealth to the Third World if it was only to help feed "ever-increasing numbers of hungry children."[17]

If there was little in Trudeau's statements to bolster Canada's cherished image as an international good guy, he was at least commendably direct, which represents something of a departure in Canadian foreign policy statements. In the case of the Canada–West Indies relationship, the naive and good-hearted sentiments that are its traditional expression survive long after events have passed them by. A Canadian Senate Committee report of 1970 on Canada–Caribbean relations said that "Canada should decide to manifest special concern for the area and such a policy would be valid, valuable and in the best interest of all concerned .... The Committee recommends that Canadian policy, while placing increased value on relations with all countries of the area, continue to reflect this country's special links with the Commonwealth countries of the region."[18] In 1975 an External Affairs official said that "the Commonwealth Caribbean continues to occupy an important part in our perception of our role abroad." This official, who had been in the Caribbean division for a year and was acting head of the division at the time he was interviewed, had never been to the region.

An instructive comparison is with the United States, which has no trouble seeing its foreign policy, in the Caribbean and elsewhere, in terms of its own interests, economic, political and strategic. Canadian officials will almost never talk in these terms. The United States has a clearly enunciated attitude toward takeovers of its companies by foreign governments, outlined in 1972 by former President Nixon.[19] Canada has no such clear-cut policy. Another instructive comparison is with Australia under the Labour government of Gough Whitlam (1972–75), which joined nascent bauxite

87

and iron ore cartels, set up to determine the prices of those materials and protect the interests of countries producing them. Canada, although also a major iron ore producer, refused to have anything to do with the iron ore group.

But there are signs that Canada's deference to the United States in foreign policy, abdication of any explicit world role, and complete indentification with the industrialized west may be changing. It was no accident that a visit to Cuba was the centrepiece of Trudeau's tour of Latin America in January 1976, the first by a Canadian Prime Minister. While Canada's overtures to China and the Soviet Union in the early seventies turned out to be merely preludes to American detente with those countries, closer relations with Cuba appear to constitute a more genuinely Canadian diplomatic initiative.

Unlike every other Western Hemisphere country except Mexico, Canada never went along with the American-led diplomatic boycott and economic blockade of Cuba. As a result Canada has built up a substantial trade with Cuba, amounting to $145 million on the export side, nine times what it was in the last year of Cuba's old regime, 1958.[20] In 1974, MLW–Worthington, the Montreal subsidiary of an American company, completed a sale of railway engines to Cuba with Canadian government support and despite provisions of the U.S. Trading with the Enemy Act prohibiting such a sale.

Canada has also been a less than completely reliable ally of the United States in the intricate international negotiations over the law of the sea. In fact as the conferences have dragged on it has moved closer and closer to the position of the seventy-seven Third World countries working to broaden the rights of coastal states and ensure strong international regulation of deep-sea resource exploitation. The Americans have been muttering darkly about the "seventy-seven plus one."

Whether these are aberrations or represent the beginnings of a whole new direction in Canadian foreign policy remains to be seen. If there is a new direction, however, it has yet to manifest itself in any significant way in Canada's relations with the Commonwealth Caribbean.

6/Rent-a-country

The well-known motto which appears under the coat-of-arms of the colony — *Expulsis piratis commercia restituta* — has a mocking sound under present conditions, and the sober investor, as well as the regulatory authorities whose business it is to inform and protect him, must take into account the fact that the pirates are still much in evidence on these islands, and have penetrated into every corner of their life and polity.

The Hon. S. H. S. Hughes,
Report of the Royal Commission on
Atlantic Acceptance Corporation, 1969

When the Royal Bank of Canada established a branch in Nassau, the capital of the Bahamas, in 1908, there was only one other bank in the colony, the Bank of Nassau. This bank's operations were sufficiently precarious that an embezzlement on the part of its manager caused it to suspend payment in 1916. The next year the Royal bought its assets for some £39,000 and from then until after World War II the Royal was the only bank in the Bahamas. This in itself was not the cause of any particular concern. The colony was poor and devoid of natural resources and its population was barely 50,000. More banks were hardly its most conspicuous need.

But by 1975 there would be no fewer than 168 fully active financial institutions in the Bahamas, and international bankers would be a common sight in Nassau, white and North American like the tourists who outnumbered them by perhaps a hundred to one, but distinguishable from the tourists by their suits and ties and the purposeful air with which they strode down Bay Street, Nassau's main thoroughfare. Little of the new banking bustle had anything to do with domestic requirements: in fact only nine of the 168 banks were even licensed to do domestic business.

The rest of the banking business, by far the larger portion, consisted of activities for which the Bahamas is, because of its history, unusually well suited. For the Bahamas has developed along very different lines from the rest of the Caribbean — it is often not even

89

considered part of the Caribbean, although it is not really part of anything else either. There has been no oil or bauxite in the Bahamas to attract multinational corporations, and there was no sugar industry until 1968. Slavery on a large scale only began with the arrival of the defeated Loyalists from the mainland in the 1780s. Instead, the staples of the Bahamian economy have been piracy, wrecking, gun running, bootlegging, tourism, gambling, real estate speculation, and international banking. "There has always," said one Bahamian civil servant, "been some sort of racket."

When the colony was first settled it quickly became a pirate centre and remained so until an early eighteenth-century governor named Woodes Rogers cleaned the pirates out and gave the Bahamas its uplifting motto: "With the pirates expelled, commerce is restored." After this Bahamians turned their attention to wrecking, to which they added an interesting fillip not recorded in the Turks and Caicos Islands or other places where this occupation was practised. While others waited for ships to run aground before plundering them, the Bahamian wreckers were reluctant to leave so much to chance: they directed ships toward the shoals, just to make sure. During the American Civil War the Bahamas struck it rich by turning itself into a base for running the Union blockade of the Confederacy. The Eighteenth Amendment in the United States ushered in another period of prosperity as the Bahamas, like Canada, became a rum-running centre. Between these sporadic booms there were long stretches of poverty.

There is much talk in the Bahamas about how much the islands have changed in the last two generations, and of course they have. But the endeavours that are responsible for the current era of prosperity are all within the Bahamian tradition. Their success has been largely due to the efforts of two enterprising Bahamians, both from the white elite that until 1967 ran the colony in a manner reminiscent of Family Compact days in Canada. One, Sir Harold Christie, was by all accounts one of the best of that breed and the other, Sir Stafford Sands, was close to being the worst, but there was little difference in the visions they had for their country. Both men left substantial fortunes at their deaths.

Harold Christie opened his real estate agency on Bay Street in 1922. It was his idea that if its assets were properly promoted the Bahamas could be turned into a haven for the world's rich and some of the locals could live off the crumbs. These assets were considerable. Not only is there no winter in the Bahamas but there is also no personal income tax, no corporate tax, no inheritance tax and no sales tax. There is a property tax of sorts but it is not onerous and even in the 1970s contributes less than $2 million a year to the public coffers.[1] Nevertheless, attracting a class of people whose natural habitat was London, New York and the Riviera to a small, struggling island colony was a sufficiently improbable proposition that it took all of Christie's persistence and persuasiveness and the right combination of circumstances to realize it.

In 1937 he landed a bigger catch than he could have dared to hope for. This was Harry Oakes, at that time the richest man in Canada. Oakes had been born in genteel circumstances in Maine sixty-two years earlier and had determined early in life that he would make a fortune. He went to the Klondike in 1898, later following the trail of gold to Alaska, the Philippines, Australia, the Belgian Congo, California's Death Valley, and finally northern Ontario. His lonely search lasted fourteen years, and left the once-effete Yankee tough, self-centred and crude. In northern Ontario he brought in the gold mine he had been looking for, and then another one. He became wealthy beyond his dreams, a legend in the gold-mining fraternity and, more or less by accident, a citizen of Canada.

But it was not in Oakes's nature to enjoy the wealth he had gained. He became increasingly suspicious of everybody around him, and Harold Christie, who became his closest friend, would later say of him, "He just can't understand anybody who isn't trying to get something out of him. He's very funny that way. If he thinks you are, it makes him mad, but when he sees you aren't, it makes him even madder."[2] His enemies grew in number, and the more he was disliked, the more distrustful he became. In the 1930s his rage began to focus on one specific evil: taxes, and particularly the burdensome mining taxes imposed by Prime Minister R. B.

Bennett, which Oakes suspected were directed expressly at him. In Palm Beach, Florida, where Oakes maintained one of his numerous residences, he met Harold Christie, whose song of the tax-free Bahamas had now finally found an appreciative audience. As easily as he had adopted Canada as his home Oakes abandoned it in favour of the Bahamas.

Oakes never fit into the respectable, provincial, exclusive society of Nassau. He even preferred the company of the local blacks to that of the narrow and colonial whites. He distressed proper Bahamians by swaggering down Bay Street in his prospector's outfit. Through Christie he bought up substantial chunks of New Providence Island — at the time the only one in the Bahamas with more than a scattering of people — and had houses built. Once a lover of trees, he now amused himself by levelling the trees on his properties. According to legend he was once snubbed by a waiter in the British Colonial Hotel, the largest in Nassau, so the next day he bought the hotel and fired the offending waiter. And the hated name could still arouse the old passions. "Bennett!" he shouted to a visiting Canadian reporter, Gregory Clark. "Stalin takes it all. Bennett takes all but fifteen per cent. The difference between them is fifteen per cent. Bennett wouldn't like to hear it put that way, would he?"[3]

Sometime during the night of July 7, 1943, Harry Oakes, Sir Harry by now, was murdered in his Westbourne residence just outside Nassau. Christie, who had spent the night at Westbourne, as he often did, came into Oakes's bedroom the next morning to wake up his friend and found the body, burnt and with its head battered. As rumours of the murder spread, the Duke of Windsor, exiled to Nassau as Governor of the Bahamas to keep him out of trouble in Europe, clamped a news blackout on it. He also called in a Miami detective of his acquaintance, Edward Melchen, to deal with the case. By the next day Melchen and a Miami Police fingerprint expert he brought with him, James Otto Barker, had found their man: Marie Alfred Fouquereaux de Marigny, a member of the minor colonial nobility of Mauritius who had come to Nassau and married Oakes's adolescent daughter against her parents' will, was arrested and charged with the murder of his father-in-law.

De Marigny was eventually acquitted, after a long and highly publicized trial in which it was found that the fingerprint evidence that Barker had constructed could have been fabricated. The murder was never solved, at least partly because much of the evidence that might have led to a solution was destroyed in the course of building the case against de Marigny, and many questions surrounding the case remain unanswered. There are some in Nassau who still believe de Marigny was guilty, despite the verdict. Others have speculated that the murder was a contract job planned from Miami, and one writer, Marshall Houts, quoted unnamed sources as having told him that the contract was taken out by Meyer Lansky, the Miami underworld king, because Oakes was opposed to allowing him to open a gambling casino in the Bahamas.[4] It is an interesting theory but Houts does not even come close to proving it. Perhaps the key question is why Barker built a case against de Marigny that was at best shoddy, and at worst dishonest. Was he incompetent? Did he simply want to nail a suspect, any suspect? Or was he trying to cover up for somebody?

The only sure thing is that Oakes did have enemies, many of whom were not sorry to see him dead. Afterward, de Marigny was stopped in Toronto by an old miner who said, "Did you kill Sir Harry Oakes?" De Marigny said he had not. "Well, that's what I call a pity," said the miner. "I was always sure you did, and I looked forward to meeting you because I wanted to shake you by the hand."[5]

For Harold Christie, the death of Oakes was only a temporary setback. After the war he became acquainted with another Canadian, a brewery tycoon named Edward Plunkett Taylor, and tried to convince him of the merits of a swampy, uninhabited area called Lyford Cay at the other end of New Providence Island from Nassau. Lyford Cay was partly owned by the Oakes estate, with the rest owned by Christie himself, and it played an important part in the promoter's plans. "I remember him taking me over there in 1947," said Col. Oakley Bidwell, who now does public relations for the Lyford Cay Co., "and telling me about the possibilities of the place. He showed me where the golf course would be, where the tennis courts would be. All I could see was a cloud of mosquitoes

— I was slapping at mosquitoes and wishing we could get back. But everything he said has come to be."

Christie first went to work on Taylor in 1951 and, said Col. Bidwell, "it took him five years of going after Mr. Taylor until he got enthused, but once he did you couldn't stop him." It was Taylor who turned Lyford Cay into a physical realization of the tax-haven status of the Bahamas. He and his friends, eager as they are to escape taxes, are also accustomed to living in a certain style, and Lyford Cay allows them to do precisely that. New members of the Lyford Cay Club have to be accepted by their peers but once they are they may buy a lot on the site for $35,000 to $100,000 and build on it; they are entitled to the use of the golf, tennis, sailing and other recreational facilities; and they have the exclusive right to get past the guard stationed at the gate to keep Bahamians and other undesirables out.

This exclusivity is perhaps the most controversial aspect of Lyford Cay. "People in the government sometimes sound off about it," said Col. Bidwell, "but it's pure politics. After all, they're all honorary members of the Club. We try to explain patiently that a private club is an extension of a man's right to a private home." He was vehement about the value of Lyford Cay to the Bahamas. "There's a wholesome respect for the dollars they have put in," he said. "The Lyford Cay members have poured $100 million into the economy. The 140 houses on the site were all built by Bahamian labour. All the materials for the houses had Bahamian duty paid on them, and in fact everything the residents bring in has Bahamian duty paid on it."

Among the Canadian members of the Lyford Cay Club are Earle McLaughlin, chairman and president of the Royal Bank of Canada, Peter Nesbitt Thomson of Power Corporation, Fraser Elliott and Heward Stikeman of the prestigious law firm of Stikeman, Elliott, Robarts and Bowman; Donald Fleming, who after being defeated for the leadership of the Progressive Conservative Party in 1967 took a position with the Bank of Nova Scotia as general counsel for its Caribbean operations, based in Nassau; and Steve Roman, the uranium multimillionaire whom voters in the suburban Toronto riding of York North have twice declined to elect as their representative in the House of Commons. Roman's Lyford Cay house, which cost him a million dollars to build, is the most lavish in the development. It was all completed except for the landscaping, when one night a barge from Florida docked at Lyford Cay and by the next morning the entire generous expanse of Roman's grounds was neatly planted with trees, shrubs, grass and flowers.

Taylor himself is now a permanent resident of Lyford Cay and actively directs his Bahamian interests, which include the Lyford Cay Club, the Lyford Cay Company, which owns the unsold land on the site, and the New Providence Development Company, which is developing two housing projects near the Lyford Cay site and owns a total of five thousand acres of land on New Providence, along with a dairy, a construction materials factory, a hotel and golf club, a tree and plant nursery and a large portion of the New Providence water system. He has also embarked on a new international venture, International Housing Ltd., which he bought from Daniel K. Ludwig, the shipping magnate who, after the deaths of H. L. Hunt, Aristotle Onassis, Howard Hughes and J. Paul Getty, succeeded to the title of the world's richest man.[6] Through International Housing, Taylor hopes to sell low-cost houses built with poured concrete and Meccano-like aluminum forms to the teeming millions of the Third World. In addition, he is chairman of the board of a Nassau-based subsidiary of the Royal Bank, Royal Bank of Canada International Ltd., and according to a senior employee of Royal Bank International, rarely misses a board meeting. In March 1975, the Bahamas Chamber of Commerce named Taylor a Distinguished Citizen for his service to the community through business.[7]

Canadians have also been involved in the other mainstays of the modern Bahamian economy: tourism, gambling, and international finance. The principal Bahamian architect of these activities was Sir Stafford Sands, a large, obese man with a demeanour to match his physique. He sustained contradictions at which weaker men would have balked. In 1964, while Minister of Finance of the Bahamas, he co-authored with New York tax expert Sidney R. Pine a book called *Tax Ideas,* which detailed how Americans

95

could avoid taxes by setting up shop in the Bahamas. In 1966, while still Minister of Finance, he was appointed a director of the Royal Bank of Canada.

But his real passion was tourism. Sir Stafford looked at everything in terms of its possible effect on the tourist trade. When the Bahamas switched from pounds, shillings and pence to decimal currency in 1965, there was some discussion of what the best name for the new currency would be. But there was no doubt in Sir Stafford's mind. "Imagine what an American tourist would say if an article cost, say, ten conchs or five wahoos," he told the Chamber of Commerce. "Immediately he'd ask, 'How much is that in real money?' The dollar is the only logical and sensible name for the new currency."[8] But just to give Bahamian money a soupçon of exotic flavour, Sir Stafford introduced a diamond–shaped 15-cent piece and a three-dollar bill. There were 45,371 tourists in the Bahamas in 1950, the year Sir Stafford took over the Development Board (later the Ministry of Tourism), and 915,273 in 1967, the year he left office.[9]

The growth of Bahamian tourism was largely the result of a high-pressure promotional campaign — it was only after the election of Lynden Pindling that the government of the Bahamas began to spend more on health and education each year than it did on tourist promotion[10] — but Sir Stafford presided over improvements to the physical plant as well, the most important of which were the creation of Freeport and the introduction of casino gambling. Freeport, now the second largest town in the Bahamas, did not exist in 1955, the year the Bahamian government granted 50,-000 acres of land around Hawksbill Creek on Grand Bahama island, with an option on a further 50,000 acres, to a company called the Grand Bahama Port Authority. The head of the Port Authority was Wallace Groves, a Virginian who had done time for mail fraud in the early 1940s. Grand Bahama became Groves' personal empire, but it also attracted a variety of other promoters who smelled the possibility of wealth. One of these was Louis Chesler.

Lou Chesler grew up in Peterborough, Ontario, and by the time he was a student at the University of Toronto in the 1930s the stock market was already his main activity. He quickly dropped out of school and joined a brokerage firm, and before long he branched out and got involved in mining ventures, in which he made and lost millions. But eventually he became associated with Thayer Lindsley, the mining lord whose far-flung interests included Falconbridge Nickel, and put his future on a more solid basis. Soon he had his own underwriting and investment company, Alan H. Investments, which he sold in 1955 for $4 million, the better to turn his attention to the United States, where he developed interests in everything from Florida real estate to Hollywood movies and political connections that included Robert Anderson, the Texas oil lobbyist who became Dwight Eisenhower's Secretary of the Treasury.

According to a *Wall Street Journal* profile of him in 1964:

> Mr. Chesler has perhaps even better contacts with the Democrats. A scene that occurred one summer day in 1960, a few weeks before the Democratic National Convention, illustrates the point: Mr. Chesler was standing on the sidewalk with a small group of friends when a limousine drew up and parked. In the back seat sat one of the contenders for the Democratic Presidential nomination. Mr. Chesler peeled off five $1,000 bills, stuffed them in the breast pocket of the politician's suit and, calling him by his first name, said: "This is for the convention."[11]

Among the other acquaintances Chesler developed were members of the underworld, including associates of Meyer Lansky, the Miami-based gambling boss who has been a major figure in the American underworld for forty years. These connections would play an important role in Chesler's entry into the Bahamas.

When Chesler came on the scene in 1961, the development of Grand Bahama, although well advanced, had not lived up to Groves' expectations. The Hawksbill Creek Agreement, drawn up by Sir Stafford, had given the Port Authority what a later commission of inquiry described as "almost feudal powers"[12] — including control of immigration — and in return the Authority undertook to dredge a deep-water harbour at the mouth of Hawksbill Creek and create an industrial complex based on the absence of taxes and a special exemption from customs duty (the Bahamian government's only significant source of revenue) for everything except

97

consumer goods. By 1960 the harbour had been dredged with the help of Daniel K. Ludwig, who was rumoured to be Groves' shadowy backer, but only one industry of any size, the Freeport Bunkering Company, had been started, the lack of residential and entertainment facilities being cited as the main difficulty in attracting investors. That was where Chesler came in.

Chesler and Groves formed the Grand Bahama Development Company in 1961 to undertake the residential and tourist development of 100,000 acres of the island. Chesler had come to Groves' attention through his notable success in the Florida real-estate market, but it turned out he had other things to offer as well. It was, Groves told the 1967 commission of inquiry into gambling in the Bahamas, Chesler's idea to open a casino in Freeport. "Chesler talked about it a lot," said Groves. "He was a very big talker."[13]

Before 1959, the offshore gambling haven of the American mob had been Cuba, where a long-standing agreement between Meyer Lansky and Fulgencio Batista had allowed the former and his cronies to ply their trade unmolested while keeping the latter in power and making him rich. On the last night of 1958, as Batista fled to the Dominican Republic in fear of Fidel Castro's advancing guerrilla forces, another plane carried Lansky from Havana to Florida. Reporting on the Bahamas gambling inquiry nine years later, Boyce Richardson of the Montreal *Star* said that "the only man who comes well out of the report is Fidel Castro, who fired all the gamblers out of Havana. That was a major blow to American criminals, and for some time after that they were in a depression. The opening up of the gambling in the Bahamas marked their recovery."[14]

Although gambling was illegal in the Bahamas, it had existed on a small scale since 1920 on the basis of certificates of exemption granted by the governor-in-council. One of the major projects of Grand Bahama Development was the Lucayan Beach Hotel, the plans for which included a 9,000-square-foot area designated as a handball court. On April 1, 1963, the governor-in-council granted a certificate of exemption to a company called Bahamas Amusements Ltd., another Groves–Chesler joint venture. The "handball court" became a casino.

On the government side, the protagonist in the realization of the casino was again Sir Stafford, who acted as attorney to the applicants for a certificate of exemption while at the same time participating in the decision to accept the application as a member of the government. Indeed, Chesler later attributed the initial impetus for the casino project to the government, presumably in the person of Sir Stafford. But other clues to Sir Stafford's enthusiasm for the idea were uncovered by the commission of inquiry, which found that he received a total of $1,800,000 over a period of five years from companies concerned with the application. Other members of the government, including its leader, Sir Roland Symonette, were given substantial "consultancy fees" although the commission could find no evidence of any consulting work having been done. Even Sir Etienne Dupuch of the Nassau *Tribune* was on the casino forces' payroll.[15]

Chesler replied "absolutely none" when asked if the U.S. underworld had any connection with Bahamian gambling, but he admitted to having asked Meyer Lansky, whom he described as the "dean of gambling," for advice on the staffing of the casino.[16] When the names of the prospective casino employees were presented to the commissioner of police just before the establishment opened, the list contained a number of known Lansky associates, including gamblers who had been involved in Havana operations. After discussions with American authorities, the commissioner found nine of the twenty-six prospective employees unacceptable, but he was persuaded to let several of these stay, and three of them — Frank Ritter, alias Red Reed, Max Courtney, also known as Morris Schmerzler, and Charles Brudner, alias Brud — remained until they were finally thrown out by Pindling in 1967.[17]

Despite the casino the Lucayan Beach Hotel was not, in its early years, a success. Chesler and Groves sold it in 1963, before it opened, to Toronto-born stock promoters Allen and Cecil Manus, who had the backing of a large Canadian finance company, the Atlantic Acceptance Corporation Ltd. From then on, the involvement of Atlantic Acceptance and its associated companies deepened steadily, and at the time of the spectacular collapse of Atlantic in 1965 they had more than $11 million tied up in the hotel and related ventures, with little in the way of security. Mr. Justice Samuel Hughes of the Ontario Supreme Court, who served as a one-man provincial Royal Commission investigating the Atlantic failure, found that of all the questionable ventures that helped cause the collapse, "none was more considerable than that which involved it in the affairs of Grand Bahama Island."

Atlantic founder and president C. Powell Morgan was, said Hughes, "enchanted with the hotel and everything connected with it, from the time that he first visited Freeport at the invitation of [Allen] Manus in September 1963; and, as usual, his interest in his own personal enrichment predominated over his sense of duty to the companies that he served, and the directors and shareholders of which looked to him for guidance." Hughes found that the financing of the hotel was "a quite inappropriate venture for a company engaged in the acceptance finance business, and it was pursued at every step by inappropriate means."[18]

The hotel went through a series of ineffectual management teams from the time of the sale to the Manus brothers until it was finally taken over by the Montreal Trust Company as receiver for Atlantic Acceptance. American gamblers continued to be treated majestically at the hotel despite the resentment of Allen Manus, who referred to Ritter, Courtney and Brudner as "the three mongrels,"[19] and his successors. Chesler and Groves remained in control of the casino until 1964, when they had a falling out and the Canadian abruptly departed, returning eventually to Toronto where he lives in a Bloor Street penthouse.

He still did not completely lose interest in the Bahamas. He retains an interest in Sentinel Holdings Ltd., formerly Security Capital Corp., whose main asset is its eighty-eight per-cent ownership of General Bahamian Companies Ltd. of Nassau, with interests including liquor, cars, pharmacies, and computer software. Despite Sentinel's small size and poor profit record, it has been the object of a continuing battle for control, involving Chesler, Norman LeBlanc, the Canadian accountant whom American authorities have accused of helping financier Robert Vesco loot the IOS mutual funds empire, and Shirley Oakes Butler, daughter of the late Sir Harry, whose American husband Alan owns the Bahamas-based Butlers Bank, one of the key financial instruments used by Vesco in his takeover of IOS in 1970.[20] Allen Manus, meanwhile, took up residence in Monaco, which declared him *persona non grata* in 1975, and London, and continued to promote stocks, notably that of International South African N.V., a company incorporated in the Dutch Caribbean island of Curaçao, whose major assets were mining rights to lands in South Africa that might or might not contain diamonds.[21]

Sir Stafford Sands left the Bahamas for Spain within weeks of the election of Pindling in 1967 and spent the rest of his life in exile, never staying in any one country long enough to let the tax authorities catch up with him. He died in 1972. Wallace Groves continued to spend much of his time in Freeport, although he retired as chairman of the Port Authority in 1969. He closed the casino in the Lucayan Beach Hotel in 1967 but opened another one, El Casino, in an incongruous moorish-style building on Grand Bahama. His interests expanded to include a piece of a new casino on Paradise Island off Nassau (it was called Hog Island before being renamed by its longtime owner, A & P potentate Huntington Hartford).[22]

While the commission of inquiry appointed by the Pindling government was highly critical of the methods by which gambling had been introduced, gambling itself has become an accepted part of Bahamian life, or at least its tourist life, for as a concession to the churches the government prohibits the entry of Bahamians into the casinos. "These are all overseas companies," said Donald Tynes, secretary of the government's Gaming Board. "All their profits go out anyway. Why should they take money from us?" In 1974 ten Bahamians were convicted of gambling and fined $250 each. The two casinos' total win reached $37 million in 1973, and the government's share of that, $8.5 million, represented a modest but not inconsiderable portion of its total revenue.

While thousands of dollars changed hands under the dim lights of the Paradise Island casino, millions were being handled across the bridge on Bay Street. The main branch of the Royal Bank of Canada, the same one that once sufficed for all of the Bahamas' banking needs, occupies a prominent position on Bay Street, right near the parliament buildings and Rawson Square, the heart of town. The Canadian Imperial Bank of Commerce and the Bank of Nova Scotia are close by. A few blocks to the west is the office of the Royal Bank of Canada International, the Royal subsidiary elegantly presided over by that prominent Nassauvian, E. P. Taylor. Turn left and you quickly approach the head office of the Bank of Montreal (Bahamas and Caribbean) Ltd.

Go west again for a few miles and you come to an elaborate modern structure that identifies itself as the Trust Corporation of the Bahamas building, and inside are the offices of TCB and Roy-West Ltd., in both of which the largest single shareholder is the Royal Bank of Canada. This building is also the nominal head office of a large number of corporations of obscure origin and purpose; these have names such as Financial Growth International Ltd., Development Corporation of the Americas Ltd., Casablanca Investments Ltd. and, perhaps most suggestive of all, the Baffin Island Trust Company Ltd.

What the ordinary Bahamian gets out of all this is unclear. Although wages are high by Caribbean standards, prices are even higher: with the absence of taxes, the government has to depend heavily on import duties for its revenue, and everything is imported so everybody feels the pinch. And since it's the same size pinch no matter what your means, it's the poor who feel it most. The Bahamas' dependence on customs duties also prevents the government from undertaking a serious program of import substitution to promote local agriculture. Even at that the government is seriously underfinanced, and its total budget in 1973 was only $107 million, or $595 per Bahamian,[23] a little more than half of what the government of Ontario spent per Ontarian in the same year — and that's only part of government spending in Ontario since the federal government spends vast sums in that province too. Still, Nassau's growing community of international bankers has turned the town into something of a minor Zurich and, despite the naturally secretive nature of their trade, is becoming more and more

102

conspicuous there. Actually the international bankers are quite happy to talk about their business, so long as the conversation is off the record and doesn't get too specific. When it does the banker will often interrupt you and say "Listen. What we're doing here is perfectly legal . . ." There follows a pregnant pause. ". . . In the Bahamas." He will then give you a knowing look and you are expected to follow another line of questioning.

The Bahamas' historic absence of taxes has much to do with the emergence of Nassau as a banking centre, but there are other factors as well. While the banking laws of the Bahamas don't provide for numbered accounts, as in Switzerland, they do allow banks to keep to themselves the names of their account-holders, so it amounts to more or less the same thing. In fact they do not only permit secrecy, they insist on it.

Bahamian laws also encourage foreign banks to set up "non-resident" subsidiaries in the country. These banks are not permitted to take domestic Bahamian business; what they do instead is trade in foreign currencies, mostly with each other. This is the mysterious Eurocurrency — mostly Eurodollar — market, of which Nassau has become a thriving centre. This activity is not subject to Bahamian exchange control regulation, or to much regulation of any sort.

According to Frank Davis of the Central Bank of the Bahamas, the government has been working on revisions to its banking legislation to improve the country's attractiveness to foreign banks. Prime Minister Pindling rarely misses an opportunity to reassure the banking community that no changes in the tax laws are being contemplated. "Let me . . . dispel any notion of an impending change in our status as a tax haven," Pindling told the Nassau Chamber of Commerce in March 1975, adding that "we have to work hard in order to maintain and increase the respect and trust of international investors."[24]

These reassurances are important because the main thing the Bahamas has to offer is an elusive and ill-defined commodity called confidence. There is no point putting money into a tax haven if there is even a chance that the government may decide that taxes are a good idea after all in a year or so, or if the government may be displaced by another with a different sense of priorities.

Since this confidence was so vigorously promoted by Sir Stafford Sands and his colleagues, the change of government in 1967 made investors apprehensive about the future. But while many of the internal policies of the government changed, its friendliness toward foreign investment did not. A brief monetary crisis in 1972 and the coming of full independence in 1973 also caused brief flurries of concern, but they too died down.

Add to this the Bahamas' proximity to the United States, which allows Nassau residents to watch Miami television and to direct-distance-dial to anywhere in North America (notably, for the bankers, including Wall Street) and an advanced infrastructure built up to accommodate the tourist trade; and one begins to ask, what more could an international banker want? The answer to that is the presence of other international bankers, and by now Nassau can of course offer that too.

The happy outcome of the Bahamian experiment has led other Caribbean states to try to imitate it. In late 1974 Grenada was abuzz with rumours that Prime Minister Gairy would turn the country into a tax haven. Since most of Grenada's labouring population is made up of subsistence farmers it's impossible to collect taxes from them anyway, and that meagre revenue would easily be exceeded by the money that would come in from foreign corporations attracted to a tax haven — so went the reasoning. However, the proposal was quietly shelved: perhaps the realization struck Gairy that international "confidence" in Grenada was not at a high point.

More successful as a tax haven has been the tiny Cayman Islands, which like many other Caribbean states has suffered from the decline of the traditional basis of its economy, in this case the turtle industry. The Caymans, where the Union Jack still flies, has been the chief beneficiary of whatever nervousness there is about the Bahamas. Its entry into the international banking game was largely the work of an aggressive Montrealer named Jean Doucet, who established two banks on Grand Cayman, Sterling Bank and

Trust Ltd. and the International Bank, and went around the world promoting the pleasures of doing business in the Caymans. The banks' investments included a hotel in the Virgin Islands, a cattle ranch in Quebec and a vaccine for tooth decay. In April 1974 the two banks claimed an estimated $52 million in assets.

In September of that year, however, Doucet suddenly left the Caymans for Monte Carlo. A few days later his two banks collapsed, and liquidators discovered that their real combined assets were about $4.2 million, as compared with liabilities of more than $40 million. Unfortunately for Doucet, there is an extradition treaty between Monaco and the Caymans, and he was arrested in Monte Carlo in May 1975 and shipped back to Grand Cayman to stand trial on twenty-four counts of fraudulent conversion. The fall of Doucet, however, hardly affected the status of the Caymans as a banking centre. When reporter Walter Stewart visited the islands in late 1975, he found 186 financial institutions and roughly 5,000 registered corporations, in a colony with a population of barely 12,000.[25]

But the most important financial centre of the Caribbean is still Nassau, and its most important activity is Eurodollar trading.

Despite its name, a Eurodollar is not strictly speaking a dollar, nor is it necessarily resident in Europe. It is rather a claim held outside the United States against a dollar on deposit in a Stateside bank, and although the dollar itself never leaves the United States, the claim is lent and deposited, bought and sold all around the world just as if it were real money. So long as it doesn't come back to the United States it remains a Eurodollar.

In effect, a Eurodollar has all the advantages of a U.S. dollar without being subject to the controls placed on domestic dollars by the U.S. Federal Reserve Board. As a result depositors can generally get higher interest rates on the Eurodollar market than in the U.S. — or on the domestic market in any country. The spectacular growth of the Eurodollar market — from $9 billion at the end of 1964 to a 1975 figure of more than $100 billion[26] —was one of the major financial events of the 1960s and helped bring about the international monetary crises of the early seventies. The Eurodollar makes life pleasant for international bankers, multinational corporations and oil sheiks but difficult for central bankers trying to regulate their countries' economies through monetary policy.

In her informative 1975 book *Euro-dollars: the Money-Market Gypsies,* economist Jane Little described the Eurodollar market as "a truly international creature beyond the control of any single national authority. In trying to tame the market, central bankers have been in the untenable position of chasing an elephant with butterfly nets."[27] The only way the Eurodollar could be regulated is through international agreement, and the existence of the market in more or less its present form is too useful to too many people for that to be a likely eventuality. Even governments often find it convenient to flout the regulations they themselves have set up. The old monetary system the Eurodollar helped bring down didn't work anyway; the Eurodollar provided an easy way for bankers to get around it while still paying lip service to its continued existence.

The world centre of the Eurodollar market is, not surprisingly, London, and the main secondary centre, again not surprisingly, is Toronto. As of April 1976 Canadian banks held 28.9 per cent of their assets and 30.5 per cent of their liabilities in foreign currencies.[28] A large part of that consisted of Eurodollar deposits and loans, some held within Canada and some held in London and the other financial centres of western Europe, and in Singapore, Hong Kong — and Nassau.

Nassau differs from other Eurodollar centres in its almost total artificiality. For while London, Toronto and Singapore have long been financial or trading centres of some importance, Nassau was only a tax haven — quite a "successful" one as these things go, but still nothing more than that. And indeed, in the early days of Eurodollar trading in Nassau, in the mid-sixties, most of the bank branches here made good Jane Little's description of "a plaque, a walk-in closet, a desk, a file cabinet and a telephone."[29] All of the actual banking was done at the head offices in the United States, Canada or Britain. For a large number of medium-sized American banks that couldn't afford to get in on the big-league stuff in London, it was a way of getting into the Eurodollar market on the cheap.

Now all that has begun to change. The real-life bankers began to arrive in Nassau in the early seventies, and since most Eurodollar trading takes place between one bank and another bank, they have attracted more and more of their colleagues. The Royal Bank of Canada for instance, incorporated its Royal Bank International subsidiary in Nassau in 1961, but activated it only in March of 1972. By 1975 it employed twenty-three people in Nassau, including eighteen Bahamians, almost all in clerical positions; it also has a branch office in George Town, Grand Cayman.

Since the large sums of money in Nassau are, by and large, only passin' through, the question of where they are coming from and where they are going remains. Probably the greatest source of Eurodollar deposits in Nassau, and also the most frequent destination for Eurodollar loans, is Latin America — especially for the Canadian banks. Latin America is characterized by chronic political and economic instability, and by a small number of very rich people who want to keep their money in a safe place to guard against revolutions, inflation, currency crises and similar misfortunes. Many of them have found that place in Nassau. "You name it and we're into it," said an official at the Nassau branch of one Canadian bank when asked what sort of business his bank did in Latin America.

A somewhat different insight into the nature of the business being carried on in Nassau was given by another Canadian banker, who recounted the tale of the man who came to him with a proposal to corner the world market in platinum. The amount of platinum the man had mentioned sounded a bit odd to him, and with a little checking he found that it amounted to 257 years' production of the metal. Another potential customer came in with half a million dollars in a cardboard box. "I told him we don't want to see that," he said. "Some people in this bank and in other banks would have taken it gladly — it's perfectly legal in the Bahamas."

While all this is going on, there are undoubtedly a few people in the Bahamas who are asking themselves how long it can last. Like the Eurodollar market itself, the existence of Nassau as a tax haven and banking centre is to the advantage of too many powerful people for it to be in any immediate danger of being wiped out overnight. But again like the Eurodollar market, Nassau *could* be wiped out overnight if enough of those people got together and decided to do it. Proponents of the Bahamas as a tax haven like to make the distinction between "evading" taxes or regulations and "avoiding" them — it is the latter that is done in Nassau. Nassau exists not in spite of the authorities in its phantom residents' home countries, but with their tacit blessing, and it is on that blessing that it will always depend.

7/Money Men

Drive with care — you might hit a customer of Scotiabank.
sign on the highway between Georgetown
and Timehri airport, Guyana

The high-powered international transactions of Nassau are a world away from a Scotiabank Jamaica branch in May Pen or a branch of the Royal Bank of Trinidad and Tobago in Diego Martin. It is doubtful whether all the small branches scattered through the Caribbean are as important to the banks as their operations in that one madcap centre of international finance. From the point of view of the West Indies, however, those small branches, and the larger ones in the major cities, are an important controlling factor in their economies and, even today, by far the most significant Canadian presence in the region.

In the West Indies, as elsewhere, banking has changed in the last twenty years, and so has the relationship between the banks and the societies over which they continue to have so much influence. Beginning in the 1960s, West Indian governments made attempts to require the foreign banks to serve national goals: to tame them without actually taking them over. Partly because of these efforts and partly because of the natural evolution of banking, the banks have more of a West Indian face than they used to. But whether behind the face the banks are genuinely more indigenous institutions, or are simply more carefully organized to transfer West Indian wealth out of the region, is very much open to question.

As we have seen, the banks initially followed the trade routes between Canada's Atlantic provinces and the Caribbean. In the early days, there was little attempt on the part of the banks to generate much local business, especially on the loan side: the banks were there to finance trade, mostly in agricultural goods. In most of the islands where the Canadian banks set up shop, the British-owned Colonial Bank had already been there for a while, and

109

pretty well monopolized the financing of the sugar industry and other plantation agriculture.

The Canadian banks were, however, somewhat more vigorous in seeking local deposits. After getting a foothold in Jamaica with a branch in Kingston in 1889, the Bank of Nova Scotia opened branches in several smaller Jamaican communities before World War I: Montego Bay and Port Antonio in 1906, Mandeville in 1907, Port Maria in 1908, St. Ann's Bay and Savanna-la-Mar in 1910, Black River in 1911. The idea was to get hold of the deposits of ordinary Jamaicans, and the result was that the Bank of Nova Scotia became a very familiar institution in the colony, and was widely known simply as "The Bank". "The success of this bank," said John Smith, assistant general manager (administration) of the Bank of Nova Scotia Jamaica Ltd., in 1975, "is that it became a local bank very early." This, however, was true only on the deposit side, since loans were by and large restricted to traders.

Not all the banks expanded as rapidly in their new environments as the Nova Scotia did in Jamaica. In Trinidad, for instance, the Royal had only two branches, one in Port of Spain and one in San Fernando, until the 1950s. On the whole, however, the West Indies were, as historian Tom Naylor has said, "recognized as a 'surplus' area for the banks, the volume of deposits exceeding the volume of loans and investments in the area .... Like the Maritimes the West Indies suffered a net drain in funds that helped perpetuate their underdevelopment."[1]

A steady exodus of funds, through deposits gathered locally and loaned out elsewhere, through the repatriation of bank profits and through other means, is one of the chief dangers of a foreign-owned banking system in any country. This danger is one of the reasons why Canada until 1976 so jealously guarded the domestic ownership of its own banks. Within the country, it is one of the major grievances that western Canada, in particular, has held against a banking system controlled in Toronto and Montreal. In the west, the drain of money and the policies of the banks led to the establishment of the Bank of British Columbia and the abortive Bank of Western Canada and to the demand that provincial governments be allowed to get into the banking business; in the

West Indies, they led to the localization movement of the late 1960s and 1970s.

After the entry of the Canadian Bank of Commerce into the Caribbean in the early 1920s, there was little expansion of the Canadian banking presence in the area until after World War II. In fact there was a retrenchment as many smaller and less profitable branches were closed. The number of branches and sub-branches of Canadian banks in the Caribbean and Latin America peaked at 140 in 1926; that figure was not reached again until 1958.

While Barclays, the successor to the Colonial Bank, was and still is the largest single bank in the islands, Canada, with three sizeable banks, became the most important banking country. For many years these four banks had a monopoly on the banking business of the West Indies, and although that monopoly has been challenged they are still very much in control. In the last twenty years, several American banks — Chase Manhattan, First National City Bank, First Chicago, the Bank of America, and the Citizens' and Southern Bank of Savannah, Georgia — have come into the West Indies; an Indian bank, the Bank of Baroda, has started doing business in Guyana; and the governments of Jamaica, Guyana and Trinidad and Tobago have set up indigenous banks. Most of these are aggressive in seeking business and some have been successful. But they remain small in comparison to the long-established Big Four of the Royal, the Commerce, Nova Scotia and Barclays.

The success of its three rivals also led another large Canadian bank, the Bank of Montreal, to try its luck in the West Indies. It did this at first in the form of a joint venture with the Bank of London and South America, one of the British banks that had made several South American countries, notably Argentina, virtual financial colonies of Britain. BOLSA turned over its branches in Central America and the northern part of South America to the Bank of London and Montreal, as the new venture was called. The Bank of Montreal contributed some capital and new branches were set up in the West Indies. The head office of BOLAM was established in Nassau in 1958.

The marriage, however, did not work out, and in the divorce settlement BOLSA repossessed its Latin American branches while

111

the Bank of Montreal got the Jamaican and Bahamian ones. The branch in Port of Spain was taken over by the Trinidad government.

But it was not only the number of banks and their extent that changed after the War; there were important changes in their character as well. The 1950s and 1960s saw the entry of the banks into consumer banking on a large scale, and the new branches that sprang up throughout the islands were designed to lure whole new classes of West Indians into the banking system. There was precedent for this on the deposit side, but consumer loans were a completely new endeavour. Here again it was the Bank of Nova Scotia in Jamaica that pioneered. "Everybody thought that we were crazy," said a senior official of the bank, "and that we would lose our shirts. But we didn't. We made a fortune."

The Nova Scotia began its consumer loan program in 1965, and other banks soon followed its lead. "YOU CAN GET IT NOW," advertises the Royal Bank of Trinidad and Tobago. "Imagine! Going home with the good news . . . 'Hey! Guess what? We're getting the car! With CASHADVANCE making it so easy!' CAR. COOKER. TV SET. REFRIGERATOR, what have you . . . Get it now. With CASHADVANCE. And only Royal has it. CASHADVANCE ! The special Royal Bank loan system to help you get the good things in life. Now. While you can enjoy them." The Commerce isn't quite as hard-sell but its message is similar: "A Commerce Bankplan Loan can take the waiting out of wanting. The way we figure it, you could be enjoying the same things you're working and waiting for. A more comfortable home. A vacation trip. A car of your own. You name it. And we'll come up with a convenient way to help you do it. A Commerce Bankplan Loan."[2]

The expansion of consumer lending is by no means unique to the West Indies; consumer loans have been the most spectacular area of bank growth in Canada as well. But its effects are more clearly detrimental in the West Indies than in countries whose economies are more varied. For one of the major problems of West Indian economies from slave days to the present has been their heavy dependence on imports. And not only is the level of imports high, but it has been getting higher. In Jamaica it increased from 38.5 per cent of Gross Domestic Product in 1960 to 43.5 per cent in 1972, while in Trinidad and Tobago it increased from 34.7 per cent in 1960 to 43.5 per cent in 1972. The 1972 figures for Jamaica and Trinidad were higher than that of any country in Latin America.[3]

The loan policies of the commercial banks are of course only one of many reasons for this growth in imports, but they are a significant one. For the car, cooker, TV set and refrigerator purchased by the aspiring West Indian who reads the Royal Bank ad, are not manufactured in the West Indies. At best they are assembled locally from imported components, and more often they are imported whole from the United States, Canada, Britain, Japan or another metropolitan country. Consumer loans are only one way in which the banks encourage this tendency. Another large slice of their loans goes to the distributive trades, which use a good part of that money to import merchandise into the region. By providing the credit that makes imported goods available to West Indians, and by helping to create a taste for them through advertising, the banks are reinforcing the dependent pattern into which West Indian economies were moulded in colonial days.

In marked contrast to the banks' enthusiasm for consumer loans is their attitude toward small-business and agricultural loans. Ask a banker in the West Indies about small-business loans and he will generally tell you that they are handled on the basis of sound banking principles. "Everything has to be judged on whether it's a good risk or not," said C. R. Baggan, controller of the Royal Bank of Trinidad and Tobago, in 1974. "A bank has to be run on a sound credit-management policy, and not just to fulfil some social function." Alec Shaw of the Caribbean division of the Bank of Nova Scotia in Toronto said that "the small businessman who is a worthy credit risk can borrow money. The bank looks at every credit application on the basis of its merits."

If the attitude toward small-business loans is guarded, the hostility toward agricultural loans is unconcealed. "Agriculture is a risky business because of its dependence on the climate," said Alec

Shaw. "A loan to the agricultural sector is often an outright grant," said Hugh Woolner of the Royal Bank Jamaica Ltd., and Ray Jackson of the same bank chimed in, "All you need is a flipping drought." C. R. Baggan took the same approach: "A man wants $25,000 or $35,000 so that he can plant rice: who's going to reimburse the bank if it doesn't work?"

This attitude is borne out by the figures. In Jamaica only 3.8 per cent of bank credit goes to agriculture. The only bank in the country that makes a substantial number of agricultural loans is Barclays, which has sixty per cent of its loans tied up in agriculture. But these loans are almost entirely to sugar planters, and Barclays is no more eager to lend to small farmers than are the other banks. One of the rare exceptions to this pattern is a Bank of Nova Scotia program to lend money to cane farmers on the basis of their government cane licences in the Central American territory of Belize. But although this program would later be considered a success by the Bank, it was set up first on the initiative of one heretical local banker, without the approval of head office. The manager in Corozal near the Mexican border simply started lending to cane farmers on his own. "He threw the fear of God into us," said Alec Shaw. "But we went down and looked at it and it was working well, so we established this program."

The banks' scale of priorities may be good business for them, but it isn't very helpful to West Indian attempts to develop indigenous agriculture and industry. And an increasing number of West Indians are of the opinion that the development of these sectors is essential if the traditional patterns of dependency are to be broken. Just as West Indian tastes are geared to what can be imported from larger and richer countries, so West Indian industries — export agriculture, tourism, resource extraction by multinational corporations — are geared to metropolitan requirements. It is increasingly recognized that a stable future for the islands will be possible only if West Indian consumption can be tailored more closely to local resources, and West Indian production brought into line with local needs.

If you present this argument to a banker in the West Indies he will probably agree with you. He is not against agriculture or small business; he thinks they are very important. But they are also not his problem. His problem is to run a bank. At a profit. Economic development is the government's problem.

Governments have attempted to deal with the problem by taking some of the burden on themselves, in some cases sweetening the pill for the banks by providing guarantees for loans in the sectors that they otherwise wouldn't handle, in others setting up financial institutions outside the commercial banking system to lend to those sectors. Trinidad and Tobago has a Development Finance Corporation, which lends to local industrial and tourist projects, and an Agricultural Development Bank. The Jamaican government guarantees twenty per cent of the defaults on agricultural loans made by the banks. These programs are a start, but their success has been limited. In Trinidad, neither the DFC nor the ADB has the capital to mount an effective assault on underdevelopment. And the Jamaican program has not yet succeeded in getting the banks to divert a significant proportion of their loans to the agricultural sector.

The banks are very happy to see the establishment of these and similar government programs. If the government is willing to take the risks that agriculture and small business entail, that will take some of the pressure off them and allow them to pursue their safer and more profitable loans to multinationals, merchants and consumers. It is the same philosophy of business–government relations that in Canada allows private railways, airlines and broadcasting networks to go after the most profitable sectors of their respective markets while government-owned entries in the same fields have to maintain services that lose money but are necessary in the public interest.

Since the attainment of formal independence, there has been a series of attempts by West Indian governments to put some constraints on the operation of the banking system and make sure that it conforms to national needs. While the attempts at regulation have undoubtedly changed the context in which the banks operate,

115

they have not fulfilled all the hopes that were held out for them.

In colonial days the only institutions that regulated monetary affairs were Currency Boards in the various islands. The Currency Board system was a rigid, insensitive but administratively efficient method of monetary control used by Britain throughout its far-flung network of colonies. A Currency Board could issue coins and notes, which had to be fully backed by securities held in London. Such currencies were completely convertible with the pound sterling but local authorities had no power to influence the exchange rate or the money supply. As a result, the only local institutions that could have any effect on the money supply were the commercial banks, which could transfer their assets into or out of the country as they wished. One critic of the system pointed out that "it depends for its flexibility not on any official authority but on the actions of private profit-seeking institutions."[4] In the 1950s, minor modifications in the system were made in Jamaica, permitting the Currency Board to hold a portion of its currency reserves in local securities, but the system in its essence remained intact until the eve of independence.

Acting on a report by Graham Towers, who had been the first Governor of the Bank of Canada, the Jamaican government set up the Bank of Jamaica in 1960, to take over the functions of the Currency Board, regulate the money supply, influence credit policies, and act as banker to the government. Trinidad and Tobago established a Central Bank on the same model in 1964, to be followed in due course by Guyana, Barbados and the Bahamas. A remnant of the old Currency Board system persists in the Leewards and Windwards, where the East Caribbean Currency Authority administers the monetary system of the associate states and the independent State of Grenada.

Even in Canada, where the Bank of Canada has been in existence since the 1930s and where the major commercial banks are all owned within the country, it is often questionable who regulates whom and how much power the Bank of Canada really has to take monetary measures that are against the commercial banks' wishes. In the West Indies, where the Central Banks are new and uncertain institutions and where the banks are owned abroad, these same questions arise in a much more acute way.

Speaking for the opposition Jamaica Labour Party during the debate on the establishment of the Bank of Jamaica in the House of Representatives in 1960, Donald Sangster (who was later to succeed Alexander Bustamante as Prime Minister) said, "another question that is bound to arise among the banks here . . . and there are many of them that are branches of external banks, of worldwide organizations . . . is how is the control of their activities by the Central Bank in Jamaica going to fit into the control by their head offices?"[5]

A provision was put into the act establishing the Bank of Jamaica that gave it the power to prescribe a minimum ratio of loans and other assets held by the banks in Jamaica to their Jamaican deposit liabilities. While this provision put some constraints on the extent to which the banks could use Jamaica as a surplus area and invest deposits gathered in the island in metropolitan countries, it by no means ended that practice entirely.

At about the same time as the Commonwealth Caribbean countries began their attempts to bring the banks to heel through regulation, the government of Cuba was taking much more drastic measures: it was bringing all the banks in the country under government control, through expropriation in the case of the American banks, and through purchase in the case of the Canadian. This was part of Cuba's headlong transition to a socialist economy, in which the place and purpose of the banking system would be transformed.

The West Indian islands had neither the inclination nor the apparent need for such a move. The kind of independence they were entering did not seem incompatible with the presence of a foreign-owned banking system, so long as its more obviously harmful aspects were mitigated. Even those West Indian officials who would not have rejected nationalization of the banks out of hand on ideological grounds were reluctant to consider it on practical ones. The tiny, underdeveloped countries of the West Indies, they would argue, simply didn't have the skills to run a banking system all by themselves. Better to let Barclays, the Royal and the others run it for them and use the little expertise available in the islands to regulate them and make sure that they operated in the national interest.

But by the end of the 1960s, at least some West Indian governments were coming to the conclusion that stronger action than a regulatory mechanism would be required. In part, this was due to the inevitable disappointments that they had experienced with central banks, and the banking system's stubborn resistance to change. And in part, the governments recognized the powerful symbolic importance of the banks as one of the most visible manifestations of the foreign economic presence in the region. It was no accident that when Trinidadians were looking for a place to vent their frustations against Canada over the Sir George affair in 1970, they chose the main branches of the Canadian banks on Independence Square.

One of the measures taken by the governments was the establishment of new, indigenous banks. Trinidad now has three such banks: the National Commercial Bank, formed out of the Port of Spain branch of the Bank of London and Montreal, which the government took over in the heat of the 1970 uprising; the Trinidad Co-operative Bank, and the Workers Bank. "To serve the needs of others — the only legitimate business in the world today," says an ad for the Workers Bank, which claims that it is "inspired by the philosophy enunciated by the late Mr. A.P. Giannini who founded the Bank of Italy — 'the bank for the little people' — in San Franci co in 1904 and lived to see the Bank become the Bank of America — the largest Bank in the world."[6] Guyana has the Guyana National Co-operative Bank while in Jamaica there is the Workers Savings and Loan Bank.

But the indigenous banks are small, unable and unwilling to buck the banking philosophy laid down by the multinationals, and in some cases the battleground for some of the more sordid forms of local politics. None of the three Trinidadian banks has more than three branches. The Guyana National Co-operative Bank, while in theory infused with the spirit of Forbes Burnham's co-operative socialism, in its first few years pursued a loan policy little different from that of the commercial banks. In 1970, its first year of operation, the GNCB allotted only 2.6 per cent of its loans to agriculture, while in 1971 the figure was 5.2 per cent[7] — in both cases even less than the percentage of commercial bank loans that went to agriculture.

In Jamaica, the Workers Bank was the centre of a scandal that led to the suspension of trading in its shares on the Jamaica Stock Exchange in early 1975. Allegations against the Bank, first made by Jamaica *Daily Gleaner* columnist Thomas Wright,[8] concerned illegal loans made to friends of the government, flouting of exchange-control regulations, loans made without proper security and loans on which no interest could be collected. The Bank's 1974 accounts showed a provision for bad debts of J $856,700, and a net loss of J$853,592. The acting chairman and general manager resigned, and was replaced in the latter position by a Jamaican banker trained in Canada by the Canadian Imperial Bank of Commerce. A year later some of the worst problems appeared to have been overcome, and the 1975 accounts showed a modest profit and no provision for bad debts.[9]

The most serious attempt made by West Indian governments to deal with the inadequacies of the foreign-owned banking system has been localization. In 1966, the Bank of Nova Scotia established a Jamaican subsidiary, the Bank of Nova Scotia Jamaica Ltd., and transferred its Jamaican operations to the new company. It was the first bank in the West Indies to make such a move, but it was only anticipating what it knew was coming. For within a few years the governments of both Jamaica and Trinidad were to establish policies requiring all banks to go local and to sell fifty-one per cent of their stock to local investors.

In the eyes of some of the more nationalistic West Indian politicians, localization is just a public relations gimmick that leaves the real power relationships unchanged and control in foreign hands — Michael Manley, while leader of the opposition in Jamaica, attacked it on those grounds when it was introduced by a JLP government. For some conservative West Indians and many foreign businessmen, it is only one step short of that worst of all evils,

119

nationalization. But for the West Indian governments and the banks alike, it appeared to be a sensible compromise that would satisfy the growing nationalist spirit without disturbing confidence in the soundness of the banking system. Manley himself, once he became Prime Minister, did not hesitate to see the wisdom of his predecessor's policy.

But no less than previous attempts to put the banks under some sort of control, localization has proved to have unexpected snares. Simply accomplishing the transfer of fifty-one per cent of the shares of the banks to local interests has turned out to be more difficult than expected. Both the Jamaica and Trinidad governments provide for a five-year period between the time a bank sets up a local company and the time fifty-one per cent is required to be in local hands. But so far, no bank has even approached the fifty-one per cent figure. Even Scotiabank Jamaica, which has been local since 1966, was only thirty per cent locally owned in 1975. A number of the banks had, as of 1975, not yet gone local at all. These were mostly the American ones, which are smaller and newer and don't have the same long-standing interest in the region, but the list of recalcitrant banks also included the Canadian Imperial Bank of Commerce.

The reluctance of the banks' head offices to surrender control was only part of the reason for this slowness. In fact, with forty-nine per cent and a management contract as against a dispersed local investment, the head offices would be able to retain all the control they need. But one of the effects of the underdevelopment and foreign domination of West Indian economies is that the number of people and institutions with large amounts of capital to invest is severely limited, and putting sizeable chunks of several of the biggest corporations in the country up for sale at the same time would overload the market. With this justification, the banks have put their shares onto the market at an extremely cautious pace: Jamaica has had to abandon its original five-year timetable for localization and Trinidad will likely be forced to do the same. When bank shares do get offered, investors generally seek after them hungrily, and several offerings have been oversubscribed.

For the most part these shares, like bank shares everywhere, go to a fairly narrow group of people. With the scarcity of other appropriate investors, the island governments are widely suspected of having indirectly taken up a portion of the share offerings. And most of the rest have gone to the local business elites, small and closely knit and generally white, for whom the nationalist trend in the West Indies has opened up previously unknown areas of activity. This is reflected in the boards of directors of the localized banks. The board of the Bank of Nova Scotia Trinidad and Tobago Ltd. includes such prominent white Trinidadians as Jack De Lima, of the well-known Port of Spain jewellery firm, Y. De Lima (which opened a store in Toronto in 1975); Mervyn de Souza, Trinidad's first actuary and head of the Trinidadian subsidiary of the Maritime Life Assurance Company; and Vernon Charles, a soft-drink entrepreneur who became so enamoured of things Canadian that he eventually abandoned Trinidad to take up residence in Vancouver. Just as the American presence in Canada often operates through the Canadian managers of firms owned south of the border, so the Canadian presence in the West Indies operates through these local elites.

After Lynden Pindling was elected Premier of the Bahamas in 1967, Milo Butler, then a member of the new government and now Sir Milo and the Governor-General of the newly independent country, walked into the Bay Street branch of the Royal Bank of Canada, slammed his fist on the manager's desk and demanded to know why there were no black faces in the bank. Since eighty per cent of Bahamians are black it was a good question, and the manager didn't have a satisfactory answer. In this respect the Bahamas was behind the rest of the Caribbean, for by this time in Jamaica, Trinidad and elsewhere, the banks had blacks in all positions except the ones that counted. While in the early days of Canadian banking in the Caribbean virtually all employees except for menial staff were imported from Canada there are now few expatriates left; even in the Bahamas the black faces started to appear in the late sixties. According to an official of the Royal Bank in Montreal, this did not represent a change in policy on the part of the

121

bank. "By not having locals," he said, "we were merely giving our clients what they wanted. Those were the attitudes in the community. We didn't create them. When the attitudes changed, we changed."

This flexibility is most dramatically evident in the Royal Bank of Trinidad and Tobago, which is now entirely locally staffed, but the other localized banks are moving in similar directions and retain only a handful of foreigners. This aspect of localization is encouraged by the policies of West Indian governments, which require foreigners working in their respective countries to have work permits and are quick to deny a permit if there is a qualified national to fill the position, but it also has advantages for the banks themselves, since maintaining a large number of expatriates is not only bad from a public relations point of view but also expensive.

There are more opportunities for West Indians in the banks than there used to be, but these opportunities are still unequally applied. The top positions in newly localized banks almost invariably go to local whites: the managing director of Royal Bank Jamaica is a white Jamaican, Ronald Sasso, while the managing director of the Royal Bank of Trinidad and Tobago is Carlton de Souza, a white Trinidadian who has been in the Royal Bank organization since 1942. And it is still not uncommon to hear stories such as those related by Jamaica *Daily News* columnist Gillie Afflick about one bank where local employees were systematically passed over for promotion and placed in dead-end positions, where many were forced to resign and those who stayed worked in an atmosphere of constant frustration.[10] Afflick did not name the bank, but he was asked whether it was a Canadian institution. "No, this was an American one," he said, "but they're all the same."

On the whole, the Canadian banks, and especially the highly sophisticated Royal, have done a better cosmetic job than the American, but there are still some problems. In Trinidad, where the banks have been fighting an effort by their employees to organize a union (a problem they are just beginning to face in Canada, where only one small bank, the Montreal City and District is unionized), the Bank of Nova Scotia fired a union activist, Miguel Hospedales. The union took the case to the Industrial Court, which found that the dismissal was "harsh, oppressive and not in accordance with the principles of good industrial relations practice," and ordered Scotiabank to pay Hospedales $2,000 in damages.[11]

But the central question about localization is whether it has forced the banks to change their policies to make them more compatible with the interests of the countries in which they operate. And the most widespread criticism of localization is that this has not happened. *Tapia,* the weekly organ of the Trinidadian opposition group of the same name, said in 1975 that Prime Minister Williams "stole the clothes but the idea escaped him, so that his idea of localization turned out to be local exploitation with the key element of control still firmly vested abroad."[12]

We have seen that officials of the localized Royal Bank and Bank of Nova Scotia in Jamaica and Trinidad are highly skeptical if not openly hostile toward loans to agriculture and small business, whatever their importance to the national economy. Asgar Ally of the flow of funds division of the Bank of Jamaica has observed that localized banks tend, if anything, to be more exclusively concerned with profit than their wholly foreign-owned counterparts. Especially in their first years of operation, the localized banks feel that it is essential for them to make a healthy profit for their new local shareholders and prove their soundness as an investment. Profitability has been one of the more evident characteristics of the localized banks. Scotiabank Jamaica had a 1974 after-tax profit of $2.76 million,[13] while the much smaller Royal Bank of Trinidad and Tobago (total assets of $120 million as compared to $326 million for Scotiabank Jamaica) had a profit of $2.04 million in the same year[14] — in both cases a much higher profit in proportion to the size of the bank than their Canadian parents had.

Localization has made it somewhat more difficult for the banks to transfer money out of the region, but nevertheless the outward flow of funds continues. The behaviour of the banks in this regard has changed somewhat in any case. While the old-style British or Canadian bank with branches abroad saw those branches as simply a source of deposits to be disposed of profitably in the metropolis, today's banks regard themselves as multinationals and range the world in search of opportunities for loans and investments. In 1945, commercial banks in Jamaica had £13,654,000 in deposits but only £4,137,000 in local investments, loans and advances while £8,670,000 had been invested abroad or advanced to banks outside the colony.[15] In the late 1960s and early 1970s, by contrast, banks in Jamaica had a consistent surplus of foreign liabilities (balances due to banks abroad) over foreign assets (investments abroad and balances due by banks abroad). At the end of 1974 foreign liabilities were J$60,402,000 while foreign assets were only J$38,841,000.[16]

There are , however, other ways in which banks transfer money from one place to another, and the localized banks in Jamaica and Trinidad have resorted to a wide variety of them. The simplest is the straightforward declaration of a dividend to be paid to the bank's shareholders — which happen to include the parent bank in Canada, the United States or Britain. On its 1974 profit of $2.04 million, the Royal Bank of Trinidad and Tobago declared a dividend of $1.17 million,[17] of which $951,000 went to the Royal Bank of Canada as the owner of 81.5 per cent of the Bank's shares.

A variety of other payments are made to the parent companies as well. According to Hugh Woolner, the Royal Bank Jamaica pays $11,000 annually for a service contract from the Royal Bank of Canada. It also pays for expertise in certain areas, for training programs, for the use of the lion symbol, and for having loans above a certain amount guaranteed by the Canadian bank, for a total of about $77,000. The bank workers' union in Trinidad has charged that the banks in that country are taking much larger amounts out. "Inspectors who usually came once a year," the union said, "are now four and five times visiting the respective banks. Each time they come a bill for over [TT]$300,000 is cashed. Management fees and expenses tripled. 'Management contracts' are never less than [TT]$500,000."[18]

In any case, there is no doubt that money is leaving the region in various guises, and that the foreign-owned banking system in the West Indies still behaves in essence like a foreign-owned banking system. Spokesmen for the localized banks like to emphasize how autonomous they have become. "Before localization, we were a loose network of branches, under the jurisdiction of an office in the Bahamas," said Hugh Woolner. "There were many people making decisions who had never seen the shores of Jamaica. Now we're a bank. We're very independent."

Bank spokesmen in Montreal and Toronto, on the other hand, prefer to talk about how the localized banks are "still part of the family." This kinship is perhaps most effectively expressed in the requirement that the Canadian parent guarantee any loan that exceeds ten per cent of the local bank's paid-up capital — in the case of the Royal Bank Jamaica, this means that any loan over $412,500 has to be guaranteed. Loans under the legal limit but over $220,000 are routinely sent to Canada for "advice and counsel." For loans guaranteed by head office, the Royal Bank Jamaica pays a fee of one half of one per cent. Royal Bank officials in both Kingston and Montreal are enthusiastic about the importance of this service supplied by the parent, and note that head office rarely turns down a loan approved by the local bank. "We sometimes suggest a different form," said Joseph Hutchison, head of the Royal Bank's Caribbean region, "but people know what we will and will not approve."

In discussing the advantages of the West Indian brand of localization, bankers in Kingston and Port of Spain are inclined to bring up the benefits brought by the international connection — monetary stability, confidence in the banking system, more than a hundred years without a bank failure: all the virtues so beloved of the Colonial Office in London. The Canadian banks have played a central role in propagating these virtues, along with their accompanying ills of foreign domination, dependency and underdevelopment. Even as the Canadians themselves leave, the system they helped implant continues, and that is perhaps the best indication of how thoroughly they did their job.

Canada's involvement in the financial affairs of the West Indies is

125

not limited to the banks. In the areas of trust and insurance, Canada is equally prominent.

Trust companies are hybrid institutions that do diverse kinds of financial business, from acting as the executors of wills to managing investments to mortgage financing. In Canada there are strict laws separating trust companies from the chartered banks. Banks cannot own shares in trust companies, and interlocking directorships between the two types of corporations are forbidden. These laws have the effect not so much of preventing links as of concealing them, and close informal relationships such as the one between the Royal Bank of Canada and the Montreal Trust Company or between the Bank of Montreal and Royal Trust remain.

In the West Indies there are so such restrictions to worry about, and so the trust field is dominated by the banks. All three of the Canadian banks with large-scale operations in the region also have trust subsidiaries scattered throughout the islands. In the case of the Royal and Nova Scotia in Jamaica and Trinidad, these are associated with the localized bank; where no such bank exists, they fall under a head office in Nassau, which reports to the parent bank.

The first Canadian insurance companies entered the West Indies around the same time as the first Canadian banks, and as we have seen, Sun Life was a leader in the movement for closer Canadian–West Indian ties in the early 1900s. But although foreign — mostly Canadian and British — companies dominate the insurance industry, they don't monopolize it in quite the same way as they do banking. Insurance has its multinational giants just as banking does, but smaller, local insurance firms have proved to have a greater capacity for survival than small banks. In the West Indies, an indigenous insurance industry began to develop soon after the end of slavery, and the first Jamaican life insurance company, Jamaica Mutual Life, was founded in 1844; it is now the largest life insurance concern in the region. Nevertheless, the entry of the foreign companies severely hampered — "stultified," in Asgar Ally's phrase — the growth of this indigenous industry.[19]

At the same time as they have moved to localize the foreign

banks, and for essentially the same reasons, the governments of Trinidad and Jamaica have tried to persuade the foreign insurance companies to localize their operations. Insurance companies are perhaps the most important source of long-term capital and are heavy investors in such things as mortgages and government securities.

Like the banks, the insurance companies have responded to government policies favouring localization in a variety of ways: some have pulled out of the West Indies, some have set up local subsidiaries, some have simply stonewalled. In 1970, the Toronto-based North American Life Assurance Company stopped writing new business in Jamaica; at the same time a new Jamaican company, Life of Jamaica, was formed. In 1975, NALACO turned all its Jamaican operations over to the new company.[20] By contrast, Manufacturers Life, also of Toronto, set up its own Jamaican subsidiary, Island Life, which took over ManuLife's Jamaican business in 1972 and began writing its own policies two years later.

In Trinidad, the company most successful in accommodating itself to the new climate was Maritime Life (Caribbean) Ltd., a subsidiary of a middle-sized Canadian firm based in Halifax. Maritime Life (Caribbean) was fortunate in obtaining as its managing director in 1966 a bright, ambitious young Trinidadian named Mervyn de Souza, who had returned from England five years earlier as the only qualified actuary in the West Indies and gone to work in the Ministry of Finance. As a civil servant de Souza was responsible for drafting Trinidad's landmark Insurance Act, the main provision of which was a requirement that all insurance companies invest at least sixty per cent of their assets locally; this minimum was later increased to seventy per cent. But by the time the Act was passed, de Souza had left the government to take the Maritime Life position and do a little consulting on the side.

So while much older and larger Canadian insurance companies such as Sun Life and Manufacturers Life were announcing plans to pack up and leave Trinidad as a result of the new legislation,[21] Maritime Life quietly registered under the new Act, the first company to do so. Meanwhile, de Souza was preparing the firm for what he knew was the next stage: a government policy favouring the sale of insurance companies to local investors.

Although this policy was announced in 1972, as of 1975 Maritime Life was the only foreign-owned insurance company to have gone local; local investors owned forty per cent of Maritime Life (Caribbean). The company was also growing extremely fast — too fast for de Souza's own taste. "In 1974 the company grew at a rate of forty per cent of the previous year's business," he said. "I would prefer a steady growth of ten to fifteen per cent a year." Maritime Life had employed nine people in 1966; now it employed seventy. "CLIMB THE STEPS OF SUCCESS WITH MARITIME," lettered on the staircase leading up to the company's principal office on Prince Street in Port of Spain, was forgivable hyperbole. At the 1975 Trinidad carnival, it was somehow fitting that a steelband sponsored by the company, Maritime Life Hatters, were the champions of Panorama, the most important steelband competition. And de Souza's consulting business was also going well. Working on government contracts, mostly on pension matters, he had achieved a status he had never had as a civil servant. "I can call up a minister and get him right away," he said. "What civil servant can do that?"

But while all this was happening, some important changes were taking place at Maritime Life's head office in Halifax. In 1969, the forty-seven-year-old company became the Canadian subsidiary of the Boston-based John Hancock Mutual Life Insurance company. The participants explained that the sale would be to the advantage of both sides: John Hancock would get a greater Canadian presence, and Maritime would get the capital it needed to continue its expansion program. Three years later, a further advantage of the relationship manifested itself when Maritime's president, Fred Richardson, left to take a job in Britain, and no suitable Canadian replacement was available. So Orville Erickson, second vice-president in the district agency department of John Hancock, was named president of Maritime — for an interim period, until a Canadian successor could be trained. (Michael Hepher succeeded Erickson as president in 1975).

Although a report of the sale of Maritime Life appeared in the

Trinidad *Guardian,* along with a comment by Mervyn de Souza about the benefits of the change for Maritime Life (Caribbean), it was not widely noticed, and people continued to think of Maritime as a Canadian company. For Canadians who worried about such matters the sale of Maritime Life might appear a small but illustrative instance of the dependency of their own economy. But from the perspective of Trinidad, a country perhaps even more familiar with dependency, an international connection was an international connection, and whether that connection led ultimately to Halifax or to Boston was not of much concern.

8/Bauxite and Power

Our father who is Alcan
hallowed be your name.
Your kingdom has come
in Kitimat as in Jamaica.

Tom Wayman,
Alexander: 5

In late 1970, less than a year after the Canadian banks in Port of Spain had been the scene of Black Power demonstrations, a second drama involving conflicting Canadian and West Indian interests was building up. The protagonists this time were Forbes Burnham and his Guyanese government on the one hand, and Alcan, a large multinational corporation based in Montreal, on the other. The drama centred around Alcan's Guyanese subsidiary, the Demerara Bauxite Company (Demba), in which Burnham had announced his government would seek what he called "meaningful participation": majority government ownership plus other measures to ensure effective government control.

Nationalization in one form or another of the local operations of multinational corporations by Third World countries was not a new phenomenon. Mexico had nationalized its oil industry in the 1930s, Iran had tried to do the same in the early 1950s. Pro-Western leaders such as Eduardo Frei of Chile and Kenneth Kaunda of Zambia had bought fifty-one per cent of their respective countries' copper industries. But this was both the first time it had happened in the Commonwealth Caribbean and the first time a Canadian corporation had been involved, so that for the Canada–West Indies relationship it was an important test case.

Guyana, far from North America and a little less subject to the North American influences that were so dominant in the island territories, was the one West Indian country where such a confrontation might have been expected. In its relative isolation, Guyana had developed a political culture in which proposals such as nationalization were not rejected out of hand. And Demba was by far the largest industrial enterprise in the country, and a more appropriate symbol of the foreign presence than any other company with the possible exception of the giant sugar concern, Bookers.

The presence of bauxite in British Guiana was first identified positively by the colony's Geological Survey Department in 1910, and it soon came to the attention of the Aluminum Company of America, which had established a monopoly of aluminum production in the western hemisphere. Alcoa had begun life in 1888 as the Pittsburgh Reduction Company, when Charles Hall, who had invented the electrolytic reduction process that made the commercial production of aluminum possible, interested a group of Pittsburgh financiers in forming a company to exploit the process. The next year, an ambitious Pittsburgh banker named Andrew Mellon acquired control of the Reduction Company in exchange for $250,000 credit from his bank, and Alcoa became the basis of the Mellon family fortune, one of the largest in the United States.[1]

The key resources needed for the production of aluminum are bauxite and electric power, and although both of these are found within the United States, the Pittsburgh Reduction Company from its early days looked for sources outside the country as well. For electricity, it turned its attention primarily to Canada, and for bauxite, primarily to the Guianas. When the Shawinigan Water and Power Company, which would grow to dominate the electric power industry in Quebec, opened for business in 1898, its first customer was Pittsburgh Reduction's Canadian subsidiary, Northern Aluminum; later, Alcoa developed its own power on the Saguenay River in north-central Quebec. And when Alcoa president Arthur Vining Davis heard about the British Guiana bauxite deposits, he first dispatched the company's chief engineer to investigate the deposits, and later sent a Scottish-American adventurer, George B. Mackenzie, to acquire as much of the suitable reserves as possible. Mackenzie quietly travelled around the Demerara River district, buying lands at bargain prices, telling the coffee planters of the area, who were in some distress because of low prices, that he wanted the lands "to plant oranges."[2] In 1916

Alcoa incorporated the Demerara Bauxite Company in the colony. Alcoa was at this time engaged in beating back a series of challenges to its monopoly position, and several of these aspiring competitors made attempts to get their hands on a share of the rich lode of British Guiana bauxite. The first of these was the Merrimac Chemical Company, which Alcoa disposed of by buying out its Guianese interests. In 1919 the Uihlein family, aiming to get into the aluminum business, acquired bauxite lands in the area where Alcoa had set up its operations. Alcoa countered with litigation, claiming that it had a previous option on the property: the suit eventually failed but by the time it did Alcoa had held the Uihleins up for four years.

According to Joseph Uihlein, Alcoa also put pressure on the British Guiana government to prevent his company from obtaining bauxite rights; in the 1920s, the government pursued a policy of ensuring that the bauxite remained a "British" asset, a proposition that dealt a serious blow to the Uihleins but handsomely suited Alcoa, which had established Demba's citizenship in the British Empire not only by incorporating it in British Guiana, but also by making it a subsidiary of its Canadian company, Northern Aluminum. Alcoa also bought out a company, Sprostons Ltd., which was negotiating for bauxite lands and which Alcoa believed the Uihleins had their eye on. And finally it put an end to the Uihleins' challenge by buying out their corporate instrument, the Republic Carbon Company.

Perhaps the most serious threat came from a collaboration of Sir William Price of the Quebec pulp-and-paper family, J. B. Duke, the North Carolina tobacco magnate, and an American machine-tool manufacturer, George Haskell. Duke and Price had established the Duke-Price Power Company to develop hydroelectric power on the Saguenay River. The Uihleins had been interested in buying Duke-Price power to smelt aluminum but their defeat at the hands of Alcoa ended that scheme. Now Haskell was interested in producing aluminum and he too approached Duke and Price. He negotiated with Duke initially in an attempt to reach a power purchase deal, but later the talks included the possibility of Duke-

133

Price participation in his new enterprise. Determined not to repeat the mistake of the Uihleins, Duke set up the Quebec Aluminum Company and equipped it with a board of Canadian directors for the purpose of campaigning in London for British Guiana bauxite rights, an endeavour in which it received the support of that old West Indian hand, Lord Beaverbrook. In 1925, however, plans were abruptly cancelled and negotiations with Haskell were broken off: control of the Duke-Price Power Company had been sold to the Aluminum Company of America.[3]

The acquisition of a Saguenay power source marked a major expansion of Alcoa's capacity, and the company built an aluminum smelter, an alumina plant (alumina is an intermediate stage between bauxite and aluminum), and a new town, Arvida — honouring Arthur Vining Davis — on the river. The alumina plant allowed it to fulfil a condition under which it had set up its bauxite operation in British Guiana, which was that it process the bauxite into alumina on British soil. In British Guiana it had been widely expected that the alumina plant would be built in the colony, and there was some grumbling when it was established in faraway Quebec instead, but the Arvida plant technically fulfilled Alcoa's obligation.

In 1928 Alcoa set up a new Canadian corporation, Aluminium Limited, and issued its shares to Alcoa shareholders in proportion to the stock they held in the mother company. The directors and managers of the new company were to be completely separate from those of Alcoa. Aluminium Limited was given almost all of Alcoa's holdings outside the United States, and the Aluminum Company of Canada (Alcan), the former Northern Aluminum, became its chief operating company. (The name "Alcan" came to be applied to the whole complex, and Aluminium Limited formally changed its name to Alcan Aluminium Limited in 1966.)

The implications of Alcoa's unusual move were far-reaching. On one level, it was part of the company's strategy of maintaining monopoly control of the industry while staying one step ahead of the antitrust authorities: it was forestalling the development of possible competitors by creating its own. On another level, it was consolidating the "British" character of subsidiaries such as Alcan and Demba. And perhaps most important, it was creating an instrument through which it could participate in the European aluminum cartels; Northern Aluminum had been a member of the original cartels at the beginning of the century but American law had prevented Alcoa from entering the latest one, set up in 1926. Now this problem was solved, and Aluminium Limited formally entered the cartel in 1931.

Although Alcan and Alcoa remained largely under common ownership for another three decades, their development followed separate if parallel paths, and they were united as much by their common interest as large aluminum producers as by their ownership links. After World War II, two new companies, Reynolds and Kaiser, were brought into the game, so that in place of the initial Alcoa monopoly there was now an oligopoly of four firms, still showing all the familiar characteristics of market control and lack of competition.

World War II was a major turning point for the industry. Aluminum was a crucial war metal and so governments took drastic steps to ensure its supply. The United States government established its own capacity, which it turned over at the war's end to private concerns, mostly to Reynolds and Kaiser, allowing those companies to get their start as major producers. As by far the largest producer in the British Commonwealth, Alcan was an important element in the Allied war effort. With loans of US$173 million from the Allied governments, it increased its ingot capacity from roughly 90,000 tons at the start of the war to five times that figure at its end. This expansion included new construction in the Saguenay valley and at several other locations in Quebec: Shawinigan Falls, La Tuque and Beauharnois.[4] Alcan emerged from the war as a full-fledged giant in its own right. In 1951, an American antitrust ruling finally forced a separation in ownership between Alcan and Alcoa, to be completed within ten years. An increasing number of Alcan's shares were held in Canada, and at one point in the early seventies more shares were held in Canada than in the United States, although as of early 1976 the count stood at forty-two per cent Canadian, forty-three per cent American.[5] Where actual control lay remained unclear.

British Guiana was Alcan's chief source of bauxite supply until the 1950s, when a coincidence of two events made the company turn elsewhere. One change was that the development of the vast bauxite reserves of Jamaica had now become feasible. The commercial possibilities of Jamaican bauxite were first investigated in 1942, and Alcan began the construction of its Kirkvine works, near Mandeville, in 1949. Contrary to its long-standing policy in British Guiana, Alcan undertook to produce alumina in Jamaica, shipping it to the company's new aluminum smelter at Kitimat in northern British Columbia as well as to Arvida and to its smelters in Europe. In the next few years Kaiser and Reynolds entered Jamaica to mine bauxite, making the island the largest bauxite producer in the world by 1957, and later Alcoa came in with an alumina plant.

In British Guiana, meanwhile, the People's Progressive Party of Dr. Cheddi Jagan and Forbes Burnham had begun to show a strength that was, from Alcan's point of view, disquieting. It was not hard to see that the PPP, with its anticolonial stance and Marxist rhetoric, could become a threat to one of the largest and most visible foreign industrial enterprises in the country. In the bauxite town of Mackenzie, where segregation between the white, expatriate managers and the mostly black labourers had always been rigidly enforced, tension began to grow. In one incident, a British Guiana policeman refused to let a PPP politician into the managers' area of town.

Partly in response to these developments, Alcan changed its strategy. Guyanese bauxite is of a very high quality, and can be calcined to make a product that is used in the refractory and abrasive industries. By concentrating on calcined bauxite in Demba's expansion plans, the profitability of the British Guiana subsidiary could be maintained at the same time that the dependence of Alcan's worldwide network on it could be reduced.[6] With the precedent of its Jamaican alumina plant, Alcan also built a small alumina plant at Mackenzie, primarily to take advantage of the bauxite wastes that had accumulated over nearly forty years. At the same time it took advantage of the evolving political situation, seeing in the dethroning of the PPP after only a few months in office in 1953 and the re-establishment of direct colonial rule an opportunity that might not soon come again. It demanded for its alumina plant tax concessions that were meant to apply to new industries, and the colonial authorities happily said yes.

For the next decade Alcan rode the political waves, as did Reynolds, which had come into British Guiana in the favourable climate that followed the dismissal of the first PPP government. But the smooth sailing lasted only a few years, as new elections were called in 1957 and voters again chose the PPP. The entire term of office of the second PPP government was marked by high political tension as Burnham, now in opposition, tried with undercover CIA and British help to topple the Jagan regime, a task in which he finally succeeded in 1964. But to form a government he had to establish a coalition with the right-wing United Force, once again creating a temporary political situation favourable to the aluminum companies, which quickly obtained new taxation and mining agreements.

Although Mackenzie was in many ways isolated from the main streams of Guianese life, it was by no means immune to the country's political crisis. Resentment grew, segregation became more difficult to enforce, and incidents became more frequent.[7] In response to the outcries against it, the company began to develop a Guianese middle-management group, and even to invite the new local managers into the Watooka Club, until then the exclusive preserve of the expatriates (but not to make them feel comfortable there: they soon began to drift back to the Mackenzie Sports Club, where the welcome wasn't as icy). By 1970, more than half of Demba's middle managers were local, although the top rung remained resolutely foreign.

In that same year, with the spectre of nationalization looming large, the company set in motion an elaborate public-relations campaign designed to demonstrate that Demba's presence had been good for the country. The president of Demba, J. G. Campbell, went on the radio in Georgetown to "set the record straight" about his company.[8] Thousands of copies of a little blue booklet, *Where did the money go?*, purporting to show that only a small part of Demba's dollars had gone to the company's owners, were distributed.[9] A calypso, also called "Where did the money go?", was composed. At a local exhibition in the little town of Skeldon, in the extreme eastern part of the country just across the Correntyne River from Surinam, Demba mounted a huge display, dwarfing the handicrafts exhibits and ginger-beer-and-pepper-sauce booths around it. But the campaign was undone by its very intensity. It was too much too late. The campaign was cut off as suddenly as it had been launched. Plans to make a record of the "Where did the money go?" calypso were abandoned.

By this time Alcan was facing, in Forbes Burnham, not a reluctant ally forced by circumstances and his own hunger for power onto the same side as the company, but a skilled, self-confident and ruthless adversary. In 1966, Burnham had led the country into independence as the state of Guyana. In 1968, in an election that the opposition PPP, not without evidence, accused him of having rigged, he had won an absolute majority and had been able to ditch the United Force. In 1970, he proclaimed Guyana the world's first Co-operative Republic, declaring that co-operativism would be the Guyanese road to socialism.

With the increasing number of Third World nationalizations, the international climate was changing too. Strong arguments for the nationalization of bauxite were provided by a Jamaican economist, Norman Girvan, whom Burnham would bring to Guyana to be part of his bargaining team, once he had decided to enter into negotiations with Alcan. In a remarkable series of essays,[10] Girvan argued that the relationship of the Caribbean to the overseas companies that were exploiting the region's bauxite was not greatly different from its older relationship to the foreign masters who dominated the sugar industry. This relationship, he wrote, had led "to a cumulative process of development and enrichment for the aluminium companies, and the metropolitan economies where they are based, and a cumulative process of underdevelopment and dependence for the bauxite countries, which provide most of the raw materials."[11]

Furthermore, this situation was not accidental, or a result of the greedy decisions of malevolent managers, but inherent in the whole nature of the aluminum companies, "I am sure," wrote Girvan, "that the managements of Alcoa, Alcan, Reynolds and Kaiser would like to be in a position to feel that the operations of their companies lead to the economic development of Jamaica, Guyana and Surinam so long as this is consistent with their business strategy. The trouble is, that it is not."[12]

The typical aluminum company is multinational and vertically integrated, and its local subsidiaries are organized to serve the global economy of the company rather than the national economies of the countries in which they are located. This shows up in the agreements that are made between the aluminum companies and local governments, in the pricing arrangements between the bauxite subsidiaries and their parents, and in the companies' policy by and large of doing only the minimum amount of processing in the countries that produce the raw materials and the maximum amount in the countries where their head offices are and at other metropolitan locations.

The only solution to these problems, Girvan concluded, is nationalization. Because the defects in the bauxite relationship are structural, they can only be removed by changing the structure. Through nationalization, not only could the Caribbean states get a "better deal" out of bauxite but, much more important, they could gain control over the industry. Girvan also argued for full as opposed to partial nationalization, even though it would be more likely to arouse the companies' opposition and mean that the takeover would involve some disruption and dislocation. This, he said, "should be looked upon as part of the learning process — it is these difficulties which can stimulate the internal effort necessary to successfully run the industry. Ultimately the only way of learning is by trial and error in the process of actually *doing* the management and marketing ourselves."[13] More colloquially, the Guyanese economist Clive Thomas was urging Burnham to "tek all."

Burnham, however, opted for the easier course of partial nationalization, or, as he put it, "meaningful participation" in Demba. This took the form of a set of six nonnegotiable points on which the negotiations between Alcan and the Guyanese government would be based, announced by Burnham in a speech on November 28, 1970. The points were:

● The government would have majority rights in Demba.

● These rights would be obtained through purchase of shares in the company.

● The price for these shares would be determined by the valuation of the company for tax purposes.

● The government would pay for the shares out of its portion of future after-tax profits of the company.

● The government would exercise effective control over the company, as befitting its position as majority shareholder.

● The agreement would go into effect January 1, 1971, regardless of when it was signed.[14]

In spelling out these points, the government was making it clear that it wanted to avoid the Chilean or Zambian situation, where despite fifty-one per cent participation by the government in the local copper subsidiaries, effective control had remained in the hands of the multinationals and partial nationalization had been a severe financial burden on the state. Within Guyana, Burnham's position won wide support. The only serious opposition came from the PPP, which wanted the government to take over all of Demba and Reynolds as well, and other radicals who considered Burnham's position too moderate.

The negotiations began on December 7 in the Bank of Guyana building in central Georgetown amid much publicity. Alcan had already given notice that its appearance at the negotiations didn't imply that it accepted the nonnegotiable demands. In fact it was somewhat taken aback at the toughness of the government's position. In another place or at another time, the company might have been better prepared for a situation such as this and better able to handle it, but in tiny, poor Guyana in a year when Third World countries had hardly begun to flex their muscles, it dismissed Burnham's stance as unacceptable cheek. Norman Girvan wrote later:

It would be naive to pretend that the attitudes of those present at the negotiating table did not reflect the profound antagonism that exists everywhere between the Third World and metropolitan capitalism. From the standpoint of the Alcan representatives, they were dealing with 'natives,' for whom they felt deep contempt. Some of the Alcan people did nothing to hide the feeling, while others made heroic efforts that only became increasingly weaker under conditions of exhaustion, fatigue, and provocation.[15]

Alcan proposed that it and the government form a new partnership in which it would have a fifty-one per cent share and the government forty-nine per cent. Alcan would contribute the total assets of Demba to the partnership and Guyana would kick in G$50 million, which would be raised from the World Bank or some other source and would be used to finance the expansion of calcined bauxite production. This would be the only expansion the company would undertake for the next fifty years. The new company would compensate Alcan for Demba's inventory from its depreciation fund. Managerial responsibility for the company would lie with a chief executive officer, who would be appointed by Alcan and have wide powers.

It was a long way from Burnham's nonnegotiable position. Alcan would still have majority participation and almost total control. Guyana would be shut out from having an aluminum smelter or an expanded alumina plant. The government would have to go into debt to finance the deal and the provision that payments be made from the new company's depreciation fund meant that Alcan would be paid whether the company made a profit or not. Although Alcan modified the proposal several times in the course of the negotiations, it never budged on the essentials. It continued to insist on the right to appoint the manager of the company and on an expansion exclusively in calcined bauxite.

Later, there would be suggestions from each side that the other had bargained in bad faith. From the point of view of Alcan and its friends, the government had never intended to come to an

141

agreement with the company about meaningful participation and had simply made its proposals to create a public climate in which full nationalization would be acceptable. From Guyana's point of view, Alcan's counterproposal was an attempt to call Burnham's bluff and force him to back down. The company never thought he would carry through with his threat to nationalize if no agreement could be reached.

On February 20, 1971, the government formally broke off negotiations with Alcan. Three days later, at a mass rally in Georgetown's National Park marking the first anniversary of the Cooperative Republic (Burnham has a fondness for such occasions), the Prime Minister announced his intention of nationalizing Demba. The takeover bill was introduced in the Guyanese Parliament later that week and passed on March 4 with the full support of the PPP, obtained after a series of meetings between Burnham and Jagan in which the Prime Minister made some unaccustomed political concessions to his chief rival.

Negotiations continued on the sticky subject of compensation. Burnham designated July 15 as "Vesting Day," the day on which nationalization would take effect, creating a prearranged deadline beyond which the government would once again take unilateral action. Like the previous negotiations, the talks on compensation reached an impasse, which this time was resolved by the intervention of Arthur Goldberg, the former U.S. Supreme Court Justice and Ambassador to the United Nations, fresh from an unsuccessful attempt to be elected Governor of New York. Goldberg, who was both a long-time adviser to Reynolds and a friend of Burnham's, and had taken an active interest in the talks, worked out a compromise which was agreed to by both sides on July 14, the day before nationalization was to occur. According to the agreement, Guyana was to pay Alcan US$53.5 million — somewhat higher than Burnham had originally offered — over twenty years at six per cent interest, to come out of government revenues and not out of future profits.

Despite the rancour that had accompanied the negotiations the actual transition went smoothly. With nothing more to lose, Alcan did not see it as being in its interests to try to sabotage the new

142

enterprise. Instead, it established a working relationship with the Guyana Bauxite Company (Guybau), as Demba was now called. Alcan has been a steady customer for Guybau bauxite and, to a lesser extent, alumina. By contract between the two firms, Guybau bauxite is stored at the Alcan transshipment terminal in Chaguaramas, Trinidad, and Alcan's Saguenay Lines is one of the shipping companies that takes the bauxite from Mackenzie down the Demarara River and across the Caribbean to the terminal.

In Guyana, the Demba nationalization set the country on a course that has since led to the takeover of Reynolds, of Sprostons Ltd., the last remaining Alcan interest, of the Jessels sugar estates, and finally, in the spring of 1976, of Bookers, the giant firm that had historically dominated the country's economy. But in Mackenzie itself — now united with its sister communities of Wismar and Christianburg and renamed Linden after Prime Minister Linden Forbes Sampson Burnham — there is a surprising degree of continuity with the old way. In its emphasis on sound business principles and modern management techniques, Guybau somewhat resembles such socialistic enterprises as the Canadian National Railways and — perhaps more closely — Hydro-Quebec, which like Guybau symbolizes the new technocratic capability of a people that for generations was told that it couldn't do those things.

Linden remains a segregated town, but between black manager and black worker now, and so without the same explosive implications that the division had before 1970. But there is still some grumbling on the part of workers who feel that the great national enterprise should be able to do better than that. "The town was built that way," said Haslyn Parris, a member of the government negotiating team who became Chief Executive Officer of Guybau once the takeover was effected, "and we can't change it overnight." Despite the criticisms, however, and despite the wilder speculations on the part of the PPP that the takeover was a plot hatched by Burnham with the Americans, who wanted to punish Canada for its intimations of economic independence,[16] Guybau has made a difference. Perhaps the most important change is that it has allowed Guyana to diversify its markets, a measure recognized by proponents of Caribbean independence since José Marti[17] as a key step in reducing foreign economic power over the region. Guybau has sold alumina to the Soviet Union, Hungary and China as well as to Demba's traditional western customers, and it has continued to sell calcined bauxite all over the world.[18] The nationalized bauxite companies will also give Guyana the means to participate in a Caribbean aluminum smelter if that project gets off the ground.

Noticeably missing from all the complications surrounding the nationalization of Demba was the government of Canada. Guyanese observers were extremely sensitive to any hint of interference from Alcan's home government, so much so that when a Department of External Affairs official came out in favour of "fair and equitable" treatment for Demba, the Guyana *Evening Post* commented that "in the statement credited to the External Affairs spokesman one cannot escape the same contempt for Guyana as was revealed by the Alcan representatives."[19]

The official's statement was typical of the few remarks made by Canadian government representatives during the confrontation. The former Secretary of State for External Affairs, Senator Paul Martin, visited Guyana in November 1970 and later reported to the Senate that he had indicated to Guyanese officials "that what the Government of Guyana did in the exercise of its sovereign right was a matter for its own decision. Canadians would expect their corporate nationals would be treated justly and in a nondiscriminatory way."[20] In February 1971 Prime Minister Trudeau sent a message to Burnham expressing his hope that Alcan would be treated in a "fair and nondiscriminatory" manner.[21]

This condition of non-discrimination was fulfilled, in the Canadian government's eyes, by Burnham's repeated promise to nationalize Reynolds as well, a promise that was carried out in 1974. The only other attitude expressed by the Canadian government on the Guyana–Alcan negotiations was the hope that Alcan would be reasonably compensated for Demba. This too was fulfilled in its eyes, even if Alcan accepted the compensation agreement with some reluctance. And if Canada had not been satisfied that Guyana was treating Alcan fairly, what would have happened then? Would there have been strongly worded diplomatic notes, a recall of the Canadian High Commissioner, threats to cut off Canadian aid, perhaps Canadian troops in Georgetown? The world never got a chance to find out. There were no attempts to prevent Guyana from doing what it had set out to do, or to punish it afterward for what it had done.

Except for one. Coastal Guyana, the settled part of the country, is below sea level and is kept from being flooded by a system of dikes (the country was first settled by the Dutch). Guyana had applied to the World Bank for a loan of US $5.4 million to shore up its seawall, and the application came to a vote in June 1971, while the negotiations between the government and Alcan over compensation were going on. The American Executive Director of the Bank abstained, as the strongest sign of disapproval that was diplomatically possible. Since the negotiations were in progress, the American reasoned, and since the World Bank had acknowledged that it was too early to judge the impact of nationalization on Guyana's economy, presentation and approval of the loan were premature. The U.S. Undersecretary of the Treasury observed that there was little indication that Guyana was making a "reasonable effort" to compensate Alcan.[22] "After all, Guyana is a small country," Haslyn Parris of Guybau commented later. "It only has three quarters of a million people. If they were all drowned it wouldn't be such a big thing. More people than that get killed in floods in India."

Despite the American objection, the World Bank approved the loan. One of those routinely voting in favour was the Canadian Executive Director, who represents, among other countries, Guyana.

From the beginning, Alcan in Jamaica behaved as if it were determined to learn from its mistakes in British Guiana. It established and maintained a policy of processing all its bauxite into alumina locally, and has never shipped raw bauxite out of Jamaica except for testing purposes. It leased part of its expanses of unused bauxite lands to tenant farmers and cultivated much of the rest itself. It contributed money to visible socially useful facilities such as schools and hospitals. Its labour relations were businesslike if

145

not cordial. Its Jamaican towns, Mandeville and Ewarton, avoided the worst excesses of Mackenzie. By incorporating a local subsidiary, Alumina Jamaica Ltd. (Aljam, later Alcan Jamaica Ltd.), it placed itself in a position in which it paid local taxes on a more realistic basis than the other aluminum companies.

And yet only a few years after the nationalization of Demba, Alcan found itself faced with a Prime Minister of Jamaica who was demanding substantial increases in his government's revenue from the aluminum companies, insisting on government participation in the running of the industry, and playing a leading role in organizing the bauxite-producing countries into an association designed to resist the multinationals.

One of the chief fears Alcan and the other aluminum companies entertained about the Demba nationalization was its possible demonstration effect: if Guyana could nationalize the bauxite industry and get away with it, what about Surinam, Jamaica, even the Dominican Republic and Haiti? If this weren't nipped in the bud, who knew what might happen?

In Jamaica, there was little to fear from the somnolent government of Prime Minister Hugh Shearer. But the Opposition Leader, Michael Manley, was rather a different proposition. Manley had visited Guyana in September 1970, and had expressed his support for Burnham's plan to seek meaningful participation in Demba and called it the most important single economic step undertaken in the Caribbean.[23] He had a Burnham-like disdain for fixed modes of thinking and could not be counted on to treat the multinationals in the accepted fashion if elected.

The 1972 election swept Manley and his PNP into office. Although he moved cautiously in the early part of his term, events were happening elsewhere that would soon force him to act. In 1973, the world suddenly became aware of a body called the Organization of Petroleum Exporting Countries, which seemed to have the power to raise the price of oil at will. In the industrialized countries, the dominant reaction to OPEC's new strength was one of fear and outrage that countries such as Abu Dhabi that no one had ever heard of were dictating to the Americans, British and

French. But in the non-oil-producing countries of the Third World, the rise of OPEC had two effects. On the one hand, the higher price of petroleum was a severe economic burden on many of those countries, and created a critical shortage of ready cash for their governments. On the other, OPEC emboldened many Third World leaders to think that if the oil producers could control the price of their commodity, why couldn't the copper producers, or the iron ore producers, or the sugar producers, or the banana producers do the same?

Or the bauxite producers. At a meeting in Conakry, Guinea, in early 1974, seven bauxite-producing countries — Australia, Guinea, Guyana, Jamaica, Sierrra Leone, Surinam and Yugoslavia — agreed to form the International Bauxite Association. Later in that eventful year the IBA Council of Ministers met in Georgetown, and, while the drama of Burnham's intense struggle with the soon-to-be-nationalized Reynolds Guyana Mines was enacted around them, decided in principle to set a minimum price for bauxite similar to the minimum price for oil established by OPEC. It also admitted three new members, Ghana, Haiti and the Dominican Republic, so that seventy-five per cent of the world's bauxite was now produced in IBA member countries.

Since then, the IBA's task has not proved easy. At its second annual meeting in Kingston in November 1975, the Council of Ministers postponed the establishment of a minimum price and recommended to the members that they adopt interim pricing strategies. A month later, Australian voters turned out the Labour government of Gough Whitlam and gave the far more conservative Malcolm Fraser, an opponent of Australian participation in commodity organizations, a commanding majority. Both because of its vast bauxite reserves and because it is a white, developed country, Australia's presence had been an important plus for the organization. Adding further to the IBA's difficulties was the soft world market for aluminum, which reduced its bargaining power.

The IBA also aroused the open opposition of the United States. In November 1974 William D. Eberle, President Ford's chief trade adviser, accused the bauxite producers of having violated agree-

147

ments by raising their prices, and spoke of a developing administration strategy for punishing export cartels, including the IBA.[24] In 1975 a State Department spokesman predicted that the IBA wouldn't repeat the success of OPEC — it didn't have the internal solidarity, both political and cultural, that OPEC did, and it didn't have as important a commodity as its weapon: aluminum could be produced from other ores, including ones that were available in the United States. This was an echo of what the aluminum companies had been saying, and the bauxite countries were no more interested in listening to it from one source than from the other. Then in January 1976, Assistant Treasury Secretary Gerald L. Parsky, letting it be known that his department was a bit apprehensive that Secretary of State Henry Kissinger might be willing to compromise American free-market ideology to appease the Third World commodity producers, came out against any minimum-price commodity agreements with producing countries. He warned that the U.S. must not "sacrifice economic principles for the sake of political gains," and conceded only that the U.S. would be willing to join "producer–consumer forums" to discuss problems of copper, and possibly bauxite.[25]

It was evident that the bauxite countries were on their own.

Nevertheless, they had made some important gains. In the course of 1974, the Chamber of Deputies of the Dominican Republic passed an additional levy on bauxite of US$5 per metric ton. Normally docile Haiti negotiated a new agreement with Reynolds by which the company would pay a substantially increased levy, and the Surinam Aluminum Company, a subsidiary of Alcoa, agreed to pay the government of Surinam US$27 million more in yearly taxes.

The most dramatic changes, however, were being negotiated in Jamaica, where Prime Minister Manley proposed new production taxes that would not only increase his government's take from bauxite, but transform the whole system by which Jamaica is compensated for the ore taken out of its earth. The issues of pricing and taxation have been central in the recent bauxite controversies because they are central to the way the multinational corporations operate. Traditionally, payments by aluminum companies to bauxite-producing countries have been of two kinds: royalties paid on each ton of bauxite, and taxes paid on the profits of the bauxite subsidiary. The royalties have generally been modest: Jamaica was collecting a royalty of twenty-six cents(J) a ton, giving it approximately J$2 million (C$2.2 million) from 13.4 million tons of bauxite in 1973.[26] And the tax on profits has been subject to the vertically integrated corporation's capacity to declare its profit at whichever point along the line it finds most advantageous.

This was the key point at issue in the "Where did the money go?" controversy in Guyana. "Mr. Campbell [the Demba President] says," wrote "Economist" in the Guyana *Graphic* on August 27, 1970, "that Demba's total sales since 1919 have been $905 million. What he does not say is that these sales have been at prices which Demba's parent company, Alcan, have seen fit to grant Demba." Alcan says that it has always tried to simulate "arm's-length" transactions — transactions between an independent buyer and an independent seller — in the bauxite transfers between one of its companies and another. But arm's-length transactions are the exception rather than the rule in the aluminum industry. In the context of a vertically integrated corporation it is doubtful whether one can fairly determine a price for each component of the final product. Manley argued that Jamaica has a stake in the actual aluminum ingot that is ultimately produced by the multinational, and that his government's revenue should be determined on the basis of that ingot.

Manley proposed to the companies a levy of 8.75 per cent of the price of aluminum ingot produced from Jamaican bauxite, in addition to a royalty on bauxite of fifty cents (J) a ton. The companies, which chose to negotiate as a team (Alcan, although its legal and tax status was different from that of the American-based companies, insisted on being part of the team too), made a counter-proposal of 3.5 per cent of the price of ingot. No agreement was reached and so Manley introduced the levy by legislation: 7.5 per cent of the price of ingot in 1974, 8 per cent in 1975 and 8.5 per cent in 1976. This formula increased Jamaica's bauxite revenue from slightly less than J\$25 million in 1973 to more than six times that amount in 1974.[27] A few months later Forbes Burnham of Guyana, equally hard hit by the oil crisis and desperate for revenue, announced a similar levy to be collected from Reynolds in its last few remaining months as a private company. Reynolds protested, and the battle was raging fiercely when the IBA ministers reached Georgetown.

In Jamaica, Manley had also begun entering into negotiations with the companies for the purchase of equity in their bauxite operations and repossession of their bauxite lands. First agreement was reached with the two raw bauxite exporters, Reynolds and Kaiser. Next came the smallest of the alumina producers, Revere. In late 1976, the government reached an agreement with Alcoa, while talks with Alcan, which had begun more than a year earlier, were still in progress. The atmosphere in these talks was a new one. The initiatives of Manley and Burnham and the formation of the IBA had had their effect. The companies were no longer trying to stonewall, but simply to get the best deal that they could.

Alcan said that it was standing a loss on its Jamaican operation since the introduction of the new levies, although again that reflected internal pricing formulas set by the multinational. The company's bauxite future now lay in Australia and Brazil, both of them countries with no-nonsense right-wing governments. Alcan's Jamaican experience has, perhaps, been instructive. It did make an effort to avoid needless antagonism. The contributions to schools, the tenant-farmer program and the rest may, as union representative Lloyd Goodley suggested, have "come out of their public-relations budget," but it was more than one had come to expect from multinational corporations doing business in the Third World. It may even have been as much as such a company could do. The lesson of Alcan in Jamaica is that that is not enough.

9/In Business

A rich multi-national corporation like Bata which enjoys millions of profits every year, should not use its wealth and power to keep from paying poor workers a few extra cents an hour.

Transport and Industrial Workers Union,
Trinidad, 1973

(i) The Shoemaker

With the possible exception of the Royal Bank of Canada, the most pervasive Canadian institution in the West Indies is the Bata shoe company. A company whose profits come from the age-old industry of manufacturing shoes may seem unworthy of comparison with firms engaged in such up-to-date enterprises as aluminum reduction and international banking — especially Bata, built on old-fashioned paternalism and the Protestant work ethic. But in at least one important respect the shoe company is as modern as its more glamorous contemporaries: there are few Canadian concerns that are as aggressively transnational as the Bata empire and none that is more widespread.

As with Alcan and other multinationals based in Canada, Bata's Canadianism has an element of chance to it. The company is of Czech origin, and between the two world wars was the largest industrial enterprise in Czechoslovakia. Thomas Bata, Sr., who became known as the "Henry Ford of Europe," inherited the family shoe business from his father at the turn of the century and, emphasizing mechanized production methods and discipline among his workers, built it into a multinational giant. By the time he was killed in a 1932 airplane crash in his company town of Zlin, it was the biggest shoe company in the world.[1]

After Bata's death the company continued to expand, and it was in this period that it first entered the West Indies, with a chain of retail outlets established through British Bata. It also made its first appearance in Canada in the late 1930s, when Thomas Bata, Jr.,

151

heir-apparent to the company, set up a shoe factory in the new company town of Batawa in central Ontario. At the same time Jan Bata, Thomas Sr.'s half-brother and the company's regent until young Tom came of age, supervised the establishment of a Bata factory in Belcamp, Maryland.

This penetration of North America was more than a simple business move. The European political situation had placed the future of Bata's interests in Czechoslovakia in some doubt, and Jan Bata wanted to hedge his bets. Although not sympathetic to the Nazis himself, he was more than willing to do business with them, and the company's factories in Czechsolovakia continued to produce throughout the German occupation. Meanwhile he set up shop in North America, just in case. This effort to play both sides ultimately caused Jan Bata's downfall: both the Americans and the British blacklisted him, and after the war the Czech court convicted him in absentia of collaboration. But Tom was younger and deemed to have had less responsibility and Canada was more tolerant, so that control of the empire passed, more or less by default, to him. Jan Bata lived out his days in Brazil, trying without success to get the company back through endless litigation.[2]

Although the headquarters of the worldwide Bata network was now the head office of Bata Ltd. in Toronto, Canada never became the centre of the Bata empire in the same sense that Czechoslovakia had been, and it was estimated in 1972 that only five per cent of Bata's world production was in Canada.[3] Instead Bata developed into a genuine multinational, loyal to itself rather than any country, and moving factories and stores like chess pieces across the globe. It continued to expand and spread out and now operates in about ninety countries, most of them low-wage countries in the Third World. Its West Indian interests grew to include factories in Jamaica, Trinidad and Guyana as well as the retail outlets.

In late 1973 Trinidad Footwear Ltd., the local Bata manufacturing company (incorporated separately from the retail interests to take advantage of the benefits accruing to 'pioneer' industries, although the two are run by the same management), introduced a new weapon to the arsenal of labour relations in Trindad: the lockout. "We're the pioneers of locking out in Trinidad," said M. Oldroyd, production technician and deputy manager of the company, with a little laugh. "I don't believe in locking out, and it's not the organization's policy, but sometimes you have to do it."

Bata was embroiled in a struggle over wages with the Transport and Industrial Workers Union and its president Joe Young, a resourceful and militant labour leader who would later be a founder of the United Labour Front that aimed to end the long reign of Dr. Eric Williams. The union was fighting for an increase of sixty-five cents(TT) an hour on wages that ranged from TT$35.20 to TT$45.20 for a forty-five-hour week; the company had offered twenty-eight cents(TT). A "drop in production" was cited as the reason for the lockout,[4] but talking about it later Oldroyd was more forthright: "They started destroying things and became quite naughty, so we locked them out."

The TIWU countered by setting up picket lines outside the Bata retail outlets and launching an island-wide "Don't Buy Bata" campaign at the height of the Christmas season. In one incident, a woman picketer and a TIWU official were arrested after a scuffle between a policeman and a pregnant woman outside a Bata store on Frederick Street in downtown Port of Spain.[5] Although according to Oldroyd the boycott "didn't hurt us as much as we had feared," the result of the conflict was a union victory and a wage increase of sixty cents(TT) an hour. A year later, faded "Don't Buy Bata" signs could still be seen on walls in Port of Spain as a reminder of the battle.

"Ninety-nine per cent of the people in the factory," said the British-born Oldroyd, "are decent people, but one per cent are very militant, and they're in control of the outside union leaders." Of these outside union leaders, he found Joe Young particularly difficult to deal with. "At a meeting he won't even take a biscuit and coffee: he thinks it might be a bribe. He'll make a demand and that's it — he won't budge. I could understand it if he did that in front of his men; after all he has to keep their confidence. But he's the same in private."

Told of Oldroyd's characterization of him, Young reacted with a mixture of amusement and anger: "I'm not interested in being

153

friends with no boss. I'm not going to get anything for the workers in the factory by being friends with no boss."

Bata has leaned toward the East Indian side of the Trinidad racial equation: most of its shop managers are East Indian (as are most shop managers in the country) and many of the factory workers are East Indians who have come into town from the sugar belt. The factory workers are also mostly women. Oldroyd is one of only two expatriates on the staff, the other being the company's designer. The company manager is Czech-born but has been in Trinidad since the early 1940s.

The Bata organization put Oldroyd through college and he has worked for Bata companies in Britain, Sudan, Libya, Singapore and Guyana as well as Trinidad. As of early 1975 he was quite happy to be in Trinidad since he didn't want to go back to Britain "until the oil starts flowing." Using the same standard of measurement that old Thomas Bata himself would have applied, he considers Trinidad quite a well-off country. After all, almost everybody has a pair of shoes.

(ii) The hockey supplier

Jack Cooper presides over a smaller empire than Tom Bata's, but he has found it no less advantageous to manufacture a substantial proportion of his products in countries where wage rates aren't the burden they are in North America. In his trade, sporting equipment, production began to shift to Asia in the 1950s, and although he resisted the move, Cooper himself eventually began to buy baseball gloves and other items in Asia. He still does, but he also found another, complementary solution: he struck a deal with the government of Barbados.

A white-haired, leathery-faced, depression-reared, waste-not-want-not, came-up-the-hard-way executive with a fondness for the details of his business, Cooper found stolid and hard-working Barbados much to his liking; in fact he admitted, in a rare outpouring of romantic feeling, that he "fell in love with the place." Also to his liking were Barbadian wage rates — one-eighth the Canadian rate for comparable work when Cooper Barbados Ltd., a subsidiary of

Cooper Canada, began operation in 1969 — and the terms on which he was invited into the country. Cooper Barbados got a ten-year tax holiday, freedom from all customs duty on raw materials, and a choice factory site right near Bridgetown harbour at a reasonable rate.

The arguments in favour of the deal were persuasive ones for Barbados as well as for Cooper. The new industry created badly needed jobs — employment at the plant would rise as high as three hundred — and the concessions the government was making didn't really appear to be concessions at all, since the new production was entirely for export and wouldn't compete with any existing Barbadian firm. Nor was any Bajan entrepreneur likely to come along who wanted to make the plant's main product, hockey gloves; interest in ice hockey in Barbados is not notably high.

(Some Bajans, however, soon found other uses for the gloves. Jack Cooper reported that on one of his periodic trips to Barbados to inspect the plant he paused to relax in a rumshop near a construction site. A bricklayer wearing a pair of Cooper hockey gloves cut off at the cuffs walked into the rumshop and Cooper asked him where he had got them. "They're made in Barbados," said the bricklayer. Cooper said he knew where they were made, but where had he got them? The bricklayer replied, in the universal euphemism for such transactions, that "his friend had found them in the garbage.")

Cooper has tried to reduce the strangeness of the product by showing his Barbadian employees films of National Hockey League action, complete with Kate Smith singing "God Bless America". But according to the present-day logic of factory location followed by transnational companies both large and small, there is really nothing strange about producing hockey equipment in a country that never sees ice except at the bottom of a glass of rum. People in economically favoured countries are less and less inclined to do dull, repetitive work. Those who will do it ask such high wages that the products they make can't compete with imports from the Third World. Even immigrants, who could once be counted on to do the jobs that others wouldn't, become infected with the prevailing attitudes in their new countries.

155

As a result, production in a wide variety of low-technology, low-wage industries has increasingly shifted to poorer countries. In some cases, the new industry is based on local needs as well as export markets, and on local resources; in others it is simply a creature of the production strategies of metropolitan-based corporations and is completely divorced from the local economy. Industries of the first kind can in some way contribute to the development of the countries where they are located, while industries of the second kind cannot. But both kinds can provide visible signs of apparent progress and at least temporarily meet the most crucial imperative of any government, the need for jobs, and so they are welcomed into many countries with open arms and chequebooks.

Jack Cooper describes the Barbados plant as his "baby", and he is proud of it. And with reason, for according to the standards by which such operations are judged, Cooper Barbados has been a decided success. It has allowed Cooper to remain competitive in certain markets, such as medium-priced hockey gloves (even Barbadian wages are too high for the production of low-priced gloves, which Cooper continues to buy in the Orient), and has given Barbados those coveted jobs. Not surprisingly, Cooper said his relations with former Prime Minister Errol Barrow were "friendly," and it is likely that he will get along just as well with new Prime Minister Tom Adams.

As a result of mechanization, employment at Cooper Barbados has dropped from a high of three hundred in 1974 to a hundred and fifty in mid-1976, but an expansion program is expected to bring it back up to three hundred by the end of 1977. In this expansion, the plant will be diversifying, and such products as handbags, luggage and cricket equipment will be produced for local consumption as well as for export. To be approved as a manufacturer for the local market Cooper has had to renegotiate its agreement with the Barbados government, giving up some of its tax advantages. But there is little cause for worry since most of the benefits remain intact, and the operation was given a further boost at the beginning of 1976 by new United States tariff regulations that abolished duties on certain products from selected underdeveloped countries — including sports equipment from Barbados.

Jack Cooper is pleased with the progress of his baby, and at a time when most of the statements emanating from Canadian businessmen with interests in the West Indies are complaints, his attitude toward the whole proposition of doing business in the region is unusually, almost uniquely, positive.

(iii) The school

The cocktail party, a fund raising event for the local hospital, is clearly a major event in the social life of the tiny island of Carriacou. A visitor to the island, looking for Canadians, figures that if there are any Canadians in Carriacou they will be at the party. There are a couple of nuns in a corner but they turn out to be from the United States. Then someone asks, "Where are you from?"

"Toronto. Where are you from?"

"Toronto. This is ridiculous. Let's try that again."

His name is Bill Allison and he is a teacher at the Canadian Junior College, located in a camp at Carriacou's southern tip. This is the other end of Carriacou from its centre of activity, the town of Hillsborough, and it is an indication of how close the contact is between the Canadian Junior College and the people of the island that in two days of repeated questions about whether there were any Canadians in Carriacou no one had mentioned its existence.

The Canadian Junior College is a school for Canadians and a successful year there fulfils the requirements of Ontario's grade thirteen program. It is also a commercial enterprise, run from Toronto by the man who dreamed it up and brought it into being, Belgian-born Bill Van Reit.

Van Reit studied classics at the University of Toronto but he is imbued with the spirit of the entrepreneur. He agrees with the common criticism that Canadian businessmen are conservative and unwilling to gamble, and it was a characteristic of his adopted country that he was not interested in picking up. As things turned out, no one could accuse him of following a well-trodden path. By his own account, he was still a student, and sitting in the Swiss

157

Chalet chicken restaurant on Bloor Street near the University of Toronto, when he was struck by the idea of starting a Canadian private school in Switzerland.

The Canadian Junior College in Lausanne opened a few years later. It offers a standard senior high-school program, with perhaps a slightly heavier emphasis on languages than is usual in most Canadian schools, and charges a fee of $7,000 a year. "I have been reproached," Van Reit said, "for running an elitist type of education. This is true."

In 1968, with his Lausanne program underway, Van Reit visited Grenada and was so taken with it that he immediately started looking for a suitable piece of land to buy there. There was nothing that he could afford; however, he then saw a seven-acre plot in Carriacou advertised in the Toronto *Globe and Mail.* He flew down and bought it immediately.

Carriacou is a dependency of Grenada but it has its own character and very definitely regards itself as distinct from its larger neighbour. The appeal of Grenadian Prime Minister Eric Gairy has never penetrated Carriacou and it remains the stronghold of Opposition Leader Herbert Blaize; during the crisis that surrounded Grenada's independence in 1974 Carriacou was a refuge for opponents of the Gairy regime who feared for their safety on the mother island. Many of the ten thousand Carriacouans felt at the time that if Grenada were going to be independent of Britain there was no reason Carriacou shouldn't be independent of Grenada, but the separatist movement never got beyond the stage of talk. Since the island's traditional citrus industry was all but destroyed by the worldwide drought that hit many parts of the Caribbean in the early seventies, the main source of income has been remittances from abroad; an elderly woman in a straw hat at the teller's window in the Hillsborough branch of Barclays Bank with a cheque written on the Canadian Imperial Bank of Commerce in Toronto and a British ten-pound note clutched tightly in her hand is a vivid image of Carriacou's economy. It is too far from the path of the big jets that come from North America and Europe to have a mass tourist industry, but its beaches are superb, its hillsides green and enticing, its sunsets incomparable, its ambience gentle and comforting, and its Big Drum Ceremony a unique creation that has gained some international attention. Most of those who have found their way to Carriacou have been charmed by it.

One such was Bill Van Reit. His original idea was to develop his property as a school in the summer and a tourist camp in the winter. The school would specialize in marine biology and be more or less an appendage to the Lausanne location. When the facility opened in 1972, however, the tourist business went badly while the school business went well, so that Van Reit decided to turn it into a school year round. The Canadian Junior College Research Centre for Studies in Marine Sciences and Oceanography began its senior high-school program in 1974. With fees at $4,500 it is not quite as restrictive as the Lausanne school but it is still not exactly open to the broad masses of Canadian high-school students. While the surroundings and the dress of both students and staff at the school are unmistakably tropical, the faces and the atmosphere in the classrooms are straight from a collegiate in one of the better areas of Toronto. Students get most of the standard Ontario curriculum, plus a physical-education program emphasizing swimming, diving and sailing and courses in such things as marine geography, island ecology and "people and cultures of the Caribbean."

But outside of this last course, the students' opportunity to learn anything about the peoples and cultures of the Caribbean is severely limited, and apart from the thirty-odd Carriacouans who are employed at the camp in menial jobs they rarely get to meet anyone from the region. The students are simply too young, their experiences too widely separated from those of people who have lived all their lives on the island and their attitudes about such crucial things as sex too different for anything but a strict separation between the school and the island to be possible.

Van Reit is not greatly worried by this. He had done his bit for the island, providing jobs for Carriacouans as well as education for Canadians. He has had nothing but goodwill from the government of Grenada and most of the people he has come in contact with.

And if a few of the younger Carriacouans have begun to resent the presence on their island of an institution that is neither for them nor run by them, well that can hardly be helped.

(iv) The developer

The Sir George Williams affair, as was pointed out in Chapter 4, dealt a serious blow to Ken Patrick's plans for the West Indies,[6] but the worst was yet to come. Marigot Investments, his Caribbean development company, was in trouble, and only three years after the arrests in the Sir George computer centre in 1969 he would lose control of it.

The company had acquired a varied and rather impressive array of West Indian interests. It had taken advantage of a financial crisis in Antigua's largest trading company, Geo. W. Bennett, Bryson & Co., to gain control of it in 1965, and had also picked up a banana-packing firm in St. Lucia, an investment house in Trinidad and some hotels, as well as the real-estate investments that formed the heart of the operation. "The idea," one of the company's senior employees said later, "was to use the profits from the trading company to provide a cash flow for the real-estate investments. It was a good game plan but it didn't work. The trading company didn't consistently make a profit, and the real-estate investments ate up tremendous amounts of money."

Patrick conceived of developing his tracts of land primarily as retirement colonies for North Americans, and three such developments actually reached fruition, one in Antigua, one on Marigot Bay in St. Lucia, and one at Blanchisseuse on the north coast of Trinidad. At first business went well but as the political climate in the West Indies changed and attitudes toward North American visitors became less welcoming, the retirement homes became harder and harder to sell. "I didn't like the business," said one former retirement-home salesman. "We were selling romantic dreams to elderly people, many of whom couldn't afford it."

By the early seventies, the company was strapped financially and the maintenance of the properties suffered, a serious matter on

Caribbean islands, with their tropical rainstorms and rich plant growth. "I went down there," recalled the ex-salesman, "and the roads were washed out. There hadn't been enough money to hard-surface them. Everything was overgrown — I bumped into a hydrant that was hidden under the grass." Eventually Marigot had to start to sell its properties. It sold hotels, it sold all three of the retirement properties, it sold undeveloped land. It was fortunate to sell a piece of land in Grenada to an investor from Wilmington, Delaware, in mid-1973. Six months later that country's "disturbances" broke out and the Wilmington man was stuck with a property he couldn't give away.

By this time Ken Patrick was out of Marigot Investments. In the sixties he had sold off pieces of the company to raise money, eventually going public in 1967. Patrick and a group of his friends were left with fifty-five per cent of the company. Among the people Patrick had managed to interest in an investment in Marigot were members of the Bronfman whiskey family, who had bought thirty per cent of its stock. In 1972, in an effort to refinance the company, Patrick issued new stock in a rights offering to the existing shareholders. Some of his backers failed to subscribe and the Bronfmans ended up with control. Patrick continued with the company for awhile under its new owners but his heart wasn't in it any more and he eventually left.

Although the Bronfmans had initially got involved in Marigot on the basis of its Caribbean properties, these were now the last thing they were interested in. With so many of its assets sold off, the company now had cash in the till, and it was valuable to the Bronfmans primarily as a financing instrument and tax loss. As of 1975 Bryson's and one piece of raw land were all that was left of the once extensive West Indian holdings. The Bronfmans also changed the name of the company at the time of the takeover, rechristening it Mico Enterprises.

Ken Patrick's Caribbean empire had come apart before it had a chance to come together. But he is not one to indulge in bitter recriminations and he still speaks about the West Indies in the same hopeful tones he always did:

It's not that we have a moral responsibility — no one believes that horseshit any more. But we do have an opportunity to solve a human problem. We've got to do it not just in consultation with the West Indian governments but in partnership with them. You can't produce a Canadian solution; a Canadian solution is crazy. The politicians there are articulate as hell and have lots of ideas. I defy you to find a better parliamentarian than Errol Barrow. The real know-how is down there. They may not be rich but they're competent.

Most of his attention now is devoted to the aerospace industry in his capacity as the Canadian representative for Boeing and to the care of his extensive farm in the Eastern Townships. "There will," said an associate, "be no tag days for Ken Patrick." Nevertheless, there is some evidence that he did not emerge from his West Indian experience entirely unchastened. Despite repeated attempts, the government of his native New Brunswick failed to persuade him to try his hand at saving the Bricklin.

(v) The innkeeper

Almost as much as the Chevrolet, Coca-Cola or Kentucky Fried Chicken, the Holiday Inn bespeaks America. Like the others, it is plastic, uniform and accessible to almost everybody, and like the others it has spread far beyond the borders of the country that gave birth to it and can be found anywhere from Toronto to Taiwan. A region so dependent on tourism as the West Indies is a natural habitat for Holiday Inns and they have sprung up in the Bahamas, Jamaica, Antigua, St. Kitts, St. Lucia, Grenada, Barbados and Trinidad. All but the first two were brought to the region by Canadians.

The Eastern Caribbean Holiday Inns are owned by a company called Allied Innkeepers (Bermuda) Ltd., which in turn is owned in equal parts by Canadian National Realties, the real-estate arm of Canadian National Railways, by Britain's quasi-governmental Commonwealth Development Corporation, and by Commonwealth Holiday Inns of Canada, Ltd., a large Canadian hotel chain that holds a string of Holiday Inn franchises in Canada and elsewhere. Allied Innkeepers is the result of a 1972 merger of the West Indian hotel interests of the CDC and Commonwealth Holiday Inns; at the time of the merger it was thought to be a good idea to get a major airline involved in the operation, and the airline that bit was Air Canada, which participates in such ventures through CN Realties. Management of the hotels is handled by Commonwealth Holiday Inns.

Commonwealth Holiday Inns is the creation of a London, Ontario, entrepreneur named David Rubinoff, who jumped on the Holiday Inn bandwagon in the early sixties, only a decade after the chain was founded by Kemmons Wilson in Memphis, Tennessee. Rubinoff started with a franchise in the London area, then got exclusive franchising rights for all of Ontario, and by 1968 was ready to expand abroad. The areas he chose for expansion were Britain and the West Indies; the British hotels have, on the whole, worked out relatively well, the West Indian ones somewhat less so.

A publicity brochure issued in early 1975 showed everything increasing for the company and at a healthy rate: total rooms, sales, net earnings. But by the end of that year the bloom had faded, and while sales were up twenty-five per cent over 1974, profits had declined from $2.4 million in 1974 to only $413,000,[7] and there was worse news still to come. For the fiscal half ending April 30, 1976, the company lost $4.8 million, more than double the loss in the first half of fiscal 1975.[8] Part of the trouble was that the company expanded too quickly in Canada, and was stuck with a surfeit of hotel rooms in the middle of a recession. Another part of the trouble was the poor performance of the West Indian properties, which by early 1976 David Rubinoff was openly saying he wanted to sell.

There were many reasons advanced for this disappointing outcome, including the name Holiday Inn itself: the connotation of plastic, comfortable, standardized accommodation that attracted customers when it was attached to a roadside stop in Kansas was much more difficult to sell to people who were looking for an exotic Caribbean vacation. But the most important reason for the results of Commonwealth Holiday Inns' West Indian experience is much simpler: it got into the wrong business in the wrong place at the wrong time.

Perhaps the most imaginative and inviting of the West Indian Holiday Inns is the one in Grenada, a low building that seems to blend into the surrounding palm trees and looks out onto one of the finest beaches in the West Indies, Grand Anse. Since late 1973, the Holiday Inn, like many other tourist hotels in Grenada, has been half empty, on its good days. The demonstrations that accompanied Grenada's transition to independence drove the tourists away and they have not returned in anything near the numbers in which they came before the disturbances. Those who have come have been mostly West Germans, occupying at least some of the hotel rooms that the more skittish North Americans have abandoned.

The number of West German tourists has been increasing all through the Caribbean. After a vacation at the Holiday Inn in St. Lucia, one Canadian, who vowed he was never coming back, complained that one of the hotel employees had told him that he would have to wait for his dinner as the staff had been instructed that "we have to give de preference to de Germans." Others reported hearing the St. Lucia police band, all properly dressed in their British-inspired uniforms, strike up "Deutschland über Alles."

But Canadian tourists still make up the bulk of Commonwealth Holiday Inns' clientele in the West Indies — in part the result of an aggressive sales campaign in Canada; in part the result of the Inns' dependence on the package-tour trade (up to eighty-five per cent of their business), which has developed quickly in Canada because of liberal air-charter rules; and also perhaps in part the result of the company's efforts to stress that the Holiday Inns are Canadian hotels. Relations with Holiday Inns Inc. of Memphis, which owns twenty-eight per cent of the Commonwealth Holiday Inns stock, are close. Like other franchise holders, Commonwealth Holiday Inns is required to pay a fee and meet standards set by Memphis in exchange for permission to use the Holiday Inn symbol and the worldwide reservation system operated by the Memphis company. It was the first franchise holder that Memphis allowed to use the phrase "Holiday Inns" in its corporate name.

Both because of the nature of the hotels and because of their heavy emphasis on the charter market, the West Indian Holiday Inns have tended to attract the less adventurous tourists, and also the less affluent ones — "we get a lot of blue-collar people from Hamilton," said John Peskett, the company's director of sales. This is the class of tourists that is most sensitive to political changes in their resort havens and to economic changes at home. As both these factors have made a Caribbean vacation seem somewhat less enticing in the mid-seventies, they are the people who have decided either to go somewhere closer or not to take a trip at all.

For tourists, hotel operators and the governments and countries of the host countries alike, the high hopes that were held out for Caribbean tourism have largely vanished. Commonwealth Holiday Inns came in at the end of the euphoria, and just in time for the bust.

(vi) The airline

> If you want to tour the world go with Air Canada
> And put your trust in the Heavenly Master.
>
> *The Mighty Junction,*
> *Antigua guest-house owner and calypsonian*

The Air Canada holding in the West Indian Holiday Inns is only one aspect of a substantial and diverse network of interests in the region's tourist industry. The airline's own Caribbean routes keep planes busy in the wintertime when they would otherwise be idle, and thus help maximize the use of expensive equipment. Air Canada also holds an interest in a new airline which aims to bring large numbers of tourists to Jamaica. And it has made a number of not entirely successful forays into the charter and inclusive-tour fields, activities which helped provoke a judicial inquiry in 1975.

Much of this was part of a diversification program which Air Canada undertook with vigour after 1972. The idea, according to

165

Judge Willard Estey, the government's commissioner of inquiry, was that

> Air Canada, in order to remain competitive with other airlines, should become involved in the leisure field industry and offer its customers additional services as part of a total package. ... It was hoped that additional profits would be generated from a greater involvement on the part of the airline in offering these services, particularly in the leisure field. This gave rise to a marketing concept, known as the 'total travel experience' (T.T.E.), which provided the customer with a package which included the air ticket, reception service at airports, ground transportation, ground accommodation, sightseeing and other amenities.[9]

In particular, Air Canada was interested in gaining back some of the passengers it was losing to the charter tours — between 1970 and 1974 charter bookings from Canada would increase tenfold — both by getting into the charter business itself and by selling a scheduled service that offered many of the features of charter travel.

The aspect of Air Canada's Caribbean participation that most concerned Judge Estey was the manner in which it got involved in providing tourist accommodation at the Sunset Crest development in Barbados. Sunset Crest is a complex of apartments, villas and shopping and other services on the sheltered west coast of the island. Most of the apartments and villas were sold to North Americans for use as vacation dwellings. When the owners were not using them, the Sunset Crest developers arranged to rent the accommodations out, either to individuals or on a block basis to charter operators.

This arrangement caught the attention of Air Canada, and particularly of its vice-president for marketing, Yves Menard. Air Canada had entered the charter business through a new subsidiary of CN Realties called Econair Canada Holidays Ltd. (later Venturex Ltd.), of which Menard was president. In late 1972, Menard discussed with Fred Laforet, Sunset Crest's prime mover, the possibility of Econair's leasing a hundred apartment units in the development. At the same time Mike Lezama, market development manager for Air Canada's southern routes, was negotiating the rental of twenty-five villas for the airline's Sun Living program. Sun Living is the airline's effort to offer a charter-style inclusive tour, but with scheduled flights. Since the scheduled air fare is considerably higher than charter rates, Air Canada has to make sure that the cost of accommodation is low for the whole package to be competitive.

With Sunset Crest, this meant renting out accommodation at less than its cost to the airline. Both the villa and the apartment deals went through, and Air Canada began operating Sunset Crest vacations in the winter of 1973-74. By this time, for reasons that remained unclear to Judge Estey, the apartment as well as the villa leases had been assigned to Sun Living rather than Econair.[10] The experiment was not a success. Air Canada expected to lose money on the apartment leases, and it did — almost three times as much as it had projected. As for attracting passengers to Air Canada, which was the goal of providing the accommodation, Judge Estey reported that during the months of February and March of 1974, when the apartments were ninety-five per cent full, only twenty-six per cent of the Air Canada seats set aside for Sun Living were used.[11] The leases were renewed for another year in 1974, but allowed to lapse in 1975. The Judge was highly critical of the decision-making process within Air Canada that let such a dubious program be launched and get as far as it did without proper financial scrutiny or control by the airline's top management and board of directors.[12]

He was also critical of the at least apparent conflict of interest in the purchase of a Sunset Crest villa by Yves Menard in 1973. Barbados was Menard's favourite vacation spot, and after his brother-in-law, Jean-Marc Audet, bought a villa in Sunset Crest in 1969, he made frequent visits to the west-coast development, and made the acquaintance of Fred Laforet. He became interested in Sunset Crest not only for use of the airline, of which he was a senior executive, but as a personal investment as well. His negotiations for buying and financing his own villa were going on at the same time as the airline's negotiations for the villa and apartment leases. "It is

167

puzzling," wrote Judge Estey, "that no one in Air Canada who was aware of Menard's villa ownership recognized this as a potential conflict of interest situation."[13]

Menard resigned from Air Canada in February of 1975 in anticipation of a Montreal *Gazette* story on his Barbados transactions. Judge Estey's report later that year, which detailed a serious malaise in the airline, of which the Sunset Crest venture was only one symptom, led to a second resignation, that of Chairman Yves Pratte.

A far less controversial aspect of Air Canada's Caribbean involvement has been its participation in the formation and nurturing of Air Jamaica. This has been cited as a praiseworthy instance of a big brother organization helping a little brother to grow and become self-sufficient; Bob Burchill, commercial counsellor with the Canadian High Commission in Kingston, called it "an excellent example of how these things can work."

Air Jamaica was started in 1966 with planes leased from the British Overseas Airways Corporations. Two years later it was reorganized as Air Jamaica (1968) Ltd. and it was at this point that Air Canada entered the picture. Air Canada subscribed to forty per cent of the company's $1 million of voting stock (the Jamaican government bought the rest). It aso provided $7 million in the form of a purchase of preferred stock, with the money to be covered by a loan from the Bank of Nova Scotia; it was arranged that Air Jamaica would buy back the preferred stock as Air Canada's debt to the bank came due. In addition, the Bank of Nova Scotia lent $20 million directly to Air Jamaica. Air Canada provided the pilots for the new airline, and most of the managerial personnel. The first president of Air Jamaica (1968) was a Canadian named John McGill, who until then had been Air Canada's general sales manager.[14] As of early 1975, Air Jamaica had routes from Kingston and Montego Bay to Toronto, several destinations in the United States, and London, with an imminent extension to Frankfurt. It had a fleet of nine DC–8s and DC–9s. It was introducing computer reservations. It had had a steady record of profitability since 1971, its third year of operation. And increasingly, this was accomplished under Jamaican management. By this time the airline had a Jamaican president, Guillermo Machado, appointed in 1974. Only two of the Canadian managers remained, and half of the pilots were now Jamaican. Air Canada had also begun to reduce its equity participation and aimed eventually to keep only a ten per cent share.

The only problem with all this was the kind of airline the Jamaicans and Air Canada had created. Like most of the other airlines serving the West Indies, it is oriented toward travel between the region and metropolitan countries, and particularly toward bringing tourists from North America and Britain to Jamaica. Meanwhile, communication within the region itself is a continuing nightmare. Air Canada or Air Jamaica can take you nonstop from Toronto to Montego Bay and Air Canada or the Trinidad-government-owned BWIA International can take you nonstop from Toronto to Antigua. But to fly from Antigua to Jamaica requires not only a change of planes but an overnight sojourn on the ground. The one airline that does maintain connections among the islands, including the small islands of the Leewards and Windwards, is LIAT, and it is in constant financial trouble and always the target of barbs for its poor service: its initials are said to stand for "Leaving the Islands Any Time."[15] After discussing the matter with the West Indian governments in 1974 Air Canada decided not to get financially involved in LIAT.[16]

But the internal transportation problems of the West Indies are not of great concern to Air Jamaica. "We have no thought of any inter-Caribbean business in the next decade," said the airline's public-relations director, Jim Nelson, in 1975. "The only reason we have remained profitable is that we're a one-distination carrier. We sell more than a seat — we sell a destination. We would only have inter-Caribbean service if we could sell the Caribbean as a destination."

Air Jamaica had hitched its jets firmly to the tourist business — more than sixty per cent of its revenue was coming from North American and British tourists bound for a Jamaica holiday — and it was on the buoyancy of that business that its future profitability

169

would depend. When the airline had been launched this had appeared to be a good gamble, at least from a financial point of view: there had always been critics who had carped about the social effects of such a policy. In the early years of operation, the gamble had shown signs of paying off. But in the mid-seventies there was gathering evidence that for Air Jamaica, Air Canada, and all the other enterprises involved in the Caribbean tourist industry, the bright days were drawing to a close.

10/Dubious Ambassadors

Efforts will be made to shield tourists.

Jamaica Daily Gleaner,
June 24, 1976

There are few enterprises on which the West Indies have embarked with as much enthusiasm as they showed for mass tourism at its beginning in the late 1950s. It seemed the ideal industry. It required no rare mineral or sophisticated technology but only warmth, water and and a few palm trees, things that West Indians had and took for granted. It didn't involve the backbreaking work and the association with slavery that had soured people on sugar. For those who cared about such things, it was even non-polluting.

In 1959 Abe Issa, chairman of the Tourist Board of Jamaica and president of the Caribbean Tourist Association, visited the islands of the Eastern Caribbean to investigate the tourist potential of the area on behalf of the federal government of the West Indies. His report was not only glowing in its estimation of the possibilities but also hortatory in its emphasis on what should be done. The federal government, he wrote, should undertake the "task of establishing a proper 'climate' for the development of the industry," that is, an "investment climate," which "consists of incentive legislation offering tax holidays and other concessions to encourage the investment of capital in Tourism. Tax holidays and other capital inducements, such as freedom from the import duty, are necessary to attract capital, both local as well as overseas, for building hotels and for developing other tourist facilities and amenities."[1]

He warned against the dangerous "attitude of indifference to the industry on the mistaken ground that we don't need it. There can be no question of our being able to afford to do without it. When we see how such highly developed industrial countries like Britain, France, Italy and Canada develop and promote Tourism, it must be obvious that this is a valuable industry. How much more vital is

171

it, then to our countries of the Caribbean, whose industrial development is way below that of these countries!"[2]

It was a particularly opportune time to consider a major development of tourism. The imminent introduction of the big jets would make getting to and from the West Indies faster and easier. Postwar prosperity in North America seemed likely to continue indefinitely, and foreign travel, once an exclusive pleasure of the rich, was now accessible to average Americans and Canadians. And Cuba, the traditional haven for American tourists, had fallen into the hands of a new and different regime and the future of the industry there was uncertain, so that many North Americans would be looking for alternative destinations. To Issa and many other West Indians, there appeared to be no reason why they shouldn't look to Jamaica, Antigua, Barbados or Grenada.

Not all of the details of Issa's prescription were followed, but the broad outlines of his plan were adopted. As he confidently predicted, tourism became one of the major industries of the West Indies, with the active encouragement of the short-lived Federation and its successor governments. But the riches that Issa argued would follow in the industry's wake were slower in coming, and the dollars that the tourists did bring were counterbalanced by social problems unimagined by Issa and his supporters. By the early seventies many West Indians, including some within the tourist industry, were wondering whether the whole enterprise was worth it. For in committing their countries to tourism, West Indians were continuing the historical pattern in which the agricultural and extractive industries were developed for the benefit of outside interests. They were selling off at bargain prices the most precious asset that they had to offer — themselves.

Perhaps the most striking indication of the extent to which enthusiasm for tourism has declined is the readiness of people working for tourist boards, ministries of tourism, hotel chains and other tourism-oriented outfits to question the value of the industry they are promoting. "This is not for your book," said one in the midst of what until then had been a rather stiff and formal interview, "but my own opinion of tourism is that it tends to pervert any society it comes in contact with. You only have to look at the places that are dependent on tourism to see what I mean." Later he said, "Tourists are not the best ambassadors. They have a tendency to say the wrong things and ask the wrong questions. They'll ask a taxi driver, 'Do you live in a house? Do you have a washing machine? Do you have a television set?' And when he says no they'll say, 'Well everyone in New York — or Cleveland, or Toronto — has those things' and make him feel like a real idiot."

A Barbadian tourist official has become vexed with the "intellectuals" who are opposed to tourism: "I ask them, 'Have you got an alternative?' and they can't answer. I say if you come up with something better we'll stop it tomorrow." A hotel-company manager admitted that "the problems of tourism are inherent in the business" and said sadly that "the islands will remain poor."

Tourism has come under attack on economic, social and cultural grounds — in fact on just about any grounds that can be imagined. For Ken Patrick the problem is relatively simple:

> No hotel in the Caribbean is an economic proposition. It's catastrophic. If you're only full two and a half or three months of the year, you'll lose money even if you charge two hundred dollars a night and pay your employees ten cents an hour. They haven't understood that in the West Indies. Also, for each bed you have to have an airplane seat and vice versa. They haven't understood that either. I don't blame them for that — the hunger to hear the good news is so great that they shut out the rest.

Others have attacked tourism because it contributes much less to West Indian economies than it seems to, because of its heavy import content. In the more bullish days of the 1960s there was much talk about the tourist "multiplier", the factor by which you could multiply the tourist dollar to calculate its real impact on the local economy. It was argued that money spent by tourists went to local residents in the form of wages and that they then spent it on local goods and that the merchants from whom they bought the goods recycled the money still further, so that each tourist dollar really counted for two or three or more. A study of tourism in the Eastern Caribbean done in 1969 by the consulting firm of H. Zinder and Associates, under contract to the U.S. Agency for International Development, estimated the multiplier at 2.3.[3] But such

173

estimates failed to take account adequately, or often to take account at all, of "leakages" of income from tourism through foreign ownership of hotels and imports of food and other goods. The tourist industry is notoriously dependent on imports — especially the kind of tourist industry prevalent in the Caribbean. Tourists are served steaks flown in from Miami, Idaho potatoes, French wine and Scotch whiskey. Before it has had a chance to multiply, most of the tourist revenue has left the country. Some of it, such as money siphoned off by a foreign hotel owner from his share of a package-tour price paid in North America, never even enters the country. In their critique of the Zinder report, Kari Levitt and Iqbal Gulati, accepting the rather generous assumptions used by the Zinder firm but taking account of import leakages, recalculated the multiplier at 1.27. When Levitt and Gulati used more realistic assumptions, the multiplier fell to 1.07.[4] In other words the tourist dollar is not much more or less than what it appears to be — a dollar.

But what the host country gives up to get that dollar can't be measured in economic terms only. It is no accident that the most vital and creative parts of the West Indies have been precisely those that have been least touched by tourism. In Jamaica, the north coast has largely been turned over to the tourist while the country's national life, political and cultural, is almost entirely carried out on the south coast. Trinidad has succeeded in preserving much of its unique way of life because its beaches have not been regarded as suitable for mass tourism and have not attracted hotel operators from the North Atlantic. Despite all its difficulties, Guyana has gone further than other West Indian countries in political experimentation because it has been almost entirely free of tourists. Islands that are host to a mass tourist industry, on the other hand, become stodgy and subservient like Barbados, debased like Antigua, or deeply corrupt like the Bahamas. The irony of this is that these qualities eventually begin to repel the tourists who helped them happen in the first place. "Tourism," said a Barbadian tourist official, "is an industry that bears the seeds of its own destruction."

Antigua is, arguably, the country most seriously ravaged by

174

tourism. The tourist industry developed less because of any inherent advantages of the island than because the big jets from North America could land at the airstrip the Americans had built to serve their military needs during World War II. (The other small islands of the Leewards and Windwards are still without direct air communication with North America, and the bother of changing planes is enough of a deterrent to scare off most tourists.)

One of the first large tourist developments in Antigua was Mill Reef, which caused some controversy on the island because it was closed to the local population. "Personally," wrote Abe Issa in his 1959 report:

> I think the proprietors of Mill Reef are a little undiplomatic in carrying exclusivity to the degree to which they have taken it. A barred gate and an uniformed guard are, I think, somewhat unnecessary. . . . But I suggest that the Mill Reef ownership and management are within their rights to operate the club as a private concern and to restrict the free access of the public to its grounds, buildings and beach. The Antiguan Government was within its rights to grant this complete concession to encourage a development of this nature and need have no heart-burning over Mill Reef.

Issa went on to judge "Mill Reef and any other development of this nature as a good thing for Antigua. The fact is that this resort has given tremendous publicity to Antigua and has helped to put it on the tourist map. Certainly, Antigua is well known now in North America because of Mill Reef. To regret it and say it should not happen is to be unnecessarily chauvinistic, in my view."[5]

Antigua's once significant sugar industry has withered, and since 1972 no sugar at all has been grown on the island. As of 1974 between sixty and seventy per cent of its GNP was accounted for by tourism. In the centre of St. John's, Antigua's rather dowdy capital, a white North American can hardly move without being accosted by one of the town's taxi drivers.

"Do you want a taxi?"

"No; I'm not going anywhere."

"Maybe later?"

"Maybe."

"Come and see my car." He points out his car, a station-wagon.

175

"Actually, I've got a lot of business in town today. I really don't think I'll be needing a taxi today."

"What about tonight? I can show you some night-life."

"I'll see. What kind of night-life is there?"

"Well, when I say night-life, I mean girls. And men. We have girls who like men, men who like men, men who like girls. Something for everybody. You're laughing but that's the way it is. In Antigua we live the way we like. My name is George and this is where you can find me."

The tourist has his own particular psychology, and the North American on vacation is by no means the same creature as the North American at home. He expects to indulge in pleasures that would horrify him if he saw them back in Waukegan or Thunder Bay. And the entire host society is expected to organize itself to provide him with those pleasures. It is also expected to ensure his safety and comfort and is taken to task if there is any breach of that promise. In a searing critique of tourism in the West Indies, historian Louis A. Perez, Jr., of the University of South Florida noted that "increasing energies ... have been diverted to curb mounting popular disaffection with tourism. Rudeness, hostility, and abuses, Jamaica's public relations firm warned, created a 'situation that is working in counterpoint to our promotion efforts and expenditures.' "[6]

Perhaps worst of all, Perez wrote, was the effect of tourism on national identity and culture:

> The collective historical consciousness — the vital basis of national consciousness — has been defined by the requirements of tourism. The remains of the colonial past serve as the props of the neocolonial present. The colonial regime reappears as an exalted tourist attraction. Colonial buildings, missions, forts and fortresses, colonial residences, and the remains of defunct plantations pass, appropriately polished, into travel brochures. Tourist literature on the Great Houses in Jamaica, for example, neglects to describe the organization of colonial society or the quality of the human condition over which the plantation mansions presided. Instead, one reads about restorations to the "original 18th Century splendor" and is encouraged to visit plantations

176

"running much the same way for hundreds of years."
The very culture passes into dependency on tourist patronage. Art, music, dance, and literature become the patrimony of an expanding tourist economy. In the process, artistic expression in the West Indies loses its integrity and, indeed, its relevance to the West Indian experience."[7]

When a conference on Caribbean tourism sponsored by the Barbados-based Caribbean Tourism Research Centre convened in Caracas, Venezuela, in January of 1975, a few of the delegates were concerned with such problems. Rather more of them were concerned with the strictly economic problems of tourism as they related to Caribbean societies, and particularly with promoting interconnections between tourism and other sectors of the economy such as agriculture so as to reduce dependence on imports — instead of leakages, linkages. But most of the delegates were concerned with why the hotels and tourist operators weren't making more money.

The language of the conference was mostly the jargon of the marketing profession. Fred Ruoff of Hilton International expressed some dissatisfaction with the way the Caribbean was marketing itself as a tourist destination. (For Ruoff there were no places, only "destinations".) He said things such as: "the ground experience becomes a culmination of the total product that is placed before the consumer" or "sightseeing as an infrastructure item in Venezuela is outstandingly strong." Charles Bell of the same company presented profit statistics in which Hilton hotels in the Caribbean showed up unfavourably when compared with Hilton hotels in Canada and South America.

But the most impressive performance was given by one John Duncan, III, executive vice-president (sales) of Robinsons Inc. of Orlando, Florida, a company that describes itself as providing "marketing services to the travel/hospitality/leisure industries." Robinsons, in collaboration with Cornell University, had been engaged by the Organization of American States to do a survey of the attitudes of travel agents in the United States, and Duncan had the preliminary results of this survey ready to present to the conference.[8] Armed with graphs and charts, all cross-tabulated and colour-coded, to which he pointed authoritatively with the inevitable long stick, and burning with a belief in the power of modern statistical methods (to one Antiguan delegate he was reminiscent of an encyclopedia salesman), Duncan explained what American travel agents thought — and what they thought their clients thought — of various tourist geographies (what was a "destination" for Ruoff was a "geography" for Duncan).

The geography that fared best, according to the criteria used in the survey was, of all places, Australasia; the Caribbean came in fourth, behind Western Europe and Mexico. The Caribbean got passing marks for attractiveness, cleanliness and activity, but fell down badly in safety and particularly friendliness. Only the Middle East was perceived as being less friendly than the Caribbean. When the survey asked what the travel agents thought their clients wanted in a vacation, the dominant answers had to do with things like good hotel accommodations, reliable reservations and low cost. Five of the top ten criteria were related, in Duncan's words, "to man's fear of the unknown": Travel agents want to give their clients vacations that are orderly, predictable and safe.

Duncan's presentation was so well received that the chairman of the conference, Tourism Minister Peter Morgan of Barbados, asked him to do it all over again the next day for delegates who had missed it the first time. Duncan was only too happy to oblige.

But despite Duncan's graphs and figures, the conference didn't come up with any solutions for ills that have now become chronic. At the close of the conference, a bearded American tourism critic named Herbert Hiller moved that the conference propose a five-year moratorium on hotel construction, and the mood of the delegates was such that the conference easily passed the resolution (which it had no power to back with any concrete action). The seeds of tourism's destruction have sprouted like weeds in a garden patch and nobody knows how to stop them.

Canadians have played an important part in the West Indian tourist picture for a long time, not only as operators but also as consumers. In Barbados, Canadian tourists make up the largest single group, having surpassed the number of visitors from the United States for the first time in 1974. In 1973, nearly 69,000 Canadians visited Barbados, while 127,000 went to the Bahamas, 37,000 to Jamaica, and just under 10,000 to Antigua.[9]

The particular affinity Canadians seem to have for Barbados is often ascribed to Air Canada's long-standing relationship with the country, and also to aspects of the Canadian and Barbadian personalities. With perhaps a tinge of jealousy, David Harris, representative of the Jamaica Tourist Board in Canada, credited Air Canada with having directed Canadian tourists to Barbados rather than to the country he is trying to sell (British-born, Harris represented the Bahamas in Canada before he switched to Jamaica). "Where the airlines spend the money, that's where the tourists go," he said. He admitted, however, that a large part of his budget had to go into countering the "bad word of mouth" to which Canadians are especially sensitive — the reports of violence and other activities in Jamaica that scare tourists away — and lamented the fact that Jamaica had to spend $17 on promotion for every Canadian tourist it attracted, as compared to $5 for the Bahamas and only $2 for Barbados.

Prim and conservative, and with a less fragile society to start with than Antigua or the Bahamas, Barbados does not show the effects of tourism quite as badly as some of the other "destinations". Canadians find its lack of tension appealing, and are more comfortable with eager-to-please Barbadians than with the self-assured people of Jamaica. Canadians are also not terribly adaptable and want to make sure that when they pick up the receiver, the telephone will work and when they turn on the tap, water will come out. In Barbados these things are not problems.

Discussions of the differences between Canadian and American tourists usually revolve around the Canadians' lesser inclination to assume automatically their superiority to whatever is around them. It is unlikely that any Canadian would have stood in the Cable and Wireless office in St. John's, Antigua, as did tough, no-nonsense, grey-moustached American Telephone and Telegraph employee George Alexander, and tried to browbeat the unimpressed lady behind the counter. He was insisting that he be allowed to make a station-to-station call on his credit card, which the lady was saying was against the rules, and he was quickly losing his patience. Soon he stopped talking to her altogether and instead turned to the person behind him: "I can't understand what she's saying. She's talking too fast for me. What did she say?" Finally he came up with the clincher. He turned back to the counter, faced her eyeball-to-eyeball, and said firmly: "I'm in the communications business. In the *States*. And I know." The lady suppressed a giggle with some difficulty.

Canadians abroad can be just as insensitive to local customs and contemptuous of local people as Americans but they are usually too polite or too hypocritical to say so. However, the boorish behaviour of some Canadian tourists has led to increasing talk of an "ugly Canadian" syndrome in the Caribbean.[10] But perhaps the most serious complaint registered against Canadians has been their relative reluctance to do what tourists are supposed to do: spend money. Writing in the Nassau *Guardian* in March 1975, Norman Solomon, an opposition member of the House of Assembly, was worried not so much about the shrinking number of tourists coming to the Bahamas as about who they were:

> What concerns this columnist more than the decline of 10 per cent in numbers, is the drop in tourist standards, by which we mean the decline in the purchasing power and economic status of the incoming visitor to the Bahamas. An increase in gross volume may be quite meaningless in real terms. Both January and February of this year have registered for the Bahamas an increase in tourist arrivals. But of what real use are arrivals who have little money to spend after they arrive? . . . And now that we are in March we observe large groups of Canadians who are flying down on cheap charters to take advantage of special rates — special rates being offered in what is supposed to be a prime and peak tourist month."[11]

For a tourist destination so close to the United States, this seemed to Solomon to be little short of a disgrace: "On our doorstep we have the largest accumulation of the easiest spenders in the world. You need to go some 14,000 miles to Japan? Or 5,000 miles to Germany? Or even to Canada? Why not let us welcome everyone but concentrate on the one nationality so close to us that has what we want — dollars and the will to spend them freely."[12]

The inclusive-tour charter has been a major factor in defining the Canadian tourist in the minds of West Indians. Although tourist operators consider ITCs simply a "marketing tool," charters have also changed the nature of the tourist population. The charter marks the final decline of the aristocratic activity known as travel that flourished in former centuries into the commodity we know as the tourist package. While the traveller was expected to broaden his horizons and learn from the cultures of the countries he visited, the absolute minimum of intellectual effort is demanded from the tourist, and particularly the charter tourist. Much less is demanded from him financially as well, so that the ITC has been responsible for the creation of whole new tourist markets. Held back in the United States by the restrictive regulations that the scheduled airlines promote, the package-tour trade faced no such problems in Canada and in the 1970s it accommodated a rapidly growing percentage of the total number of tourists. As a result the "cheap charter tourist from Canada" has become an identifiable figure in tourist mythology. "You have Mr. and Mrs. Smith who have been coming for ten years," lamented Anders Wiberg of the Bahamas Hotel Association at the Caracas conference, "and then they arrive on the same day as an ITC from Canada and that's the last you see of Mr. and Mrs. Smith."

The charter tourist is sold the sun-sea-sand-and-sex dream at bargain rates through elaborate, glossy colour booklets distributed by such organizations as Suntours-Canada, a wholesale charter agency in which the Royal Bank of Canada has a minority interest. And for those who can't immediately put together even the four-or-five-hundred-dollar price of a package tour, the booklet includes an advertisement for the Royal Bank's Travelplan loan service. By 1975 there were 200,000 passengers a year on Suntours flights, according to the firm's president, Dennis Gill.

A growing favourite of Canadian charter tourists in recent years has been Cuba, which re-entered the tourist market in the early 1970s after being out of it for more than a decade. The new Cuban tourism is based on the ideal of *un turismo sano* or a healthy tourism, but, after several years of trying, the Cubans have only partially achieved their goal.

The tourism of the pre-1959 era is vividly remembered in Cuba, and many of its artifacts are still standing. Large segments of the Cuban population and economy were mobilized to serve the desires of the American visitors. The luxury hotels were built to accommodate them. They occupied the best beaches with their villas and estates; the du Pont estate at Varadero, which in its heyday had its own private golf course, is kept up as a reminder of this aspect of the American presence. Gambling and prostitution were everywhere. Much of the operation was under the control of gangsters, and many of the internal squabbles of the American Mafia were resolved on the streets of Havana.

After the revolution the tourists all went elsewhere and Cubans became unused to seeing any foreigners except Soviet and East European technicians, diplomats, American hijackers, Black Panthers and members of the Front de Libération du Québec. In the early seventies the tourists started coming back, although not in the same numbers and not entirely for the same things. By this time the tourist euphoria that had swept other Caribbean countries after the closing of Cuba had faded, and so Cuba went back into the business in a new and more sober atmosphere, and acutely aware of the dangers.

If there was any country in the Caribbean in a position to realize the dream of *un turismo sano* Cuba was it. First of all, its relatively large population — eight million — ensured that the country wouldn't be swamped by the tourist influx. Second, the existence of a substantial domestic market for tourism meant that the industry would not be entirely dependent on the whims of foreigners. And third, the Cuban government was more determined than any other to keep tourism under control.

As a result, tourism has become a significant but not crucial source of foreign exchange for the country, and has in the process disrupted Cuban life only slightly. The tourist in Cuba is still basically expected to accommodate himself to the Cuban way of doing things (within limits) rather than the reverse. Such phenomena as the beach boys of Barbados and the casinos of the Bahamas have not manifested themselves in Cuba. There has been a little but not much prostitution. Begging began with children asking for Chiclets outside Havana's Hotel Nacional and has escalated to people requesting more elaborate consumer goods such as watches, but it has still not reached the level of many other Caribbean countries.

There has been some grumbling about the privileges that the tourists get, such as cheap drinks and food that is not available to Cubans — of course, if they did not get them they would not come. Tourism has also intensified the problem of hotel and restaurant service: complaining about it is a Cuban national pastime but with the increasing number of foreign tourists there is more and more the feeling that something should be done. The spectacle of a taxi driver outside the Hotel Capri in Havana, meticulously cleaning his windshield while a group of tourists wait, willing to serve them when he's ready to and not before, provides a sharp contrast to the supplicating taxi drivers in Antigua. The driver's independent spirit is admirable but it's not good for business. There has been talk of bringing back pay incentives, which were abolished in Cuba in the early sixties under the guidance of Che Guevara, and there have even been rumours around Havana, vigorously denied at the official level, of a reintroduction of tipping. Already some tourists have reported that in some places tips were not only accepted but expected.

Still, tourism has been enough of a success in Cuba that at the same time as there was serious talk about a moratorium on hotel construction is some other countries, the Cubans were launching a program of building sixty-two new hotels. These hotels, designed for domestic tourism in the summer and foreign tourism in the winter (the Cubans consider the winter season too cold for bathing, but if those crazy Canadians want to come down and pay to stay at beach hotels which would otherwise be vacant, that's all right with them), will span the country and bring the industry to places where it has not been before.

Tourism officials in other Caribbean countries, aware of Cuba's natural advantages, have expressed fears about the possible effects of the competition if Cuba goes back into the industry on a pre-1959 scale. Varadero, about seventy miles east of Havana, offers gleaming white sand and clear blue water and is as close to perfection as any beach in the Caribbean. And, while a one-week package tour to Cuba is far from being a political indoctrination session, both the Cubans and the ITC operators are aware that the revolution is, in its own way, marketable. "Be the first on your block to go to Cuba," advertised Suntours in 1975. "When you come back you can hand out the same cigars Castro smokes and talk of how you walked the Bay of Pigs."[13]

If the abuses are kept under control and a genuine *turismo sano* is achieved in Cuba, it will be a remarkable accomplishment for Cuban society. If tourism in Cuba goes the same way it has everywhere else, it will be an indication of how ingrained the ills of the industry are. For the moment, the jury is still out. Meanwhile, other countries have been getting into the act as well. Haiti offers luxury hotels and gambling amid the worst poverty in the Western Hemisphere, as well as a culture unlike any other and primitive art that is now almost mass-produced, and has had some appeal for French Canadians because of the common language. Venezuela, whose lovely beaches and spectacular scenery are certain to outlast its dwindling oil reserves, has tuned up its sophisticated promotion machine for the task of attracting the North American market. On top of everything else, tourism in the Commonwealth Caribbean is facing the most common of business problems: increased competition.

It is unlikely, however, that there will be a quick end to tourism in the West Indies. There will be more "incidents", more tourists staying home because of reports of violence and political unrest, more tourists going to Miami because they can't afford to go farther (in the winter of 1974-75, while hotels in the Caribbean were going bankrupt, Florida was having its best season in years), fewer hotels being built, fewer airlines making fewer stops. There will also be fewer people, in fact none at all, talking about tourism as the answer to all the region's deficiencies. Some tourists will still come but most of them will have sought out other havens. The industry, ephemeral as it was, will have had its effects, but any real advance by the region in its struggle to face up to its history and deal with its underlying problems will not be among them.

184

11/Give and Take

I sit on a man's back, choking him and making him carry me, and yet assure myself and others that I am very sorry for him and wish to ease his lot by any means possible, except getting off his back.

Leo Tolstoy

In the pivotal year of 1970, Canada unilaterally cancelled a tariff rebate on sugar imported from the West Indies that it had first offered at the time of the Canada–Commonwealth Caribbean heads of government conference four years earlier. Although Canada was a market of declining importance to the sugar-producing countries, the cancellation was widely resented in the West Indies. Even with the rebates, West Indian sugar had been entering Canada at a price below the cost of its production, and under terms less favourable than the preferences accorded it in the American and British markets. At the time of the cancellation, only Guyana and Belize among the sugar-producing countries of the West Indies were still exporting substantial amounts of sugar to Canada, and in the next few years that trade too would shrink to almost nothing, as Canada relied more and more on distant sources such as Australia, Fiji, Mauritius and — most jarring to West Indians — South Africa.[1]

At a press conference in Ottawa three years earlier, Prime Minister Hugh Shearer of Jamaica had said that his country was not asking for handouts but for respectable terms of trade — "the form of assistance we prefer to receive from our friendly neighbour."[2] On another visit to Canada a year later, Shearer had cited figures showing that while in 1960 Jamaica had to sell 666 tons of sugar to Canada in order to pay for one Canadian tractor, in 1967 the same tractor represented 1,500 tons of Jamaican sugar. The price of Jamaican sugar, according to Shearer, had dropped by thirty-nine per cent between 1958 and 1967, but the price of Canadian cod

185

had risen by twenty-nine and a half per cent and that of some manufactured goods by eighty-three per cent.[3]

Although at that time and in that place Shearer's message fell on deaf ears, a few years later terms of trade would be one of the central issues in the Third World's campaign to cast off its old relationship with the industrialized countries, based on dependency and exploitation, and work out something better. Like other commodity-exporting countries, the sugar producers would become more conscious of their economic power and turn into increasingly hard bargainers in international negotiations. In 1975 the Latin American sugar producers would try to start an OPEC-style cartel[4] while forty-six African, Caribbean and Pacific countries would show firmness and solidarity in carving out a new and more favourable trade agreement, notably including a new sugar pact, with the European Common Market.[5]

But even with these suggestions of change sugar bore more heavily than most other industries the stamp of its colonial origins. The sugar relationship between Canada and the West Indies has long been complicated by the influence exercised in both areas by the British multinational sugar giant Tate and Lyle. Tate and Lyle is the parent firm of Redpath Industries Ltd., the dominant sugar-refining company in Eastern Canada. In 1963 Redpath and the other Canadian sugar companies were convicted of a conspiracy in restraint of trade and fined $25,000 each; a similar charge was dismissed in 1975 when Judge Kenneth Mackay found that virtually identical prices posted by the companies were due not to collusion but to the other companies' following Redpath's "price leadership."[6] The latter verdict provoked an angry outburst from Consumer and Corporate Affairs Minister André Ouellet, which led to his conviction for contempt of court and ultimately to his resignation from the cabinet. Beryl Plumptre's Food Prices Review Board found that the rate of return on invested capital in the sugar-refining industry in Canada was 29.5 per cent, almost twice as high as the average rate for other food processing. [7]

In the West Indies, Tate and Lyle was until 1970 the majority owner of Caroni Ltd., which has a near-monopoly of the Trinidad sugar industry. After the Black Power uprising the Trinidad government bought fifty-one per cent of Caroni but control of marketing was left with Tate and Lyle. The British company also held a majority interest in the West Indies Sugar Company, the largest estate owner in Jamaica, although there too it has sold a substantial part of its holding to the government. While Canada was still importing sugar from the West Indies it was common for the sugar to be carried in ships operated by Sugar Line Ltd. — a wholly-owned subsidiary of Tate and Lyle.

When Canada cancelled the tariff rebate and pronounced the death sentence on sugar imports from the West Indies, it offered $5 million for an agricultural assistance fund as compensation. This proposal did not succeed in mitigating West Indian resentment: Canada didn't bother to provide much in the way of detail and its offer was regarded as a handout rather than the fair deal the West Indies wanted.[8] But the shift from a trade preference to an aid program reflected the direction in which Canada–West Indies relations were changing.

The Commonwealth Caribbean receives more direct Canadian aid per capita than any other region of the world, and since it has not been a particular area of concentration for most of the other aid-giving powers, it has become one of the few places where Canada is recognized as a major donor country. In Canada, Ottawa's aid program in the West Indies is generally considered to be altruistic and beneficial, even among people who have serious reservations about other aspects of Canadian activity there.[9]

Since the late sixties, however, the Canadian aid program, along with the programs of other industrialized countries and multilateral organizations, has been carried out in an atmosphere of almost continuous agonizing reappraisal. The declining acceptability of the original Cold War justification for foreign aid in the United States and other countries and the disappointing results of the First Development Decade launched by the United Nations in 1961 have set the whole aid enterprise adrift on a sea of questions, reassessments and recriminations. The Canadian government's own reassessment, published as *Strategy for International Development Co-operation 1975-1980,* reflects the debates that have been going on everywhere.

The first phase of this controversy was a sudden flood of official studies of aid and development between 1968 and 1970. The United States government, the United Nations, the World Bank and other agencies set up commissions to examine their aid programs and make recommendations for reform; the World Bank study was headed by Lester Pearson, who had just escaped from official Ottawa.[10] The recommendations of these commissions had many common features. They called for a renewed commitment to international development on the part of the industrial countries and changes in the emphasis of their programs, but on the whole they did not criticize the underlying concepts on which aid was based.

In the wake of the studies came a series of critiques from the outside, most of them far less sanguine than the official reports about where international development was going and what could be done within the prevailing structures of both the developed countries and the Third World. The titles of some books published in the early seventies — *Aid as Imperialism, The Myth of Aid, The Trojan Horse, From Aid to Recolonization: Lessons of a Failure*[11] — suggest some of the flavour of this criticism. Michael Hudson, assistant professor of economics at the New School For Social Research in New York, wrote in *The Myth of Aid* that

> today's foreign aid programs are more seriously ill-conceived than even the suspicious public and disgruntled Congress have grasped. The reasons for their failure to help aid-borrowers to develop lie first in the motives that have governed foreign aid programs since World War II, and secondly in the spurious growth theories called upon to cloak these motives in the guise of altruism. Neo-classical income theory, for instance, has called for an infusion of technological capital (i.e. foreign investment) and Malthusian doctrine for a reduction in population resources, as if such policies could in themselves supplant the need for structural modification of the backward societies.[12]

A third phase of the debate was the filtering of some of the ideas of the critics, in diluted form, into the aid agencies themselves, and especially into the World Bank, where they found an unlikely champion in its president, Robert McNamara, the former U.S. Defense Secretary and architect of the Vietnam war. In particular, the World Bank became a leader in the movement away from indiscriminately looking at the Gross National Product in Third World countries as an index of development and toward paying more attention to the distribution of income in those countries.[13]

Beginning in 1973, the emergence of the OPEC countries and other Third World commodity exporters as forces to be reckoned with, the continuing financial problems and economic uncertainty in the developed countries, the growing debt crisis in the Third World, and the gathering atmosphere of confrontation between the two camps once more called into question the whole concept of development assistance.

The new international economic order that a growing number of Third World leaders were calling for in the mid-seventies implied much more than was included in foreign aid. Aid has been an attempt to apply a palliative to a situation that was to a large extent an effect of other economic policies pursued by the aid-giving countries. The call for a new international economic order entails a re-examination of all those policies and the relationships between industrialized and Third World countries that they create. It means a change in the terms of trade and in the conditions under which multinational corporations operate in the Third World. It means that aid must be fit into a coherent development strategy, and one that will be determined by the Third World countries themselves.

Along with most other aid programs, Canada's was born in the years immediately following World War II. In 1950, delegates from seven Commonwealth countries, both rich and poor, gathered in Colombo, Ceylon, to discuss the economic and social problems of South and Southeast Asia. Canada's delegate, External Affairs Minister Lester Pearson, told the conference: "Communist expansionism may now spill over into Southeast Asia as well as into the Middle East. . . . If Southeast and South Asia are not to be conquered by Communism, we of the free democratic world must

189

demonstrate that it is we and not the Russians who stand for national liberation and economic and social progress."[14]

Just as the United States had carried on the fight against Communism in Europe by launching the Marshall Plan, the Commonwealth countries would fight Communism in Asia by starting the Colombo Plan. This was the beginning of a Canadian aid program that, twenty-five years later, would extend its benefits to countries all over the world — including a Communist country allied with the Soviet Union.

But the first recipient of Canadian largesse outside the Colombo Plan was the Commonwealth Caribbean. When the West Indies Federation was set up in 1958, the Diefenbaker government undertook to provide $10 million in aid to it over five years. By the time the five years were over the Federation was dead, but the two major gifts provided under the Canadian program remained. One was a student residence, Canada Hall, at the Trinidad campus of the University of the West Indies, the regional institution that was set up by the Federation and survived the collapse of its parent: this was the first of a long series of Canadian aid projects involving the University. The second consisted of two ships, the *Federal Palm* and the *Federal Maple,* built in Canada and donated to the Federation to improve communications among the islands. The ships replaced a service operated with chartered Scandinavian freighters that the Federation had established at its inception; the most noticeable change that occurred with the arrival of the Canadian ships was a substantial increase in the operating deficit of the service. Nevertheless, they continued to run for more than a decade after the Federation fell apart.[15]

Through the sixties and seventies, Canada's aid program continued to expand, and enthusiasm for aid grew in Ottawa just as disillusionment with it was growing elsewhere, especially in Washington. Official Development Assistance (ODA), aid provided by the government, represented 0.53 per cent of the Gross National Product of the United States in 1960, 0.31 per cent in 1970, and the World Bank estimates that it will represent 0.21 per cent of American GNP in 1976. Canadian ODA, by contrast, was

0.19 per cent of GNP in 1960, 0.42 per cent in 1970 and, again according to a World Bank estimate, 0.53 per cent in 1976.[16] The authors of a critical study of Canadian aid suggested in 1973 that "perhaps Canada was realizing an opportunity to step in where the American government was being forced to withdraw. The Canadian expansion and American decline in aid-giving seem too coincidental for such integrated nations."[17] Another possible explanation is that Canada was following its usual practice of adopting American fashion, but with a slight time lag, a pattern that is observable in Canadian clothes, Canadian music, and Canadian politics.

The Canadian aid program to the West Indies was scaled up in 1964 to a level of about $10 million a year, and further increases were promised at the heads of government conference in 1966. Aid over the next five years was substantially in excess of the minimum $75 million promised. It was also in 1966 that the region was divided up into sectors for aid purposes among Canada, Britain and the United States. Canada got water resources, air transport, education and agriculture, and most of its aid projects over the next decade were concentrated in those four areas. Meanwhile, the emphasis of Canada's program shifted somewhat from the nuts-and-bolts, bricks-and-mortar sort of projects that had characterized its early years — building schools and bridges, providing lumber, bringing electricity to rural areas — toward more technical assistance and the provision of teachers.

The arrival of the Trudeau government in 1968 was accompanied by a significant upgrading of the visibility, prestige and money attached to the Canadian aid effort. A new body, the Canadian International Development Agency, replaced the old External Aid Office, and total allocations for aid continued to increase rapidly, from $253 million in 1968 to $491 million five years later. Among the more business-oriented departments in Ottawa, CIDA developed something of a reputation as a haven for house radicals. At a meeting of businessmen in Toronto in 1973, James Whiteside of the International Financing Branch of the Department of Industry, Trade and Commerce was asked about the relationship

191

between his department and CIDA. His reply was revealing:

> You have in CIDA, I hope there is no members of the press, I'd like to ask you to take this one off the record, you have in CIDA a lot of people of what we call do-gooders, bleeding hearts, you know the kind of guy who wants to do good. I see nothing wrong with that except that when I also see Canadian funds or a project coming up and the Japanese are there with their soft money, the Brits are there, the Yanks are there and old Canada isn't there, you get pretty upset. So what we at Trade and Commerce have been trying to do is to move CIDA into certain areas where they are more commercially oriented. We were saying to CIDA basically, look you take so much money and go out into the world and do good, but we would like some for export. And I think we are getting some headway, I think the people at CIDA are starting to see the need to create jobs in Canada and so on. You see aid money is often a device, a tool, to get into a market, it is a toehold.[18]

In case IT&C is insufficiently successful in impressing its point of view on CIDA, it maintains an agency of its own, the Export Development Corporation, whose activities are often confused with aid but are in fact as purely commercial as any in the government. Although there is no direct co-ordination with CIDA, the president of CIDA sits on the board of directors of the EDC, and the two agencies have sometimes got involved in different sides of the same project. In late 1974 the EDC announced that it was lending $1.7 million to the government of Jamaica to buy locomotives for the Jamaica Railway Corporation from MLW-Worthington Ltd. of Montreal. At about the same time CIDA announced that it would provide technical asistance for the maintenance of the railway. Conveniently, the JRC's largest customer is Alcan Jamaica, which is heavily dependent on the railway to ship its aluminum out of the country.

Unlike CIDA the EDC extends its credits to developed as well as developing countries; it bases its loans on commercial criteria only and its customers include Britain, the Netherlands and New Zealand.[19] There is, however, one EDC program that is intended specifically for developing countries — the Foreign Investment Insurance Division, modeled after the Overseas Private Investment Corporation in the United States. EDC insurance offers companies investing in developing countries protection against three categories of misfortunes: expropriation, government action in the host country that would prevent the conversion of that country's currency into Canadian dollars, and "war, revolution and insurrection."[20]

The EDC's program is, as would be expected, much smaller than OPIC's, and unlike OPIC the EDC has never had a claim. At the end of 1974 the EDC had twenty-four insurance policies outstanding for a total value of $43.5 million. OPIC, by contrast, had almost $10 billion in insurance outstanding at the end of fiscal 1974 and wrote 183 new contracts in that year alone. Between 1971 and 1974 it processed fifty-two claims. The Caribbean is a major area of exposure for both organizations, representing twenty-eight per cent of the EDC's insurance written between the establishment of the program in 1971 and the end of 1974, and twenty-five per cent of OPIC's in the same period.[21]

A 1975 EDC booklet said that the purposes of the investment insurance program are "to help place Canadian companies in a more competitive position relative to companies in other developed countries and to encourage Canadian private sector involvement in promoting the industrial growth of developing countries."[22] To be eligible for coverage, the investment must be economically advantageous in the EDC's eyes to both Canada and the developing country being invested in.

Fulfilling the latter criterion involves satisfying the EDC that the project "will have some significant positive impact on the economy of the recipient country, particularly with respect to the development of a self-sustaining private sector. The benefits should also include the expansion of employment, gains in production techniques and skills and an increase in the standard of living among the population."[23]

Even more than most other Canadian projects involving the Third World, the EDC's insurance program promotes one particular kind of development, based on foreign investment and tied to the economies of the metropolitan countries. But perhaps its most serious effect is that it makes the government of Canada a party to any trouble in which an EDC-insured company might find itself.

In the case of OPIC and the United States, this does not represent a serious departure, in the light of the historic American willingness to send in the Marines to protect U.S.-based companies. But for Canada, which has a *de facto* policy of non-intervention in investment disputes, the situation is somewhat different. It will be difficult for Ottawa to stay neutral in an investment dispute if an EDC insurance policy is involved; it is to be expected, rather, that the EDC will act to protect its own investment and avoid paying out a claim if at all possible, just as OPIC does.

Even with the presence of the EDC to promote Canadian commercial interests in the Third World, CIDA itself is not entirely oblivious to those interests. Perhaps the most important benefit Canadian companies receive from CIDA comes from the provision that Canadian aid be tied to purchases of goods and services in Canada. This tying of aid is by no means unique to CIDA: it is a standard feature of virtually all aid programs undertaken by industrialized countries, and although it is widely regarded as one of the most serious weaknesses of those programs, it has proved to be one of the aspects of aid that is most resistant to change.

Writing about Canadian aid to the West Indies in 1966, economists Kari Levitt and Alister McIntyre pointed out that "Canada herself is an importer of a large variety of capital goods. Thus, commodities required for projects which have high priority in the development plans of a recipient country may not be able to meet Canadian-content requirements. Alternatively, Canadian goods purchased with development loans may be of higher price or inferior quality to similar goods available from other suppliers."[24]

The Pearson report in 1969 said that "of all the limitations on the flexibility of aid, the tying of aid to purchases in the aid-giving country is the most serious,"[25] and recommended a number of measures for the gradual untying of aid. In its 1973 annual review of aid trends, the Development Assistance Committee (DAC) of the Organization for Economic Co-operation and Development, a grouping of the industrialized countries, argued for extending aid to finance the local costs of development projects.[26] And CIDA's review of aid policies in 1975 acknowledged that "the untying of aid has traditionally been regarded in the international community as a desirable objective,"[27] although it recommended only a limited change in Canadian practice in this area.

Canadian tying provisions are stricter than those of some aid-giving countries and less strict than those of some others. There has been a general trend in the seventies toward an easing of those restrictions and Canada has been a follower rather than a leader in this movement. At the beginning of 1975 a DAC Memorandum of Understanding came into effect, requiring countries adhering to it to allow aid recipients to use money from development loans for procurement in other Third World countries. Canada did not initially join in the Understanding and only announced its intention to do so at the time of the CIDA policy review in the fall of that year. CIDA assured nervous businessmen that the new policy "would have minimal effects on Canadian exporters"[28] while External Affairs Minister Allan MacEachen, noting that he didn't "buy totally the approach of the industrial community" regarding aid-tying, nevertheless said that "other things being equal, there is no reason why the aid shouldn't be spent in Canada."[29]

Perhaps the most significant changes suggested by the CIDA review were: an increasing concentration on the poorest of the Third World countries, and the channeling of a greater proportion of Canadian aid through multilateral institutions. Both of these points are highly consequential for the Canadian aid program in the West Indies.

The Caribbean receives the attention of a wide range of multilateral institutions — its own Caribbean Development Bank (CDB), the Inter-American Development Bank (IDB), and the World Bank, as well as United Nations agencies — and Canada was a participant in all of them, even before the CIDA review. The idea of setting up a development bank for the West Indies was discussed at the Canada–Commonwealth Caribbean conference in Ottawa in 1966, and unlike some of the other ideas discussed at that conference, it was actually brought to fruition. The agreement establishing the Caribbean Development Bank was signed in 1969, and Canada became one of two non-regional members (Britain was the other), subscribing US$5 million of the Bank's capital. In addition, as of the end of 1973, Canada had made available $3 million to the Bank's Special Development Fund and $1.25 million to its Agricultural Fund[30]; the latter contribution represented a down payment on the $5 million promised as compensation for the cancellation of the sugar tariff rebate.

At the time of the Bank's creation there was some hope in Canadian business circles that it would focus a large part of its resources on the private sector and particularly on "satellite" plants like Jack Cooper's Barbadian venture. But motivated perhaps as much by economic circumstance as by conviction, the Bank has lent mostly to governments and government organizations, and its projects have been concentrated primarily in the areas of agriculture and infrastructure (roads, electricity and other basic needs) with tourism and light industry getting secondary attention.[31]

Canada and the Commonwealth Caribbean are both newcomers to the Inter-American Development Bank, originally set up in the late fifties as part of the inter-American system that was designed to keep Latin America firmly within the U.S. sphere of influence. As a non-member of the IDB's big-sister body, the Organization of American States, Canada was not eligible to join the Bank, but it did its bit by setting up a $74-million Canadian Trust Fund to finance economic, educational and technical projects in Latin America; the Fund is administered by the IDB and tied to purchases in Canada.[32] The first new members of the IDB were the newly independent West Indian countries, Jamaica, Trinidad and Barbados, which joined in the late sixties. Guyana, which could not join the OAS because of the Venezuelan claim to part of its territory, was ineligible for IDB membership until after the restriction of the bank to OAS countries was relaxed with the admission of Canada as a full member in 1972. As of mid-1975 the IDB had lent almost $100 million to Jamaica, Trinidad and Barbados, most of it for infrastructure projects.[33]

The existence of such institutions as the CDB, the IDB and the World Bank is useful to aid-giving countries that want to avoid having too high a profile. With the less euphoric attitude toward aid that prevails in the 1970s, much of the public-relations value that was formerly associated with participation in development projects in Third World countries has been lost. For Canada in the West Indies, its standing reduced by the Sir George Williams, Demba and other controversies, these arguments have applied with particular force in recent years. The shifting of some aid activity to multilateral institutions, which the CIDA review proposed to accelerate, is an attempt to reduce Canada's exposure, and nowhere is it more exposed than in the West Indies.

A shifting of Canadian aid to the poorest developing countries should, in theory, mean a shifting of it away from the West Indies. Guyana's per-capita Gross National Product in 1972 was US$363, Jamaica's US$809 and Trinidad and Tobago's US$1079, as compared to US$62 for Burundi, US$64 for Mali, US$67 for Laos and US$57 for Afghanistan.[34] The West Indian countries, especially the wealthier ones such as Trinidad, are better described as middle-income rather than poor countries on the world scale. However, after the new policy was announced CIDA spokesmen were quick to issue assurances that it did not mean a phasing out of the Caribbean program. "We can't apply the same criteria to the Caribbean as we would to other areas because of our cultural, historical and other ties with the region," said Karl Johansen, director-general of CIDA's Caribbean division. "We will be in the Caribbean as a region for some time to come. Our total assistance to the Caribbean won't diminish and may in fact increase."

The new policy did entail a shift in emphasis from the richer Caribbean countries to the poorer territories of the Leewards and Windwards. But because of the existence of institutions such as the University of the West Indies that, while located in the more developed countries, serve the less developed ones as well, and because of Canada's stated commitment to regional integration, even Jamaica, Trinidad and Barbados could not be completely stricken off the list. The policy review was followed by an internal "new look" at the aid program in the Commonwealth Caribbean, but this, too, fell short of the complete rethinking of aid that CIDA always seemed to be on the verge of, but never quite got around to. While bearing out the conclusion of the policy review that more aid should go to the Leewards and Windwards, the Caribbean study still saw a need for aid in the more developed West Indian countries as well. The central finding of the study was that unemployment was now the main West Indian problem, and that Canadian aid should in future be concentrated on projects that would directly stimulate jobs.

Like all aid endeavours, the CIDA program in the West Indies has had its share of failures. A CIDA-financed fish-storage plant in New Amsterdam, Guyana stood unused for two years after it had opened. CIDA had not managed to secure reliable arrangements for the maintenance of the plant. In addition, it had not ascertained whether the fishermen, who were accustomed to selling their fish on the jetty, would be inclined to bring it to a plant about two hundred yards away; it turned out they were not. A contingent of Canadian officials showed up in Grenville, Grenada in December, 1974 for the formal opening of a similar plant.[35] More than two months later the plant stood resolutely closed. Some blamed the Canadians for inadequate follow-up; some blamed the government of Prime Minister Gairy for not paying the staff of the plant; some blamed a local dispute among two groups of rival fishermen. It was indisputable, however, that the plant was indeed closed.

In Jamaica stories are told about a science teacher from British Columbia who came down on a CIDA program and took two weeks off at the beginning to prepare a syllabus that, when finished, turned out to be an exact copy of the British Columbia science syllabus, complete with British Columbia seasons. Later he took three months off for the funeral of his father-in-law. He kept lobbying for a transfer to Kingston from the rural community where he had been stationed, and finally moved into Kingston and lived in a hotel for six months at CIDA expense.

By contrast, the Department of Management Studies at the University of the West Indies is one of the successes of the CIDA program. Management courses at both the Mona, Jamaica, and St.

Augustine, Trinidad campuses of UWI have been established with Canadian guidance, and the courses are functioning and produce graduates. Some of these graduates have gone on to managerial positions with companies and governments in the West Indies, while others are teaching new crops of students in the management department. Jim Graham, a CIDA officer in Kingston, said in 1975 that the project had "just worked out beautifully." But it is precisely because of the success of the management school that the questions raised about it are so disquieting.

Lack of expertise in entrepreneurship and management has often been cited as one of the obstacles to development in the West Indies.[36] From its inception in the 1960s, the Department of Management Studies of the University of the West Indies was intended to help correct this deficiency. A number of North American institutions were prepared to assist UWI in this endeavour. St. Augustine established ties with Cornell University, in a project financed by the U.S. Agency for International Development, the Fulbright Foundation, and later the Ford Foundation. Mona developed a close informal relationship with the University of Western Ontario, and there was a steady trickle of professors from Western's School of Business Administration heading down to Jamaica to give seminars and six-week courses. In 1971 CIDA took the Department of Management Studies in hand as part of its $10-million program of aid to UWI. CIDA wanted a university to administer the project, and because of the links that had already developed Western was the logical choice.

Western had begun its Business Administration program back in the 1920s, and had hired a Canadian who was about to graduate with a Master of Business Administration degree from Harvard, Ellis Morrow, as its first faculty member. It was the beginning of a close spiritual relationship between Western and the distinguished American institution. Western adopted the case method of business teaching that Harvard had pioneered. It also developed a habit of favouring Harvard graduates for positions on its faculty. Of fifty-three faculty members with the rank of assistant professor or higher in 1975, no fewer than eighteen had obtained advanced degrees at Harvard. In addition, twenty-five had received Harvard-style training at Western itself, including six who had completed MBAs at Western and then gone on to do their DBAs at the source.[37]

"Harvard has done for us," said Professor Walter Thompson, a veteran of more than forty years at Western, who became the coordinator of the Western-UWI management studies program, "what we're trying to do down in the West Indies, except they've done it on a friendly, informal basis." From 1971, the Western–UWI link was formal and contractual. Agreements were signed between CIDA and UWI, between Western and UWI, between CIDA and Western, and $1.6 million in CIDA money was earmarked for the management department. About a half-million dollars of that went to construct management buildings at Mona and St. Augustine; of the remainder, a quarter was to be administered directly by UWI and was to go toward scholarships and building up a library, while the rest was to be administered by Western and spent largely at Western's discretion. In 1975, well into the fourth year of the program, senior West Indian faculty members had never been able to see the agreement between CIDA and Western.

There has been general agreement in the faculty that UWI got "a good deal" out of the Western link. "It's worked out pretty well," said Fred Nunes, a lecturer at Mona. "We've learned a lot about the sheer technology of teaching business." Young Canadian lecturers were coming down on Western salaries to teach at UWI for one- and two-year periods. West Indian graduates of the program were going to Western on scholarships for advanced study. The project was working.

But the attempt by Western to create a management department at UWI in its own (and, by extension, Harvard's) image was not without its problems. Most of the questions about the project have fallen into two areas: the introduction of the case method, and the relationship between the management school and the business community. In both these areas, the underlying difficulty is the same: business in the West Indian context is simply not the same thing as it is in the North American, and many concepts which go

200

more or less unchallenged in North America are not applicable in the West Indies without serious modification.

The case method reflects a pragmatic, problem-solving approach to education, and the questions it poses generally begin with "how" rather than "why". The student at a school using the method is given a casebook in each course, containing descriptions of actual business problems which he is expected to solve. Students then report their solutions in class and discuss and argue over them until a consensus emerges.[38]

Adherents of the method are enthusiastic about its powers. "You wouldn't believe what can be done in an hour-and-twenty-minute period," said Walter Thompson. "It gives students a speeded-up experience. We've had people from business sit in on a class and say that the class went through all the options it had taken them two years to consider — and come to the same decision." At the University of the West Indies, however, while the strengths of the method are appreciated, its weaknesses are more readily apparent. "The case method allows you to rush into the environment and rush back into the classroom with a photograph," said Fred Nunes. "But while it gives you a photograph it doesn't give you an analysis of the photography." Eric St. Cyr, director of the program at St. Augustine, suggested that "cases presuppose a stable society. A university has to grow from what's happening all around it. Concepts of management and the roles and objectives of managers are undefined here."

Efforts to adapt the case method to the Caribbean context have consisted mostly of writing cases drawn from West Indian experiences, an activity which Western has strongly encouraged. "In Jamaica, they did a case about a sugar plantation," said Ainsley Mark, a lecturer at the St. Augustine campus and member of the radical New Beginning movement. "All the figures were there but the human aspect was not there." Most of the courses at UWI use a mixture of American, Canadian and West Indian cases, with the majority of cases coming from North America and the largest single slice coming from the United States. The American cases tend to be the more complex and detailed ones. "Some people feel that studying management is like studying the circulation of the blood," said Nunes. "If you understand the blood circulation of an African you understand the blood circulation of an Eskimo." Both Nunes and St. Cyr believe that it is possible to shape the case method to the West Indian environment if the cases are constructed to take account of the social context; both are also convinced that despite the number of West Indian cases that have been written this has not yet been done. Western, meanwhile, is sufficiently pleased with the West Indian cases that it has begun using some of them in its own business courses.

The difficulties of transferring North American concepts of how a business school should function to the West Indies are perhaps even clearer in the fate of UWI's continuing education program for businessmen in Trinidad and Jamaica. A successful continuing education program is a product of a secure relationship between the university and the community it serves. At Western, this relationship is symbolized by an advisory committee to the School of Business Administration that includes Paul Desmarais, chairman of Power Corporation, John Craig Eaton, chairman of the board of Eaton's, Allan Lambert, chairman of the Toronto-Dominion Bank, Alfred Powis, president of Noranda Mines, and other high-powered Canadian businessmen.[39] But in the West Indies, the university, and especially the Social Sciences faculty which includes the Department of Management Studies, has often been critical of the business community, and the business community, in turn, has viewed the university with suspicion. Despite the efforts of the department to conclude a rapprochement that suspicion has not been overcome.

"The continuing education program has been a monstrous disappointment," was Fred Nunes' judgment. "And it's our failure. The Western people have done more than their full share." He attributed the situation to weak promotion on the part of the department and "the absence of legitimacy of the university with the business community. Social Sciences has been the bane of the businessman's ass. It's difficult to ask him to attend a course in that faculty." But if the program has been a failure in Jamaica, it has been a disaster in Trinidad. The Jamaican business class is well established by West Indian standards and, because of the existence of the two-party system and the representation of business in both of the parties, has managed to avoid becoming identified as a political force in its own right. In Trinidad, by contrast, businessmen are mistrusted by everyone from the radical labour unions to Dr. Williams and are unsure of their own position in society.

In the volatile politics of Trinidad, groups may ally with each other but the alliances tend to be unstable and temporary. To enter into an alliance with the business community is both risky and morally ambiguous, and the thoughtful Eric St. Cyr is understandably hesitant about allying the university in that way. Such an alliance, argued St. Cyr, is precisely what is implied in a continuing-education program: "The critical thing for the business community is not technical expertise but political support. Until now, they have purchased their political support at Harvard and other universities abroad. With a continuing-education program we would be providing it for them." The Harvard–Western model of business education does not easily accommodate such subtleties.

In 1972 a final-year student in the management studies program at St. Augustine, Sagan Nanansingh, did a survey of the career patterns of graduates of the program from 1965 to 1971; that is, before Western took over. Of seventy-three who replied to his questionnaire, only seventeen had gone into private corporations while twenty-two were in public corporations and seven more in the civil service.[40] Although there have been no more recent surveys, observers agree that there are still more graduates going into civil-service and quasi-civil-service jobs than into business positions. "Neither the multinationals nor the local firms are interested in management," said Ainsley Mark. "The local firms want loyalty, and the multinationals give you a procedure manual when you arrive."

Of the graduates who had gone into public and private-sector jobs, twenty told Nanansingh that Accounting had been the course they had found most useful in their work; eight of those were in private corporations. By contrast only six mentioned "Caribbean Business Environment" as their most useful course, and all of those were in the public sector.[41] It was not until 1974 that "Caribbean Business Environment" was made a compulsory course, at

203

the urging of St. Cyr and others. "We need to have a large chunk of courses dealing with change," said Fred Nunes. "If we're not teaching change we're wasting the students' time. The impediment to this is not imposed by Western but it's in the minds of people who have gone to Western and come back with a Western orientation."

Western is proud of its involvement in the UWI program, so much so that it mentions the presence of the West Indian scholarship students in its syllabus as one of the attractions of its graduate program:

> The presence of these gifted people, from a developing part of the world, adds much to the richness of the experience in the classroom. While the experience and background of students from the more developed areas is rubbing off on the West Indians, the members of the MBA class, after two years' intimate contact, should have some feel for the problems of what is happening in a significant developing part of the world. It is difficult to put one's finger on specifics which evolve from this situation. The results of an exciting mixture are always difficult to describe.[42]

The soft-spoken Eric St. Cyr, a man who does not use words lightly, found it considerably less difficult to describe the situation. He called it "some semblance of academic imperialism."

Often, the most effective aid has been non-official, people-to-people assistance. When Jamaican teachers were trying to unite five organizations into a single body in the early sixties they sought the help of the Ontario Teachers' Federation, which was the result of a similar merger. It was the beginning of a relationship between the unified Jamaica Teachers' Association and Canadian teachers that seems to have worked out well for both sides. "We haven't suffered from the 'expert' attitude," said Pat Robinson of the JTA. "The Canadians have been willing to listen to our point of view. When teachers stop being willing to learn they stop being teachers."

 Canadian University Service Overseas and Canadian Executive Service Overseas, two organizations of relatively modest ambitions that are funded by CIDA but not run by it, also deal in people-to-people aid and their help has often left a better taste in the countries to which it has been extended than the official, large-scale projects. Most CUSO volunteers are in their twenties while CESO consultants are often in their sixties or seventies, and both groups are likely to approach their assignments with less cynicism and greater humility than those in between them on the age scale. But despite their formal autonomy the two organizations are integrally linked to the rest of Canadian activity abroad, and the volunteers are generally aware of it. "We're getting to be a great consulting country," said Jim France, head of the Caribbean division of CESO, "and when countries have had a CESO volunteer they tend to think of Canada for consulting." One CUSO teacher, after a year in a Caribbean country, concluded that both Canada and the host country were interested in her being there less because of what she could contribute than because she was linked to a multimillion-dollar Canadian program of aid and trade. The year after her CUSO tour of duty she was offered essentially the same job in the same country, but this time under CIDA's banner and at five times the salary. She turned it down. Many CUSO people do in fact graduate to CIDA positions. Don McMaster went from being CUSO field co-ordinator in Africa to a CIDA posting in Georgetown, where he adopted the prevailing fashion of khaki shirt-jac and trousers and, unlike many Canadians, found the texture of life much to his liking.

The overall purpose of Canada's aid effort, even more than that of most countries, is complex and probably has not been thought out at even the highest levels of Ottawa policymaking. Not even the most passionate proponent of aid would maintain that the motives behind it are entirely altruistic, but the standard selfish purposes attributed to aid-givers do not add up to an adequate explanation either. Help for Canadian exporters is undoubtedly part of the answer, but if the government were interested only in export subsidies there would be simpler and less risky ways of achieving the same objective. Aid dispensed by Britain and France may be a way of keeping some hold over those countries' old empires, and the United States and the Soviet Union may be interested primarily in ideological struggle and super-power competition, but neither of those considerations really applies to Canada.

While many Canadian aid projects, such as the UWI management department, are directed (in however bumbling a fashion) toward the strengthening of the private sector in Third World countries, Canada is sufficiently flexible in this regard that it extends aid to Cuba, where the question of a private sector was settled some time ago.

At bottom, the reason for Canada's aid to Cuba may not be all that much different from the reason for American aid to Indonesia, France's aid to Senegal or Venezuela's joining the Caribbean Development Bank. All aid-giving countries are more than anything else interested in maintaining and extending their influence. For the industrial world as a whole, aid is an attempt to continue to set the agenda for the developing countries. For each individual aid-giving country it is a concrete way of showing the flag, in pursuit of trade opportunities, political support and general goodwill that can be cashed in later.

The competition for projects is as fierce among aid donors as it is among aid recipients. "I've tried to scrounge money," said Karl Johansen, who worked as a planner for the government of Tanzania before coming to CIDA's Caribbean desk, "and I've tried to give it away, and it's a bloody sight more difficult to give money away than it is to scrounge it."

12/Some Who Stayed

He told her of the sacrifice and generosity of Christian people in Canada, who had reached out a helping hand to the East Indians of British Guiana, and had sent them "Padre Sahibs" of their own. This was Christian brotherhood indeed.

Rev. J. D. Mackay
Under the Southern Cross, *1904*

Beyond the official Canadians, those attached to some aid program or high commission; beyond the business Canadians, those with a Canadian firm, large or small, trying to make a profit in the region; and beyond the tourists, who come for their prepackaged six-days-and-seven-nights and then return home, a disparate collection of people from Canada can be found in the West Indies. Often these are the most interesting Canadians, precisely because their reasons for being there are not so simple as government service, profits, or a week in the sun. Some are there out of a genuine affection for the region, some, even now, are there as missionaries, some are there for no discernible reason at all.

Some live in the retirement ghettoes for North Americans that are to be found all through the West Indies. In their isolation from the society around them these communities are an extension of the same mentality that underlies the tourist industry, and they are faced with many of the same problems, as we have seen with Marigot Investments. Often tourist accommodation and permanent homes are combined in a single development; one such is Lance aux Epines, which occupies a hilly, gently curving spit of land overlooking the ocean on the southern tip of Grenada, at the end of the road leading from St. George's past the cluster of hotels on Grand Anse beach. With its small inns and comfortable cottages, Lance aux Epines is reminiscent of one of the quieter resorts along the Massachusetts coast. Although many of the residents of Lance aux Epines come from the wealthier class of West Indians, there are many foreigners too, most of them Canadians. Behind the bar at the Red Crab, just inside the entrance to Lance aux Epines, owner Julian Pieneczek, has time to chat as residents and tourists drift in and out. A Polish-born Canadian and former pilot, Pieneczek first came to the West Indies to fly for the government of Guyana.

A few miles from Lance aux Epines is Westerhall Point, strictly residential, a bit farther from the island's population and tourist centres, and more exclusive. And in the northeast corner of Grenada, at Chambord, Canadian entrepreneurs have started a development aimed specifically at their countrymen. But not all Canadians who come to live in the West Indies are attracted to communities of this sort.

George Strohaker found his spot in Springs, high on one of the hills that overlook St. George's, an excellent vantage point from which to view the convulsions of the society around him without being unduly disturbed by them. In the latter years of his career as a civil servant with the Ontario government, Strohaker had begun to think of retiring to that Caribbean island beloved of Canadians, Barbados. But he visited Grenada and found it more appealing, and had his spacious home built on the Springs property. Sitting on his balcony, surrounded by bougainvillea, he watched with interest the demonstrations of late 1973 and early 1974. As a foreigner he did not take sides, maintaining good relations both with friends of Prime Minister Gairy and with people who wanted to remove Gairy from power. The disturbances did not greatly reduce the white-haired and bearded Strohaker's pleasure in the little world he had chosen for himself, and he continued to model tropical fashions on the cruise ships that dock outside St. George's and flirt good-naturedly with local women.

Jim Sultan, on the other hand, was by 1974 no longer enamoured of his adopted home. He first came to St. Vincent from Vancouver in the early 1960s, as part of a Canadian team helping to build a deep-water harbour in Kingstown; he decided to stay and bought the Heron Hotel on the main street just up from the docks. But his love for the West Indies faded, and in 1974 he was thinking of returning to Canada. He described one of the North American

guests at the hotel, a regular customer, as "nice but a bit naive —
he still thinks something can be done to help these people." The
growth of radical movements in the West Indies was to Sultan
evidence of Cuban subversion. He shook his head disapprovingly
at a copy of a mimeographed publication distributed by a local
radical group: "Here, take this, it's what these people are saying. It
may be what they want, but it won't do them any good."

The twinning program between St. Catharines, Ontario, and
Port of Spain, Trinidad, was Father Lloyd Béchamp's introduction
to the West Indies. Every February a group of people from St.
Catharines, usually led by the Mayor, goes to Port of Spain for
Trinidad Carnival. On their arrival they are received at the Town
Hall by the civic officials of Port of Spain and expressions of good
fellowship are exchanged. St. Catharines has an annual event of its
own, the Niagara Grape and Wine Festival, and in exchange for
the Carnival visit a Port of Spain delegation attends that every
August. There are few even in St. Catharines who would be
offended at the suggestion that this is a particularly flagrant example of unfair terms of trade. The presence of a Trinidadian steelband enlivens a Grape and Wine parade that is otherwise made up
mostly of drum majorette groups from the neighbouring parts of
the United States.

From such an unpromising start came one of the more unusual
and potentially valuable endeavours in which Canadians have
become involved in the West Indies. Father Béchamp, who was
teaching in St. Catharines, visited Trinidad with the Carnival delegation, and through contacts made at the time eventually arranged
to come to the island to take charge of a handicrafts program in
Lopinot settlement, at the end of a twisting byway that winds
through the hills north of the Eastern Main Road. In early 1975
Father Béchamp could point to some modest success for the program. He was teaching people in the town to make decorative can-
dles and ceramics, and it was his ambition to have a store in Port of
Spain for Lopinot products; until that was realized they were being
sold to visitors to Lopinot at such events as the annual Christmas
parang.

Parang is a remnant of the Spanish influence that still persists in

209

Trinidad almost two hundred years after the Spaniards were driven out by the British and is particularly strong in some pockets, such as the area around Lopinot. Played by a band that always includes the characteristic four-stringed cuatro, parang is heard all over the island every year for a few weeks at Christmas. For Lopinot, the yearly evening of parang is a major social event, attracting many visitors; for Father Béchamp, it also represented an opportunity to invite people into his small church and sell some of the wares that the people of Lopinot had made. During his stay in Trinidad Father Béchamp was appalled at the conditions in which he saw people living, but he had also found much good: "Back in Canada so many of the people I see are haggard and worn. I don't see that here."

Although not a missionary in the conventional sense, Father Béchamp is heir to a long history of Canadian church involvement in the West Indies. The Scarboro Foreign Mission Society, which is the English Canadian Roman Catholic missionary order, maintains missions in Guyana, St. Vincent, St. Lucia and the Bahamas. In the island missions most of the priests' work consists of running parishes, while in Guyana a large part of it is devoted to education and to seeking converts among the East Indians. The Guyana mission has three schools, run by the mission but financially supported by the government, which pays the teachers. Relations with the government are touchy and many of the priests are reluctant to talk about their situation; at the order's church in New Amsterdam, on the east bank of the Berbice River in a heavily East Indian section of the country, a priest named Father Young, friendly and open about other matters, turned somewhat guarded when the question of relations with the government came up. Father Young is from Cape Breton, an area that has supplied a disproportionate number of Scarboro missionaries. As of late 1974 he had been in Guyana thirteen years and had not been back to Canada in that time, although he did take occasional furloughs in Barbados.

The Scarboro order was founded in the early years of this century for the purpose of sending missionaries to China, and that remained its *raison d'être* until after World War II. The China mission closed after the Communists gained power in 1949, but the Fathers had already begun to establish missions in other countries. There is now a Scarboro presence in Japan, the Philippines, Brazil and the Dominican Republic as well as the four West Indian states. The Guyana mission, opened in 1953, was the first in the West Indies; the next year, a mission to the Bahamas was undertaken by a veteran of the most rigorous years in China, Father John McGoey, whose health had collapsed and now did not permit a more demanding assignment than Harbour Island, just off Eleuthera.

In recent years the Scarboro Fathers have moved toward more direct involvement in the fight against oppression in the countries where they have missions. One Scarboro Father in the Dominican Republic, Arthur MacKinnon (also a Cape Bretoner) was regarded as sufficiently dangerous that he was shot to death at the height of the repression there in 1965. In an issue of the order's magazine, *Scarboro Missions*, commemorating the tenth anniversary of Father MacKinnon's murder, editor Father Gerald Curry noted that "injustice is no longer the monopoly of regimes like those described by Cardinal Mindszenty in his *Memoirs.* It is equally the act of regimes who explicity pronounce themselves to be defenders of the values of the Christian West."[1] According to Father Curry, the Scarboro Fathers believe that a missionary should "play a role in the development of the country as well as the development of the church." This attitude has led the Fathers to have a certain sympathy with Guyanese efforts to become self-reliant, despite the effects of those efforts on their own mission. It has also led them to try to inform people in Canada about life in the countries where they are working. A slide-tape presentation prepared by the Scarboro Fathers, "I Can See Clearly Now," outlines the history of the exploitation of bauxite in Guyana and deals sympathetically with the nationalization of Demba.

But among Canadian missionaries, it has been the Presbyterians who have had the greatest impact on the West Indies. In fact, there is probably no other Canadian institution that has had as deep an influence on West Indian life as the Canadian Mission. In Guyana, it was only in 1974 that the Canadian Mission changed its name to the Presbyterian Church of Guyana, although the last Canadians had left a couple of years earlier. The East Indians who were now in charge of the Church continued to keep in touch with the Presbyterian Church in Canada, and retained the sternness and propriety that the Canadians had instilled. In Trinidad the Canadian Mission sank perhaps even deeper roots; Naparima College, a large secondary school for boys in San Fernando, is one of its legacies.

On the occasion of Naparima's seventy-fifth anniversary in 1975 the School's principal, Dr. Allan Mackenzie, noted that

> when the Canadian Mission came to Trinidad nearly a century ago, the inhumane and indefensibly wicked system of indenture was at its height. . . . [The plantation masters and British officials] had no interest either in the spiritual sustenance and development of our forefathers and still less in their educational and social upliftment. To have looked after these matters would have been to have administered very badly the indenture system in which serfdom, very little different from slavery, thrived on ignorance and misery. But it was the faith and vision of our early Canadian pioneers such as John Morton and Kenneth Grant that persevered in the opening and maintenance of schools for the children of indentured immigrants.[2]

The Canadian Mission's provision of schools for the East Indians filled a gaping educational hole in both Trinidad and British Guiana. But Dr. Mackenzie's implication that the missionaries worked against the indenture system is, at best, questionable. In an unpublished but vivid and perceptive master's thesis, Zander Dunn, the last Canadian in the Canadian Mission in Guyana, wrote that "the missionaries were not ones to criticize the indenture system. Ross [Rev. George E. Ross of Rockingham, Nova Scotia, an early missionary in British Guiana] described it at its best, never mentioning any of its abuses. Only when he wrote about education for children did Ross find fault — not with the system — but with some proprietors."[3]

Even the missionaries who were more critical always blamed wicked masters rather than the system itself for the evils they saw. Signs of rebelliousness on the part of the East Indians were attributed to "heathenism" rather than social conditions. Rev. James A. Johnson of Chipman, New Brunswick, wrote from British Guiana in 1888: "The bold front which heathenism here presents could be seen in the riots which recently occurred on some of the largest estates in the colony . . . . These recent riots will probably lead the proprietors to see the advantages flowing from the establishment of mission schools and to increase their interest in the efforts put forth by the Canadian Presbyterian Church on behalf of the Indian immigrants."[4]

While the concentration on work among the East Indians was inspired by their adherence to non-Christian religions and their neglect by both civil and church authorities, it also reflected the racial preferences of the missionaries. John Morton regarded the East Indians as "our fellow citizens in the British Empire who belong also to the great Indo-European branch of the human family. They are Anglo-Saxons toasted in the Indian sun."[5] In a University of Toronto master's thesis Rudolph Grant, himself a Guyanese, suggested that the Canadian Mission's policy of maintaining schools almost exclusively for East Indians helped establish the legacy of racial division that would plague Guyana in later years:

> Though the schools were not segregated in any such sense as in the American South, the policy of the Canadian Mission led to a virtual segregation along racial lines, despite the fact that a small minority of other races attended the Mission's schools and a greater number of East Indians attended other schools . . . . It would be rash to make a necessary connection between educational policy and practice, on the one hand, and the development of political unity, on the other. Yet it is the contention here that the practice of having schools exclusively for East Indians, and employing teachers who were almost totally East Indian, was one of the probable factors which have contributed to the lack of unity among the two major race groups in Guyana today.[6]

The missionaries themselves, of course, would not have seen it that way; they regarded the racial division that existed as part of the natural order of things, beyond their power to change or influence. They were extremely devoted to their East Indian charges,

213

and the missionaries in British Guiana, in particular, in a larger, more sparsely settled and less temperate country than the ones in Trinidad and with a smaller mission, endured severe personal hardship in their efforts to Christianize and educate them. Many of them became ill with tropical diseases and died or had to return to Canada. The Guyana mission was kept alive by three missionaries of conspicuous dedication: J. B. Cropper, a mulatto from St. Lucia, the son of a civil servant who received his education in Halifax, and who became the mission's indispensable man; R. Gibson Fisher, a Yorkshireman who was the administrator and historian of the mission; and James Scrimgeour, a Nova Scotian whose special passion was education.[7]

The Canadian Mission also took on a task that was later adopted by the Scarboro Fathers: informing Canadians about West Indian life. In the early 1940s, the Committee on Missionary Education of the Presbyterian Church in Canada published a booklet called *Focus on British Guiana*, which presented a fairly even-handed portrayal of conditions in the colony and a glowing account of the work of the Canadian Mission. In the early years, letters from missionaries in the Caribbean were a staple item in such publications as the *Presbyterian Witness*. Perhaps the most remarkable observation of life in the West Indies by a Canadian missionary was a twelve-part serial that ran in the *Presbyterian Witness* in the autumn of 1904, written by Rev. J. D. Mackay of Halifax and entitled "Under the Southern Cross: A Story of East Indian Indenture in British Guiana." Mackay, who had arrived in the colony the previous year and was to be killed in an accident the next, traced the progress of his protagonist, Jugmohun, from aimlessness and ignorance in the streets of Calcutta to a hard-working but happy Christian life in British Guiana.

Jugmohun leaves his native village, his family and his girl-wife to go seek his fortune in Calcutta. But he finds nothing there, and in desperation he signs himself into indenture to work in the canefields of British Guiana. On his arrival in British Guiana he is assigned to an estate on the West Coast of Demerara, where he is put to work in the fields and proves a hard worker and a loyal servant of the plantation owners. Dissatisfied with Hinduism, he toys with Islam and Christianity, until he meets a vacationing catechist from the Canadian Mission in Trinidad who gives him a New Testament and sets him on the road to conversion.

Soon Jugmohun's five years of indenture are up, but in the absence of real alternatives he decides to re-indenture. During his second term his wife comes from India to join him and when the term is over they set themselves up as independent rice farmers in Essequibo. The happy conclusion of the story occurs with the arrival in Essequibo of a Canadian missionary to spread the gospel among those who are not so enlightened as Jugmohun — a missionary who closely resembles Mackay.

In the course of recounting the story, Mackay describes the social structure of British Guiana at the time and provides some revealing insights into his own attitudes toward that structure. On his arrival in Georgetown, Jugmohun's attention is caught by the spectacle of passing humanity in the streets:

> There was also the "Sahib tog," self-contained, active, assertive, the same he had seen in his own land. These, he instinctively felt, would be his masters in the new world, as they had been in the old.
> But there was another class that he saw in great numbers: black men, with thick lips, flat noses, and curly hair. They were poorly dressed in ragged European clothes, and spoke the "Augrezi" speech. Many of them were engaged as labourers and porters, and as many others were indolently loafing. These men, the "Kaffir tog," as he heard them called, Jugmohun felt would be his rivals in the struggle for employment. Rivals but not formidable ones, for the black man was evidently lazy, careless, and good natured, although strong and fit for hard labour.[8]

Later in the story, Jugmohun tries to dissuade his fellow "coolies", discontented with hard labour and low wages, from violence:

> When an investigation was held with the causes of the riot, Jugmohun was congratulated for the part he had played, first in advising the labourers against deeds of violence, and afterwards persuading them to return peaceably to work. He was indeed learning the lessons of honest

industry under the burning sun in the broad cane fields of British Guiana. The bonds of indenture were irksome; but training in habits of industry, constant employment, and intelligent direction, were attendant compensations. The labour of the field is as honourable as it is ancient, and still serves its divinely appointed purpose.[9]

Although Mackay's attitudes appear narrow and prejudiced now, they were not at all uncommon in 1904. There were few who questioned the hegemony of the planters, and those who did were often dealt with in the manner of the rebels on Jugmohun's plantation. These were the prevailing attitudes of the time. But times change, and when the story of the Canadian Mission is again picked up in fictional form, almost seventy years later, it is with a much darker view of its purpose and effect. In his novel *Yesterdays,* Harold Sonny Ladoo, a Trinidadian East Indian who had come to Toronto, described the plan of one of his central characters, Poonwa, to start a Hindu Mission to Canada.

Poonwa will build a school, just as the Canadian missionaries did. But

instead of having one punishment room like the Canadian Mission School had in Tolaville, he was going to have about five such rooms. Through flogging and teaching he would pound Hinduism into them. Then he would teach them to deny their culture; he would make them wear Hindu garments. Then he would get merchants from Carib Island [the fictional island, recognizable as Trinidad, where the story is set] to tie up their trade and drain their natural resources into the West Indies. But now and then he would give them a little money as aid also; and he wouldn't give them the money just like that; he would make them crawl and beg for it. Then he would teach them that white is ugly and evil; only black and brown are good. . . .[10]

Ladoo was himself educated at a Canadian Mission school in Trinidad. After he came to Canada in 1968, he conceived the idea of a series of novels spanning life in the West Indies and Canada. The first of those novels, *No Pain Like This Body,* an eerie evocation of an East Indian family's struggle with nature in Carib Island, was published in 1972, and was acclaimed by both Canadian and West Indian critics. *Yesterdays* was the second novel in the series, and also the last. In the summer of 1973 Ladoo returned to

Trinidad to attend to some family problems. A few days later his battered body was found in a ditch at the side of a road in the sugar belt.[11]

And so it will remain for someone else to tell the story that Ladoo began, even if not in the same manner. The change from the world of J. D. Mackay to that of Harold Sonny Ladoo is, above all, a change in perspective. For increasingly the initiative has shifted to the people who were the victims of the relationship that both Mackay and Ladoo describe, and the effects of that shift have only begun to be felt.

13/Strangers in Paradise

Those people from the islands — the only time you hear their voices loud
is when they're singing or when they're shouting revolution.

A school principal
Montreal

The hall is big and barnlike, there are tables around the sides
where people are sitting and drinking beer and a big open space in
the middle. The faces are predominantly black and most of the few
whites have black dates. The crowd clusters below the stage to let
itself be swept up by the loud assertive music of the brass band and
the superb smooth voice and suggestive lyrics of the Mighty Sparrow. As usual the magic works, the spell is cast, the dancing is free
and frenzied and the whole is cathartic as only a calypso fête can
be. But then Sparrow prances off into the wings, the band is silent
and as the crowd drifts out it is hit with a blast of cold air. For the
hall is St. Lawrence Market, the town is Toronto and it is a chilly
April night. An hour ago it could have been Sparrow's Hideaway
in Petit Valley or the Seamen and Waterfront Workers' Hall in
Port of Spain, but the illusion doesn't last.

Scenes like the one in St. Lawrence Market are common in
Toronto, Canada's principal gathering place for immigrants; once
a year, in the summertime, as part of the Caribana festival, steel-
bands, brass bands, masqueraders and dancers spill out into the
streets. But they do not take over the whole city, as they do Port of
Spain and the other cities of Trinidad at Carnival time, only a
carefully demarcated part of it, and they have to stop at intersec-
tions to let the traffic go by. Caribana captures much of the colour
of Carnival but there is also much lacking, and every February
many Trinidadians come home from Canada, and from the United
States and Britain, for the real thing. One University of the West
Indies lecturer in Trinidad told of his cousin who lives in New
York and returns every year for Carnival and talks wistfully of

219

buying a house in Trinidad and coming back to live. "If she didn't come home every year for Carnival," he said, "then maybe she could afford to buy that house."

Life can be hard for West Indians in Canada, and the absence of Carnival is only one of many difficulties. Some of the hardships are inherent: the winter, the homesickness, the disillusionment when the immigrant finds out that the streets of Toronto are not after all paved with gold. Others are the product of the reception that immigrants from the West Indies get in Canada. *Contrast*, the Toronto-based newspaper of Canada's black community, regularly carries reports of beatings, police harassment, and discrimination:

● "Five persons were hospitalized as racial terror swept through and continued to plague residents of Jamestown Cresc. in Etobicoke earlier this week. Up to press time one Black youth was still in critical condition in the intensive care unit of the Etobicoke General Hospital, as a result of stab wounds he received when he was attacked by several white youths on Monday night."[1]

● "A black Scarborough woman and her three daughters spent a night of terror when their home was attacked by four white men last weekend."[2]

● "Like wild Nazi stormtroopers, a Toronto policeman and two immigration officers busted into the home of a Black grandmother last Thursday, smashing her against a wall several times."[3]

● "A man on his way home about 10 p.m. Wednesday last week, was handcuffed by two Toronto policemen, bashed in his mouth and punched in his stomach until he urinated while begging, 'please stop before you kill me,' *Contrast* was told. Thirty-five-year-old Jamaican-born Alexander Joseph was just a few houses away from his Oakwood Avenue home which he owns when the incident was said to have occurred."[4]

While there are often disagreements about the details of individual incidents, there is no doubt that attacks on blacks occur, and that there have been enough of them to lead many Canadians to question their fondly held self-image of racial tolerance. Even if the White Power slogans painted on the sides of Toronto buildings represent the views of a tiny minority, they help create a psychological climate in which black Canadians feel surrounded by hostility and rejection. The loudest voices in Canada in recent years, and especially during a few tense months in Toronto in 1975, have been those of know-nothings and bigots. If there is a tolerant majority in Canada that gets on well with black immigrants and would like to have more of them come, it has by and large not been heard.

And yet, to characterize Canada as a country of unreconstructed White Power fanatics would be both dangerous and unfair. It would be closer to the truth to call Canadians a nation of innocents about race relations. One writer, Marq de Villiers, a white South African by birth, said that "most Canadians know nothing about racism. This is a good thing and a bad thing. Good because it takes a society like South Africa to really know about racism. Bad because Canadians over-simplify racism in terms of lynchings and riots, and thus miss the small hurts subtle racism can cause."[5]

To a large extent, Canadians know little of racial prejudice because they have little experience of racial diversity. Until 1967, discriminatory provisions in the Immigration Act kept Canada effectively a white country. There were few blacks and they weren't very visible and they could be patronized and patted on the head. Changes in the law in 1967 abolished the last vestiges of legal discrimination, and enshrined a merit-point system based mostly on job skills that had been introduced a few years earlier. People wanting to come to Canada from Jamaica or Nigeria or India or Hong Kong still had substantial hurdles placed in their path, but they weren't quite as severe as they had been before. Of the 770,134 people who immigrated to Canada between 1963 and 1967, all but 104,599 — 14.5 per cent — came from Europe, the United States, Australia, New Zealand, South Africa and Rhodesia. Between 1968 and 1973, 921,324 immigrants came to Canada, but only 625,392 of them came from those same countries, while 295,932 new immigrants — 32.1 per cent of the total — came from the remaining countries, mostly poor and non-white, of Asia, Africa, Central and South America, the Caribbean and Oceania.[6]

This new immigration has put the myth of Canadian tolerance to its most serious test and made at least a partial loss of Canadian

221

innocence in race relations inevitable. The preliminary indications of how white Canadians are adjusting to the limited opening up of non-white immigration are not encouraging. There are many Canadians of all races who are trying to make the transition as easy as possible. But one gunshot, one beating, one slammed door, one insult can undo months of careful work.

Ken Jeffers looked up from that morning's Toronto *Sun* with the headline "The final insult for Michael Habbib was death"[7] and out the window of the Harriet Tubman Youth Centre to a group of black children playing in the yard. "It could have been any one of those kids," he said quietly. "Who is it going to be next?" Michael Habbib was fifteen years old and Jamaican-born and he was walking across the parking lot of the Fairview Mall in Toronto when a gunman came up to him and fired three bullets at him without saying a word. One bullet hit him in the stomach, one hit him in the chest and the third missed. The front page of the *Sun* had a photograph of Habbib's mother: "Mother Pleads for Tolerance." "How does that mother explain why he was killed?" asked Jeffers. "What can we tell black kids who have reached the age of reason and see these things? What can we tell them?"

The Harriet Tubman Youth Centre, named after a runaway slave who helped many other slaves come to Canada via the Underground Railroad, is a community centre for young blacks in north-central Toronto, and Ken Jeffers, its director, came to Toronto from Trinidad via South Carolina. "We're in the business of trying," he said. "Nobody likes violence but kids are quick to see things. It's a violent history. We try to get kids not to nurture so much hatred." The Centre offers an afternoon school for black kids, sports, steelband classes, dance classes. It tries to encourage adaptation to life in Canada and black pride. Its annual budget of $70,000 to $90,000 comes from the Laidlaw Foundation, federal and provincial grants, the York Board of Education, and the YMCA, which supplied the building.[8] It has eight full-time workers to serve a black community Jeffers estimated at 60,000 people. "It's like using a razor blade," he said, "to cut down a tree."

Michael Habbib's death in early May of 1975 came in the midst of what the federal government had billed as a "national debate on immigration policy," centred around its Green Paper on Immigration issued earlier in the year. Unlike a white paper, which suggests policy, a green paper only outlines options; in choosing the green paper route to begin its rethinking of Canada's immigration program, the government professed to be aiming to let a hundred flowers bloom and hear the many voices of the Canadian people. But the route had its hazards too. "The most conspicuous and controversial feature of recent immigration has been the increase of non-white people in this country," said Alan Borovoy of the Canadian Civil Liberties Association during the immigration debate.

In its explicit avoidance of recommendations, the very format of the Green Paper throws open the whole issue. It legitimizes alternative viewpoints and policies.

While many opinions may be entitled to a hearing, they are not all entitled to a blessing. But this is the risk when Government renounces its role of leader in exchange for the role of pollster. Virtually all points of view, no matter how mutually antagonistic, acquire an instant respectability. Thus, at one and the same time, the Government officially opposes but effectively dignifies the idea of racial quotas.[9]

The national debate on immigration was bound to give a platform for those who favoured harsh, restrictive and biased immigration policies. It was bound to increase the fear already present in immigrant communities and create the suspicion that the government was trying to stir up racial tension to give it an excuse to clamp down on further immigration.

It is not a characteristic of documents written by civil servants to say what they mean simply and directly, but the Green Paper on Immigration carried mealy-mouthed obfuscation to a level unusual even for Ottawa. The Paper may have spoken only of "population change that entails after all, as regards international migration, novel and distinctive features,"[10] but it wasn't hard to figure out what it meant by "novel and distinctive," and many of the participants in the subsequent debate were not so delicate in their phrasing. The Zero Population Growth movement placed an advertisement in several newspapers featuring a photograph of a pregnant teenage girl in a maple-leaf T-shirt. "Immigration," it said. "If Canada were a girl, she'd be in trouble. Soon there'll be

223

too many people in Canada. Not because you're out there making babies. Because the rest of the world is. And they're coming here. Massing in cities. On the verge of creating the squalor that too many people can't help but create. Changing the quality of life for your children and their children."[11] It suggested an upper limit of 100,000 immigrants a year.

Most of the mail received by the special joint committee of the Senate and the House of Commons set up to hear the views of Canadians on immigration favoured keeping immigrants and especially non-white ones out (wisely, the committee chose to ignore this mail and recommend only a few relatively minor changes in Canada's immigration practice[12]). "The streets, which were once clean and neat and quiet," wrote a Toronto woman, "are littered with refuse thrown around by people who could care less. Many immigrants have the lovely habit of spitting all over the streets. Their children think nothing of relieving themselves in public in the backyards." An Edmonton writer proposed that Canada "exclude all non-whites, institute a program of deportation of non-whites in the Dominion," and "institute laws against racial pollution; such blood pollution is for ever."[13]

Someone else made a contribution to the debate by pumping bullets into Michael Habbib and adding fuel to the smouldering anger and fear of West Indian immigrants and other black Canadians. The Jamaican High Commissioner in Canada, Wills O. Isaacs, felt it necessary to issue a statement "asking all Jamaicans to remain calm and try their very best not to be resentful." He added that "I cannot, however, allow this situation to pass without commenting on the attitude of the Toronto police in their treatment to my people. In Jamaica our policemen are taught to protect the citizens, and to prevent crime in the good British tradition, but here in Toronto incidents have been reported to me which have led me to form the opinion that certain elements, and I emphasize, certain elements of the Toronto Police are extremely racist, uncultured and inhuman."[14]

Despite the provocation that led to Isaacs' remarks, they had the perhaps unanticipated effect of shifting the focus of Canadian indignation from the killer of Michael Habbib to the High Commissioner himself. External Affairs Minister Allan MacEachen called his outburst "unfortunate."[15] The Toronto *Sun*, which a few days earlier had decried "the tragic, senseless killing" of Michael Habbib and attributed it to "demented racism,"[16] now said in an editorial entitled "Rum Jamaican" that "perhaps because he is black there will be more tolerance towards Jamaican High Commissioner W. O. Isaacs' racist accusations than otherwise might be expected,"[17] ignoring the fact that Isaacs is, in West Indian terms at least, white.

If the immigration debate did strip white Canadians of some of their innocence and force them to take a more realistic look at their own racial attitudes, than perhaps it was not totally without purpose. For there has always been a good deal of evidence to suggest that Canadian tolerance is a myth. The prejudices of white Canadians, when not directed toward each other, have generally focussed on Asians rather than blacks, although that is probably only because there have generally more Asians than blacks in the country. The centre of anti-Asian prejudice in Canada has always been British Columbia, where the song "White Canada for Ever" was popular in the early twentieth century:

Then let us stand united all
And show our father's might,
That won the home we call our own,
For white man's land we fight.
To Oriental grasp and greed
We'll surrender, no never.
Our watchword be "God save the King"
White Canada for ever.[18]

In 1885, a $50 head tax was imposed on Chinese immigrants: this was the first serious restrictive provision in Canadian immigration law, and many more followed, varying in their specific targets and clauses, but all enforcing the same general hierarchy of preferences: people from Britain, the United States and the white Dominions first; the non-English-speaking but still desirable peoples of northern and western Europe second; other white people third; and everybody else a distant last. It was 1962 before the first serious effort was made to mitigate this persistent feature of Canadian immigration policy, and 1967 before the last explicitly discriminatory clauses were removed from the regulations.[19]

Although the first immigrants from the West Indies, the Maroons, had come to Canada in the 1790s, the number of West Indians in the country remained negligible for a century and a half. The first year in which as many as a thousand West Indian immigrants came to Canada was 1956.[20] The only official encouragement to West Indian immigration before 1967 was the domestic scheme, inaugurated in 1955 and designed to bring small numbers of unskilled West Indian women to Canada as domestic servants; many of the "domestics" admitted under the scheme were in fact trained secretaries and civil servants who could not otherwise meet Canadian immigration requirements.[21] West Indians seeking to better themselves economically looked traditionally to the United States and, after the restrictive McCarran–Walter Act was passed over President Truman's veto in 1952,[22] to Britain. However, white reaction in Britain and new limits on non-white Commonwealth immigration passed in 1961 diminished the appeal of that country: after so eagerly colonizing the world, Britain was ill-prepared to deal with the offspring of that colonization when they unexpectedly but logically landed in the home country.

Meanwhile, Canada's liberalized regulations of 1962 made it a possible outlet for many West Indians for the first time. Immigration to Canada from the West Indies crept up from 1,126 in 1961 to 3,655 in 1965; in the latter year, an additional 1,415 West Indians came to Canada from Britain.[23] This new liberalism, however, had its selective aspects. While only some two per cent of West Indians are white, 13.4 per cent of the West Indian immigrants admitted to Canada in 1963 and 9.6 per cent of those admitted in 1965 were white.[24] In addition, the skill requirements that were supposed to be the cornerstone of the 1962 regulations appeared to be more stringently applied for West Indians than for Europeans. In 1965, a year in which more than five times as many Italians as West Indians were admitted to Canada, 561, or twenty-four per cent, of the West Indians were professionals, as opposed to only 261 — a little over two per cent — of the Italians. In that same year 9,803

Italian construction, manufacturing and mechanical workers and labourers were admitted, compared with only 463 West Indians in those categories.[25]

Even after 1967, although discrimination was removed from immigration laws and regulations, it was not entirely removed from immigration practice. One of the factors that can make it easier for a prospective immigrant to get to Canada is the availability of a well-staffed Canadian immigration office, and the distribution of these offices around the globe is still less than equitable. The concentration and size of immigration offices depends neither on the absolute populations of different countries nor on the numbers of immigrants they have been providing in recent years. As of early 1975, India's population of more than half a billion was served by a single eight-man office in New Delhi that also had responsibility for several smaller countries around India's periphery, while for the two hundred and twenty million people of the United States Canada maintained a five-man office in New York, three-man offices in Chicago and Detroit, two-man offices in Boston, Buffalo, Los Angeles, San Francisco and Seattle, and one-man offices in Atlanta, Dallas, Minneapolis and New Orleans. England was the source of 28,828 immigrants in 1974, roughly as many as the whole Caribbean, which supplied 27,450. But England had a seventeen-man office in London, a five-man office in Manchester and a four-man office in Birmingham, while the Caribbean had five-man offices in Kingston and Port of Spain and a one-man office in Port-au-Prince, Haiti. While the correspondence between the distribution of officers and numbers of applications received was somewhat closer, there were still some serious anomalies. The one-man Port-au-Prince office received 3,243 applications in 1974 and issued 2,736 immigrant visas, while a one-man office in Bordeaux, France received 778 applications and issued 405 visas.[26]

In effect, Canada's borders were still closed to large numbers of people from the Third World who wanted to come here, and one of the results of this was that not every prospective immigrant went through formal channels. From 1967 until the end of 1972, visitors to Canada could apply for landed immigrant status while they were in the country, and many people came as visitors in the hope that one way or another they could succeed in staying. A number of cases were reported, most of them involving women from the Caribbean, in which an immigration officer led a female visitor to believe that it would be easier for her to obtain her landed status if she slept with him. "When I was at his [immigration officer Lawrence Doiron's] house," testified one woman before the commission of inquiry that investigated these and other immigration irregularities, "he told me I shouldn't be afraid, he said, 'I'm going to arrange everything for you.' He told me to bring my passport, and then he started having relations with me."

"Sexual relations?" asked commission counsel Joseph Nuss.

"Yes."

"Were you willing to have sexual relations with him?"

"I didn't want to, and I was crying. He put his arm around my neck, and told me not to cry, that I shouldn't be afraid, and that if I wouldn't do it, I wouldn't get my papers. And he told me that I didn't have enough intelligence to stay in Canada, and that he alone could give me those papers."[27]

Doiron was dismissed by the department while another employee who had allegedly engaged in similar practices, Georges-Etienne Desrochers, resigned during the inquiry.

Another result of the continuing difficulty of getting into Canada legally was an influx of illegal immigrants who, aside from being subject to the worst forms of exploitation, are often used as the excuse for the periodic scare campaigns against immigration that are carried on in the press. Even at its best, the press treats illegal immigration only as a failure of enforcement and not as a failure of policy; and at its worst, it makes only perfunctory distinctions between legal and illegal immigration and evokes fear and hostility toward all immigrants. This mood reached its peak during the 1972 federal election campaign when immigration along with bilingualism and welfare became a focus for the reaction against the "permissiveness" of the Trudeau government. The Toronto *Star* said a week before the election that "Canada's borders are like a collapsed seawall, over which flows flotsam and jetsam from all over the world."[28] The Toronto *Sun* spoke of illegal immigrants in much the same tone, and it hardly shifted that tone when it reported in a lead front-page story that "the federal government has imported 1,500 West Indians to work in Ontario at a time when 146,000 Ontarians are out of jobs. The West Indians — all men — are working in farming, mainly fruit picking and food processing, and some are earning more than $200 a week. Ottawa officials point out that Canadians don't want the jobs and apparently would rather collect unemployment and welfare." The story quoted an Ontario government official as saying that the importation of West Indian workers could become "a helluva hot issue before the election is over."[29] It failed to mention that the program under which the workers were coming in had been operating quite openly since 1966.

Reduced to minority status in the election, the government dumped its controversial immigration minister, Bryce Mackasey, and changed the regulations to make it impossible for visitors to apply for landed status while in Canada. With another storm over immigration beginning to gather in 1974, the government changed the regulations in February and again in October, both times in the direction of bringing immigration in line with immediate labour-market considerations. The new regulations had the desired effect: immigration dropped from 218,465 in 1974 to 187,881 in 1975, and in the first quarter of 1976 it dropped still further, to 32,359 from 43,448 a year earlier.[30] But as the immigration debate of 1975 showed, even that didn't please everybody.

A glaring weakness of the Immigration Debate was its failure to consider the effect of Canada's immigration policy on people outside the country. Immigration was treated entirely as a branch of domestic economic policy, as a tap that could be turned on and off at will, with the only questions to be answered being which way to turn it and how far. The relationship between immigration and foreign policy was never even considered, even though immigration policy is the most important determinant of Canada's relations with some areas of the world, including the West Indies.

The presence of a considerable and growing number of West Indians in Canada has become the strongest and most tangible link

229

in the Canada–West Indies relationship. Anywhere in the West Indies, if you say you are from Toronto almost everyone you meet will tell you that he has a brother, a sister, an uncle, a daughter, or at least a friend there. Shifts in Canadian immigration policy; pig-headed statements about immigrants by Canadian politicians or commentators; West Indians, going to Canada to visit relatives, but made to turn back at Toronto airport — all these are promi-nently reported in the West Indian newspapers. Most West Indians are aware of Canada primarily through its immigration practices and the experiences of people who have gone to live there.

If there are differing opinions on the effects of immigration on Canadian society, there are at least as many views on the effects of emigration on the West Indies. In their 1967 study of Canada–West Indies economic relations, Kari Levitt and Alister McIntyre argued that the most important effects were beneficial ones:

> Inadequate savings and foreign exchange earnings are two of the most serious constraints imposed on the development process. Indeed, as the process of economic development becomes cumulative, the foreign exchange constraint tends to attain even more critical proportions. Emigration can play an important role in helping to ease these con-straints. In the first place, to the extent that emigration helps to reduce unemployment and underemployment, it lowers the proportion of the population dependent on the regularly employed and so makes possi-ble a higher rate of savings. In the second place, the remittances made by immigrants abroad to their dependents at home are an important source of foreign exchange, which can be used to finance foreign investment goods purchases.[31]

On the other hand, emigration tends to rob the region of the people with the greatest economic potential, people with skills and those who are eager to acquire them. The very ideas of ambition and self-improvement become associated with leaving. Maureen McDonald was working as a waitress in the Broadway Restaurant and Bar near the Port of Spain waterfront in early 1975 but she wanted to go to Canada and become a seamstress or a welfare wor-ker. Couldn't she do that in Trinidad? "When you go away," she said, "you want to do something and make something of yourself. When you're in your own country you don't think about that so much."

Immigration requirements that give preference to people with education and job training, while logical from the point of view of the receiving country, ensure that most emigrants will be people their home countries can ill afford to lose. Emigration to Canada of West Indians in certain professions, such as medicine, has often coincided with shortages in those professions at home; in 1974, with the state of medical services in Trinidad a source of national dissatisfaction, there were reported to be fifty Trinidadian doctors in Toronto alone.[32]

Few West Indians who for reasons of birth, wealth or education have escaped the inevitability of a life in the canefields or the slums of West Kingston or East Port of Spain have thought in terms of using their good fortune for the benefit of their country or region. The Jamaica *Star* reported in March 1975 that "a steady emigration to Canada of its Chinese businessmen" was one of the factors causing severe economic difficulties in St. Thomas parish in eastern Jamaica: "Since 1973, more than four large Chinese business families have left St. Thomas for Canada not because of the economic decadence in the area, they claimed, but because of fear of what most of them described as 'the uncertain political atmosphere and the horror of gun crimes'."[33] Lloyd Best, the leader of Trinidad's opposition Tapia group and himself a university lecturer, criticized the tendency of West Indian academics to head for Canada at the first sign of trouble. "Toronto," he said, "is their Miami."

Vernon Charles, the sweet-drink king of Trinidad, found his Miami in Vancouver. Charles, who was described by the Trinidad *Express* as "one of Trinidad's most successful young millionaire businessmen," and had acquired directorships of the Bank of Nova Scotia Trinidad and Tobago Ltd. and Maritime Life (Caribbean) and a long string of investments in addition to his soft-drink factory, cited the attempted kidnapping of his wife in 1973 as the immediate cause of his departure. But his disenchantment with

231

Trinidad had begun three years earlier when he had tried to lease some land from the government and had been given the runaround for several months. Finally, a civil servant "called me and said that the land was available but he could not see how this would work."

> I asked why? and he said because of the price. I asked what price? He said that the land had been valued at [TT] $25 a square foot, and the rent would be $2.50 a square foot. I said that would be $200,000 for the two acres — 80,000 square feet. He said yes, but not only that. Cabinet also wanted a premium and the premium was 10 per cent of the value of the land — another $200,000. So I told him no. I told him to tell them to go to hell and keep the damn land. I don't want to have anything to do with it again. I was going to chuck in everything.

Later, Charles told the Prime Minister that he was emigrating. "[Dr. Williams] asked me, how would I go? I knew what he meant; it was my money. And so I asked him if I would be allowed to take some money with me. He said, no he might treat me as Castro treated Cubans when they wanted to leave Cuba, which was with $50." Charles eventually left with at least enough money to set himself up in Vancouver, but he retained all his investments in Trinidad and made several new ones just before his departure. "We are very happy where we are," he said. "I no longer have to carry a gun in my pocket. I no longer have to hire a watchman. I no longer have watchdogs. We don't have any burglar-proof on our windows. All our doors are open at night, except the front door and the back door, and we can leave our children without anybody and go out at nights."[34] It is only to be wished that all Trinidadians coming to Canada found the country as hospitable as Vernon Charles did.

For the average emigrant, the decision to leave is a wrenching one, involving giving up a cherished way of life and consigning himself to a state of permanent rootlessness and suspension between two worlds. He comes back for Christmas or Carnival, dressed in new clothes that say, "I've made it." He may even go back home to live, but as likely as not it will no longer be satisfying and he will be attracted once again by the richer, busier countries of the north. He tells his family and friends of the good things about life in Canada, partly because those are the easiest to communicate and partly because he is trying very hard to justify to himself the decision he made. People back home hear about the more obvious minuses — the harshness of the winters, the unfriendliness of so many Canadians, the racial incidents — but no one knows until he goes himself how hard it really is. And still the pull is irresistible: the prospect of having a better job, drawing a bigger pay cheque, being where the action is, the same things that attract Newfoundlanders to Toronto, Gaspesians to Montreal, Manitobans to Vancouver and Ontarians to Los Angeles.

"We're not a recruiting office," said Allan Findlay, one of Canada's immigration counsellors in Port of Spain, and the headlines from Canadian newspapers that were posted on the wall bore him out: "Lucky few to get access to Canada," "Canada puts tougher rules on immigrants," "Unemployment and prices to rise in 1975," "Population growth overtaking cities," "Economy demands brake on immigration." Nevertheless, the office was busy, and both it and its counterpart in Kingston are rarely otherwise. First thing in the morning, before the office opened to the public, there was a group counselling session. For independent immigration applicants, these sessions are held before a decision is made on their applications, but the applicants at this session were all sponsored by close relatives in Canada and so their acceptance was more or less automatic.

Counsellor D. S. Schellenberg's remarks were sober and low-key and concerned mostly economic and legal matters. "What we want understood clearly," he told the twenty-five prospective immigrants, "is that you're going to a country with high unemployment, a high cost of living and a severe climate." There were few questions — one about whether the government will give a person land (in Manitoba and Saskatchewan you can lease land from the government), one about how to find out before you go if the trade school you're planning to attend in Canada has government recognition (ask the immigration counsellor during your personal interview), one about whether Canada has a standard wage (there's a minimum wage set by the provinces). It is only after arrival in Canada that the really urgent questions will begin to come to mind.

Guyana's Prime Minister Forbes Burnham won't allow Canada to open an immigration office in Georgetown; with its small population and large uninhabited interior, Guyana has adopted a policy of officially discouraging emigration. Still, thousands of Guyanese leave each year. For Guyana no less than for other West Indian countries, a continuing flow of emigration is a boon in the short term even if it is a serious long-term problem. Without that outlet for some of the people for whom the local economies can't provide jobs, West Indian governments would be faced with social unrest far beyond their capacity to handle.

The countries that created and continue to maintain the economic system that puts satisfactory employment in such short supply in the Caribbean absorb its human surplus into their own labour forces. "Immigration," said the British author of the pamphlet *Workless of the World*, "is a mirror image of the world's trading and financial inequities, and ... these are the root cause of immigration."[35] There are no jobs where the people are, so the people go where the jobs are. And when this migration is international rather than internal, access to these jobs is granted entirely at the pleasure of the receiving countries. When these countries enter troubled political or economic waters, then even the option of emigrating is closed off to people in the Third World.

One of the more refined extensions of this system is Canada's seasonal workers program, which was first established in 1966 by agreement with Jamaica and was later extended to Trinidad and Tobago, Barbados, the Leewards and Windwards, and Mexico. Through the program, workers from the contracting countries are recruited to do seasonal farm work in Canada, mostly in the agricultural belt of southwestern Ontario. The farmers they work for are responsible for their transportation and housing and generally pay them the minimum wage, which is much more than they could ever hope to make in their own countries. And when the work is finished, they leave. There are no knotty problems of adjustment.

234

Contact between the seasonal workers and Canadians is kept to a minimum. They simply do their jobs — jobs that Canadians won't touch — and then they go home.

In a revealing and evocative article, Christie Blatchford quoted Blenheim, Ontario, farmer James McGuigan as saying that 5,000 Caribbean imports (5,342 workers were brought in under the program in 1974) could do the work of 30,000 Canadian transients, and do it more graciously. "People on welfare who are told to go work on a farm — it's punishment," McGuigan told her. "With students, it's a way of killing time, and who can blame them? I had two students this summer, paid them $2.50 an hour. Well, one of them had been making $6 an hour the summer before in industry; where's he going to get incentive? By Canadian standards they were doing a reasonable job. Hell, they thought they were killing themselves. But compared to the Jamaicans — and I figure they cost me a dollar an hour more with the cost of transportation and housing — they were hardly working at all."[36]

Inevitably, there is some dissatisfaction among the seasonal workers, but because of their peculiar status in the country it tends to be muted. Every year a certain number of workers run off; when they are caught they are subject to deportation. An anonymous Jamaican worker told a reporter that "we have become the new coolies in Canada — good enough to work on the land but not good enough to remain in the country."[37]

A politician in Grenada, able to contain his enthusiasm about the extension of the program to his country, was not quite as bitter but no less to the point. He called the seasonal workers a "reverse Peace Corps."

14/Allies?

Third World eyes on Canada.

headline, The Bomb,
Trinidad, December 27, 1974

Alister McIntyre, Secretary-General of the Caribbean Community and a longtime student of the Canadian presence in the region, said in 1974 that "I have always had a certain fondness for the relationship, not because of its content but because of its potential, the potential for a relationship between a relatively rich country and a poor set of countries where no imperial ambitions are at stake."

There are, of course, some Canadians who do harbour imperial ambitions of one sort or another. Earle McLaughlin wants the Royal Bank to expand its interests abroad. Ken Patrick wants Canada and the West Indies to get together for their common benefit. Max Saltsman wants to set the whole world back on its proper course. Practical or visionary, motivated by profit, power, publicity or good intentions, they represent one tendency in the Canadian attitude toward the West Indies.

But it is not the main tendency. Much of the Canadian economic presence in the West Indies, as we have seen, fell into Canada's lap, or devolved on Canada from London, Pittsburgh or Memphis. Only the financial institutions represent any sustained program of Canadian expansion. Nor is Canada's official policy characterized by anything so coherent as an imperial ambition. There is no manifest destiny or empire on which the sun never sets. People in the Department of External Affairs may harbour ambitions, but they are not on the whole imperial. In the case of the current minister, Don Jamieson, it has been reported that he wants to become Prime Minister. Most of the officials in his department want to do their jobs as well as they can, get home at five o'clock and collect their

237

pensions at sixty-five. If they entertain any high ambitions for their country they have managed to keep them hidden.

If trying to uncover Canadian imperial ambitions will not get us very far, it is perhaps more useful to talk about imperial structures. It has been Canada's lot to occupy a favoured but still subsidiary position within those structures. Because Canada has never sat in the first chair, it has avoided most of the responsibility for the military adventures, economic inequalities and cultural deprivations that have been the system's most frequent results. Because of the privileges Canada has enjoyed, it has been slow to see that the structures had to be changed. It was a pleasant and protected existence and there was nothing to suggest that it would not last.

Since the late 1960s, however, the initiative has begun to pass from Canada's traditional protectors to the countries of the Third World. Canada's old position is increasingly difficult to sustain, and nowhere is that difficulty more evident than in its relations with the West Indies. Canada has been visible in the West Indies as a trading partner, supplier of investment, source of tourists, aid-giver and outlet for emigrants. Now that the terms of trade, the effects of investment and tourism, the results of aid programs and the immigration policies of metropolitan countries have become the causes of disappointment and sometimes of anger, that new mood has inevitably been reflected in West Indian perceptions of Canada.

If the Canada–West Indies relationship is to live up to the hopes that McIntyre held out for it, the imperial structures within which it exists will have to be broken down. Canada will have to re-examine not only a few trade agreements and aid programs but also its alignment in the world. This will at best be a laborious and probably painful process, but Canada's wish to be seen as a friend of the West Indies and the other countries of the Third World will remain a pious platitude unless it is undertaken as a long-term goal. Without such a decision Canada will be as passive a player in the new international order as it has been in the old.

There are no easy steps toward changing this, but there are directions that can be mapped out and beginnings that can be made. In Canada's relations with the West Indies there are several areas where some immediate attention could help:

● The Canadian government could commit itself to a more open immigration policy and one not subject to every vicissitude in Canada's internal political and economic climate. This would correspond both to the short-term interest of the West Indies in an outlet for the people for whom no jobs are available at home, and to Canada's long-term interest in a larger and more varied population. Some effort could be made to accept young unskilled West Indians as immigrants and train them in Canada. A more active program could be undertaken in Canada to deal with the adjustment problems that immigration entails and to ease the transition both for immigrants and for Canadians.

● Canadian aid could be untied so that it would truly be aid instead of part aid and part export subsidy. Aid programs could be designed with more attention paid to the history, culture and social structures of the West Indies so that they would meet West Indian needs instead of trying to turn the West Indies into a replica and extension of North America.

● As both a host country for foreign multinationals and a home for multinationals operating abroad, Canada offers an almost unique vantage point from which to view these corporations and could be a leader in developing policies to deal with them. Canada could also make clear that it considers the relationship between a Canadian multinational operating in a foreign country and the government of the country to be the business of that government alone, and will undertake no policy, notably including insuring the multinational against political developments in the host country, that could be construed as Canadian government support for the multinational.

● Canada could adopt a much more sympathetic stance toward the movement among Third World commodity exporters to ensure a fair price for their products. In so doing it would be asserting its own power as a major raw-material exporter while at the same time providing support for one of the Third World's most important initiatives toward developing a new set of international economic relations.

None of these measures are likely to involve any great sacrifices on Canada's part. In fact they would be, on the whole, very much to Canada's benefit. At their best Canadians have wanted their country's relationship to the West Indies to be that of a benefactor and big brother. They have never been able to conceive of the possibility that Canada and the West Indies could be allies and share common interests. But if the Canada–West Indies relationship is not to be marked by increasing hostility that is precisely the direction in which it will have to develop.

Notes

Chapter 1

1. See C. L. R. James, *The Black Jacobins: Toussaint L'Ouverture and the San Domingo Revolution* (New York: Vintage, 1963), for a masterly narrative and interpretation of the Haitian revolution.
2. "Sharp rules out island take-over," Toronto *Star,* April 11, 1974.
3. In the election of July 8, 1974, only a few months after the Turks and Caicos affair had run its course, Saltsman was re-elected to parliament with a majority of 7,445, while more than half of the sitting New Democratic members lost their seats.
4. See H. E. Sadler, *Turks Island Landfall,* Vol. 1 (Grand Turk: The Fortress, 1975). Watling's Island was rechristened San Salvador by the British colonial government of the Bahamas in the 1920s in recognition of its claim to a place in history.
5. V. S. Naipaul, *The Overcrowded Barracoon* (London: André Deutsch, 1972), p. 250.
6. Roger McTair, "Dessalines talks to Toussaint L'Ouverture," *Savacou: a Journal of the Caribbean Artists Movement,* no. 9/10, 1974, p. 84.

Chapter 2

1. V. S. Naipaul, *The Overcrowded Barracoon (London: André Deutsch, 1972),* p. 254.
2. Eric Williams, *Capitalism and Slavery* (New York: Capricorn Books, 1966), p. 52.
3. *Ibid.,* pp. 7–28 *passim,* pp. 135–168 *passim.*
4. Gordon K. Lewis, *The Growth of the Modern West Indies* (New York: Monthly Review Press, 1968), p. 63.
5. Bridget Brereton, "The Experience of Indentureship: 1845–1917," in John La Guerre, ed., *Calcutta to Caroni: The East Indians of Trinidad* (London: Longman Caribbean, 1974), p. 36.
6. Sylvia Wynter, *Jamaica's National Heroes* (Kingston: Jamaica National Trust Commission, 1971), pp. 11–18.
7. Marti to Manuel Mercado, May 18, 1895. Quoted in Emilio Roig de Leuchsenring, *Marti Anti-imperialist* (Havana: Book Institute, 1967), p. 51.

8. Lord Invader, "Yankee Dollar," included on Samuel Charters, ed., *The Real Calypso 1927-1946* (New York: RBF Records, 1966), side 1, band 7.

9. See for example Peter Balroop, "Trinidad a Target for Nuclear Attack?" Trinidad *Express*, January 16, 1974, and "It Spells Danger for Us," *Tapia*, February 24, 1974.

10. Statistics from U.S. Department of Commerce, Bureau of Economic Analysis, cited in Leonard G. Campbell and Robert J. Shue, "Military Transactions in the U.S. Balance of Payments," *Survey of Current Business*, February 1972, table 2, p. 26.

11. Frank McDonald, "The Commonwealth Caribbean," in Tad Szulc, ed., *The United States and the Caribbean* (Englewood Cliffs, N.J.: Prentice Hall, 1971), p. 144.

12. See Susanne Bodenheimer, "U.S. Labor's Conservative Role in Latin America," *The Progressive*, November 1967, for a description of the AIFLD courses.

13. Philip Agee, *Inside the Company: CIA Diary* (Harmondsworth, England: Penguin Books, 1975), p. 600.

14. Ronald Radosh, *American Labor and United States Foreign Policy* (New York: Random House, 1969), pp. 400–405.

15. George Crile, "Our Man in Jamaica," *Harper's*, October 1974, pp. 87–96.

16. Caribbean Tourism Research Centre, Bridgetown, Barbados, Conference on "Caribbean Tourism — The Present and the Future," Caracas, Venezuela, January 9–11, 1975, Inaugural Address by the President of the Republic of Venezuela, Dr. Carlos Andres Perez, pp. 1,4.

17. Trinidad *Guardian*, April 14, 1975.

18. Nizam Ali, "Diplomatic Coup at Chaguaramas," Trinidad *Express*, May 25, 1975, pp. 18–19.

19. Jamaica *Daily Gleaner*, June 17, 1975.

20. Jamaica *Daily Gleaner*, July 8, 1975.

Chapter 3

1. V.S. Naipaul, *The Mimic Men* (Harmondsworth, England; Penguin Books, 1969).

2. *Granma Weekly Review*, Havana, July 20, 1975, p. 5.

3. "PM on Difference with Cuba. . . . Private Sector Has Permanent Role Here," Jamaica *Daily Gleaner*, July 24, 1975.
4. Hollis Liverpool (The Mighty Chalkdust), "Mr. Nixon's Mistake," included on The Mighty Chalkdust, *To Spree with Love* (Port of Spain: Straker's Records, 1975), side 2, band 4.
5. Gordon K. Lewis, *The Growth of the Modern West Indies* (New York; Monthly Review Press, 1968), p. 226.
6. Toronto *Globe and Mail*, August 4, 1971; Montreal *Star*, March 10, 1971; Montreal *Star*, April 8, 1974; Montreal *Star*, March 28, 1974; Montreal *Star*, May 29, 1975.
7. "Only the Master Can Move Me — Gairy," Trinidad *Express*, August 17, 1975, pp. 10–11.
8. Quoted by Greg Chamberlain, "Where Long Hair is a Shooting Matter," Manchester *Guardian*, April 1, 1975.
9. Edwin Carrington, "Industrialization in Trinidad and Tobago since 1950", *New World Quarterly*, Vol. 4, No. 2, 1968. Reprinted in Norman Girvan and Owen Jefferson, ed., *Readings in the Political Economy of the Caribbean* (Kingston; New World Group, 1971), pp. 143–149.
10. C.L.R. James, *The Black Jacobins: Toussaint L'Ouverture and the San Domingo Revolution*, Second Edition, Revised (New York: Vintage, 1963), p. 396.
11. "RCA Representative Here to Seek Local Reggae Talent," Jamaica *Daily Gleaner*, March 6, 1975.
12. Gloria Lannaman, "Shillin' a Hour," from *Dickance for Fippance*, performed by Little Theatre Movement, Ward Theatre, Kingston, December 26, 1974 to March 1975.
13. George E. Eaton, *Alexander Bustamante and Modern Jamaica* (Kingston: Kingston Publishers, 1975), pp. 21–22.
14. "Rastas Say He is not Dead," Jamaica *Daily Gleaner*, August 28, 1975.

Chapter 4
1. Quoted by William L. Grant, "Canada versus Guadeloupe, an Episode of the Seven Years' War," *American Historical Review*, July 1912, pp. 740–741, 742.
2. *Ibid.*, p. 742.

3. *Ibid.,* p. 743.
4. Peter K. Newman, "Canada's Role in West Indian Trade Before 1912," *Inter-American Economic Affairs,* Summer 1960, p. 29.
5. *Ibid.,* p. 27.
6. "Hard Times", included in *Songs of the Newfoundland Outports* (3 vols., Ottawa: National Museum of Canada, 1965), p. 58.
7. C.H. Cecil, "The Maroons in Canada," *Canada-West Indies Magazine,* September 1935, p. 25.
8. Rev. John Morton, "The Canadian Presbyterian Mission: A Historial Sketch," in *The Canadian Presbyterian Mission to East Indians, Trinidad, B.W.I.* (Trinidad: Canadian Mission Council, 1911), p. 5.
9. *Ibid.,* p. 4.
10. A.J.P. Taylor, *Beaverbrook* (Harmondsworth, England; Penguin Books, 1974), pp. 35–40 *passim.*
11. Robin W. Winks, *Canadian-West Indian Union: A Forty-Year Minuet* (London: The Athlone Press, 1968), p. 21.
12. Saint John *Globe,* January 14, 1874, quoted in Winks, *op. cit.,* p. 14.
13. Winks, *op. cit.,* pp. 16–18.
14. Toronto *Globe,* October 27, 1911, quoted in Winks, *op. cit.,* p. 26.
15. Quoted in Winks, *op. cit.,* p. 19.
16. Quoted in Newman, *op. cit.,* p. 44.
17. *Ibid.,* pp. 48–49.
18. According to notices in *Canada-West Indies Magazine,* e.g., September 1935.
19. Quoted by Courtney Tower and C. Alexander Brown, "O Canada, He Stands on Guard for Thee," *Maclean's,* July 1970, p. 1.
20. *Ibid.,* p. 7.

Chapter 5
1. "Canadian Sub-Imperialism?: Jamie Swift & Tim Draimin Reply to John Warnock," *This Magazine,* May–June 1975, p. 32. See also Draimin and Swift, "What's Canada Doing in Brazil?," *This Magazine,* January–February 1975, pp. 3–8; Jack Warnock,

"Canadian Sub-Imperialism: A Reply," *This Magazine,* March–April 1975, pp 30–32; and Steve Moore and Debi Wells, *Imperialism and the National Question in Canada* (Toronto: 1975).
2. Ruy Mauro Marini, "Brazilian Subimperialism," *Monthly Review,* February 1972, p. 15.
3. See *World Military Expenditures and Arms Trade 1963–1973* (Washington: U.S. Arms Control and Disarmament Agency, 1975), table II.
4. Quoted by Peter Lloyd, "Defence Effort Lagging Badly Canada Warned," Toronto *Star,* September 17, 1975, p. 3.
5. Roger Newman, "Defence Funds Major Irritant, U.S. Ambassador Tells Canada," Toronto *Globe and Mail,* May 13, 1976.
6. Ernie Regehr, *Making A Killing: Canada's Arms Industry* (Toronto: McClelland and Stewart, 1975), p. 11.
7. Project Brazil and Last Post Staff, "The Brascan File," *Last Post,* March 1973, p. 32.
8. Canada, Department of External Affairs, *Foreign Policy for Canadians* (Ottawa: Information Canada, 1970), p. 14.
9. Draimin and Swift, "What's Canada Doing in Brazil?" op. cit., p. 7.
10. John Deverell and the Latin American Working Group, *Falconbridge: Portrait of a Canadian Mining Multinational* (Toronto: James Lorimer and Co., 1975), p. 180.
11. A list of the "leading banks of the world" according to balance sheet total in *World Banking 1973–74: 63rd Annual Survey* (London: Investors Chronicle, 1974), ranks the Royal thirty-first, the Commerce thirty-fifth, the Bank of Montreal forty-fourth, the Nova Scotia sixty-eighth and the Toronto-Dominion seventy-ninth, (pp. 1–3). *Moody's Bank and Finance Manual 1976* (New York: Moody's, 1976), contains a list of the "50 largest banks in free world — U.S. and overseas commercial banks ranked by size of deposits," which includes the Royal in fifteenth place, the Commerce in twenty-first and the Montreal in twenty-eighth (p. a2).
12. See Clifford H. Ince, *The Royal Bank of Canada, A Chronology: 1864–1969* (Montreal: Royal Bank of Canada, 1970), pp. 85, 109–111.
13. Canada, Department of Finance, *Canadian Banking*

Legislation (Ottawa: Supply and Services, 1976), pp. 23–29.
14. Quoted by Carole Orr, "Energy: The Cabinet Learns the New Math," *Last Post,* January 1974, p. 4.
15. Canada, Department of External Affairs, *op. cit.,* pp. 14-16.
16. Trinidad *Express,* April 20, 1975.
17. Bruce Garvey, "Trudeau, the Grouchy Guru, Cools Commonwealth Radicals," Toronto *Star*, May 10, 1975, p. 3.
18. Canada, Senate, Standing Committee on Foreign Affairs, *Report on Canada–Caribbean Relations* (Ottawa: Information Canada, 1970), p. xiii.
19. United States, Office of the White House Press Secretary, "Policy Statement: Economic Assistance and Investment Security in Developing Nations," January 19, 1972.
20. Statistics compiled by Canada, Department of Industry, Trade and Commerce.

Chapter 6

1. Central Bank of the Bahamas, *Quarterly Review,* March 1974, p. 59.
2. Count Alfred de Marigny, *More Devil than Saint* (New York: Beechhurst, 1946).
3. Quoted in Geoffrey Bocca, *The Life and Death of Sir Harry Oakes* (Garden City, N.Y.: Doubleday, 1959), p. 101.
4. Marshall Houts, *King's X: Common Law and the Death of Sir Harry Oakes* (New York: William Morrow and Co., 1972), pp. 61–72.
5. Bocca, *op. cit.,* p. 233.
6. Roger Worth, "Low-Cost Housing: At 75, Taylor Begins to Build New World Empire" and "E.P. Taylor at 74: Still Excited by Business Challenges," *Financial Post,* November 22, 1975. See "Who is Ludwig? World's Richest," Montreal *Gazette,* July 5, 1976, p. 28, for a short profile of Daniel K. Ludwig.
7. "Distinguished Citizens Named," Nassau *Guardian,* March 25, 1975, p. 1.
8. Quoted in *Bahamas Handbook and Businessman's Annual 1966-67* (Nassau: Dupuch Publications, 1966), p. 193.
9. Statistics from *Bahamas Handbook and Businessman's Annual*

1960 (Nassau: Dupuch Publications, 1960), and Commonwealth of the Bahamas, *1973 Annual Report of Tourism* (Nassau: 1974).

10. Michael Craton, *A History of the Bahamas* (London: Collins, 1968), p. 291.

11. Ed Cony, "The Chesler Empire: A Mysterious Canadian Juggles Film, Casino, Florida Land Holdings," *Wall Street Journal,* June 23, 1964, p. 1.

12. Bahama Islands, *Report of the Commission of Inquiry into the Operation of the Business of Casinos in Freeport and in Nassau* (Nassau: 1967), paragraph 39; quoted in Ontario, *Report of the Royal Commission Appointed to Inquire into the Failure of Atlantic Acceptance Corporation Limited* (4 vols., Toronto: 1969), Vol. 1, p. 499.

13. " 'He was a Very Big Talker': Bahama Gambling Proposed by Chesler, Groves Testifies," Toronto *Globe and Mail,* August 17, 1967.

14. Boyce Richardson, "The Great Bahamas Coup: Gamblers Keep Pressing," Montreal *Star,* December 11, 1967.

15. Boyce Richardson, "How the Gamblers Took Over: The Great Bahamas Coup," Montreal *Star,* December 8, 1967.

16. Martin Waldron, "U.S. Mobs Didn't Control Gambling: Chesler," Toronto *Globe and Mail,* September 2, 1967, and Wallace Turner, "Bahamas Inquiry on Gambling Awaits Key Figure," New York *Times,* April 23, 1967.

17. Boyce Richardson, "The Great Bahamas Coup: Fantastic Payoffs for Gamblers," Montreal *Star,* December 9, 1967.

18. Ontario, *Report of the Royal Commission into Atlantic Acceptance, op. cit.,* pp. 494, 516, 678.

19. *Ibid.,* p. 559.

20. See John Saunders, "Security Capital Seeks Approval of New Name," Toronto *Star,* September 24, 1975; "LeBlanc Loses Majority Interest in Security Capital," Toronto *Globe and Mail,* October 1, 1975; and John Saunders, "Lou Chesler Wins a Round in Security Capital Battle," Toronto *Star,* October 17, 1975.

21. See "Manus Maketh Money," *Private Eye,* December 26, 1975, p. 18; and "Manus Loses Appeal in Union Bank Decision," *Financial Post,* January 24, 1976.

22. For a description of the interests behind the Paradise Island casino, see Donald Janson, "Bahamas Gambling Group Considers Las Vegas-Type Casinos in Atlantic City," New York *Times*, August 15, 1976.

23. Central Bank of the Bahamas, *op. cit.*, p. 61.

24. Commonwealth of the Bahamas, Prime Minister's Office, "Address by the Hon. Lynden O. Pindling, Prime Minister, at the Bahamas Chamber of Commerce Dinner Meeting at the British Colonial Hotel on Wednesday, 19 March, 1975," pp. 10, 11.

25. Walter Stewart, "Beneath the Sheltering Palms," *Maclean's*, November 17, 1975, pp. 31–32.

26. Jane Sneddon Little, *Euro-dollars: The Money-Market Gypsies* (New York: Harper and Row, 1975), pp. 7, 10.

27. *Ibid.*, p. 3.

28. *Bank of Canada Review*, June 1976, tables 7, 8.

29. Little, *op. cit.*, p. 130.

Chapter 7

1. Tom Naylor, *The History of Canadian Business 1867–1914* (2 vols., Toronto: James Lorimer and Co., 1975), Vol. 2, p. 255.

2. Trinidad *Guardian*, December 1974; Trinidad *Express*, July 7, 1974.

3. Statistics from Inter-American Development Bank, *Economic and Social Progress in Latin America: Annual Report 1973* (Washington: 1974), table 8, p. 350.

4. H.A. Gunasekera, "The Money Supply and the Balance of Payments in Ceylon," *Review of the Banco Nazionale del Lavore*, September 1954, p. 149; quoted in Charles Victor Callender, *The Development of the Capital Market Institutions of Jamaica* (Mona, Jamaica: Institute of Social and Economic Research, University of the West Indies, 1965), p. 91.

5. Jamaica Hansard, *Proceedings of the House of Representatives*, 1960–61, p. 308; quoted in Callender, *op. cit.*, p. 156.

6. Trinidad *Express*, December 15, 1974.

7. Compton Bourne, "The Political Economy of Indigenous Commercial Banking in Guyana," *Social and Economic Studies*, March

1974, p. 115; quoted in C.H. Edwards, "Canadian Banks and Underdevelopment in the Commonwealth Caribbean" (Hamilton: Society for Hamilton Area International Response, 1975), p. 73.

8. Thomas Wright, "Candidly Yours," Jamaica *Daily Gleaner,* March 6, 1975, March 7, 1975, March 8, 1975. See also "At Own Request. . . . Workers Bank Off Stock Exchange List," and "Thomas Wright Series: Banks Rap 'Breach of Confidentiality'," Jamaica *Daily Gleaner,* March 8, 1975; Thomas Wright, "Candidly Yours," March 13, 1975; Carl Wint, "Clear Up This Mess or We'll All Suffer," Jamaica *Daily News,* March 15, 1975; and other articles in the Jamaican press at the time.

9. "Turn-around at Workers Bank," Jamaica *Daily Gleaner,* June 27, 1976.

10. Gillie Afflick, "How Our Foreign Bosses Rule the Roost," Jamaica *Daily News,* March 3, 1975.

11. "Bank Must Pay Fired Teller $4,000 for Damages," Trinidad *Express,* April 5, 1975.

12. "Localisation as Exploitation," *Tapia,* June 22, 1975.

13. The Bank of Nova Scotia Jamaica Limited, *Annual Statement,* 1974, p. 7.

14. The Royal Bank of Trinidad and Tobago, *Annual Report,* 1974, p. 9.

15. Bank of Jamaica, *10th Anniversary* (Kingston: 1971) p. 16.

16. Bank of Jamaica, *Statistical Digest,* February 1975, table 9.

17. The Royal Bank of Trinidad and Tobago, *Annual Report,* 1974, p. 9.

18. Bank Workers' Trade Union, statement, "Struggle to End the Big Rip Off — Banks in Trinidad and Tobago," 1975.

19. Asgar Ally, "An Appraisal of the Life Insurance Industry in Jamaica," unpublished paper delivered to a seminar on "Life Insurance in Jamaica," 1973, p. 7.

20. Jamaica *Daily Gleaner,* June 14, 1975.

21. See for example Clair Balfour, "Insurance Act 'Terrifying': 3 Life Firms Quit Trinidad," Toronto *Globe and Mail,* March 21, 1967.

Chapter 8
1. Ferdinand Lundberg, *The Rich and the Super Rich* (New York: Bantam, 1969), p. 180.
2. Percy E. Armstrong, "Mackenzie: The Town that Bauxite Built," *Canada-West Indies Magazine,* February 1958, p. 5.
3. See Donald H. Wallace, *Market Control in the Aluminum Industry* (Cambridge, Mass: Harvard University Press, 1937), and Norman Girvan, "The Denationalization of Caribbean Bauxite: Alcoa in Guyana," *New World Quarterly,* Vol. 5, No. 3, 1971, pp. 35–48, for accounts of Alcoa's successful protection of its monopoly in the 1910s and 1920s.
4. Aluminium Limited, *Aluminium Panorama* (Montreal: 1953) pp. 61–62.
5. Alcan Aluminum Limited, *Annual Report,* 1975, p. 26.
6. Norman Girvan, "The Guyana–Alcan Conflict and the Nationalization of Demba," *Estudios Internacionales,* 1972, No. 19.
7. Cedric Grant, "Company Towns in the Caribbean: A Preliminary Analysis of Christianburg–Wismar–Mackenzie" (Georgetown: Ministry of Information and Culture, 1971; reprinted from *Caribbean Studies,* April, 1971) is an account of the political and social structure of Mackenzie and its neighbouring towns in the 1950s and 1960s.
8. Guyana *Graphic,* August 27, 1970.
9. Demerara Bauxite Company Ltd., *"Where Did the Money Go?" The Demba Record in Guyana 1919–1969* (Georgetown: 1970).
10. Norman Girvan, "Multinational Corporations and Dependent–Underdevelopment in Mineral Export Economies", *Social and Economic Studies,* December 1970, pp. 490–526; "Why We Need to Nationalize Bauxite, and How," New World Jamaica Pamphlet No. 6, 1971, reprinted in Norman Girvan and Owen Jefferson, ed., *Readings in the Political Economy of the Caribbean* (Kingston, New World Group, 1971) pp. 217–240; "Making the Rules of the Game: Country–Company Agreements in the Bauxite Industry," *Social and Economic Studies,* December 1971, pp. 378–419; "The Denationalization of Caribbean Bauxite: Alcoa in

Guyana", *op. cit.:* and "The Guyana–Alcan Conflict and the Nationalization of Demba," *op. cit.,* Girvan is also the author of *The Caribbean Bauxite Industry* (Mona, Jamaica: Institute of Social and Economic Research, University of the West Indies, 1967).

11. Girvan, "Making the Rules of the Game," *op. cit.,* p. 378.

12. Girvan, "Why We Need to Nationalize Bauxite," op. cit., p. 219.

13. *Ibid.,* pp. 235–236.

14. Girvan, "The Guyana–Alcan Conflict," *op. cit.*

15. *Ibid.*

16. See Cheddi Jagan, *The Truth about Bauxite Nationalisation* (Georgetown: People's Progressive Party, 1971).

17. "The people who buy, command. The people who sell, obey. Trade must be balanced to secure liberty. The people who wish to die sell to one people only. Those who wish to prevail, sell to more than one. The excessive influence of one country in another one's trade becomes political influence." José Marti, "On the Monetary Conference of the Republics of America," *La Revista Ilustrada,* New York, May 1891. Quoted in Emilio Roig de Leuchsenring, *Marti Anti-imperialist* (Havana: Book Institute, 1967) p. 37.

18. Guyana, Office of the Prime Minister, "Exports of Bauxite by the Guyana Bauxite Company," July 1974.

19. "Fair Treatment," Guyana *Evening Post,* February 26, 1971, p. 3.

20. Canada, Senate, *Debates,* December 8, 1970, p. 297; quoted in Isaiah A. Litvak and Christopher J. Maule, "Nationalisation in the Caribbean Bauxite Industry," *International Affairs,* January 1975, p. 52.

21. Litvak and Maule, *op. cit.,* p. 52.

22. *Ibid.,* p. 55, and C. H. Grant, "Political Sequel to Alcan Nationalization in Guyana: The International Aspects," *Social and Economic Studies,* June 1973, pg. 268.

23. Guyana *Graphic,* September 2, 1970, p. 1.

24. Interview with Washington *Star-News,* quoted in Trinidad Guardian, November 28, 1974.

25. New York *Times,* January 16, 1976.
26. *The Bauxite Industry in Jamaica* (Kingston: Agency for Public Information, 1975).
27. *Ibid.*

Chapter 9
1. See the author's " 'Our Advertising Campaign is All the Exposure We Need'," in Robert Chodos and Rae Murphy, ed., *Let Us Prey* (Toronto: James Lorimer and Co., 1974), pp. 57–68, for a profile of the Bata empire, including its early history.
2. *Ibid.* The many court judgments in these cases, e.g. *Bata et al. v. Chase Safe Deposit Co. et al.* (99 N.Y.S. 2d 535, Supreme Court, Special Term, New York County, Part IV, January 24, 1950), *Thomas J. Bata et al. v. Donald M. Hill et al.* (139 A. 2d 159, Court of Chancery of Delaware, New Castle, February 14, 1958) and *Jan A. Bata v. Thomas J. Bata et al.* (163 A. 2d 493, Supreme Court of Delaware, August 3, 1960) provide a fascinating look at the power struggle in the Bata family.
3. Eli Marx and John Burcham, *Three Leading Multinational Companies in the Textiles, Garment and Leather Industries* (London: International Textile, Garment and Leather Workers' Federation, 1972), p. 9.
4. Stephen Mohammed, "A Probe into the Bata Lockout: Why 'Experts' Say the Company's Action Wrong," Trinidad *Express,* November 28, 1973.
5. "Scuffle at Bata Branch: Woman, TIWU Man Arrested," Trinidad *Express,* December 20, 1973.
6. See pp. 70-75.
7. Commonwealth Holiday Inns of Canada Ltd., *Annual Report,* 1975, p. 6.
8. "Holiday Inns Loss Widens," Montreal *Gazette,* June 26, 1976, p. 22.
9. Canada, *Air Canada Inquiry Report,* The Hon. Willard Z. Estey, Commissioner (Ottawa: Information Canada, 1975), p. 59.
10. *Ibid.,* pp. 157–158.
11. *Ibid.,* p. 146.
12. *Ibid.,* pp. 158–159.

13. *Ibid.,* p. 190.

14. Clive Baxter, "How Air Canada Invests in Air Jamaica's Future," *Financial Post,* January 25, 1969.

15. Owen Baptiste, "Epitaph for an Airline," Trinidad *Express,* September 8, 1974, pp. 22–23.

16. Andrew Johnson, "Air Canada Not to Put $$ in LIAT," Trinidad *Guardian,* November 21, 1974.

Chapter 10

1. Abe Issa, *A Survey of the Tourist Potential of the Eastern Caribbean: Observations Made During a Tour of the Area, 16 May–3 June 1959, on the Invitation of the Federal Government of the West Indies at the Instance of Dr. Carl La Corbiniere, Deputy Prime Minister of the West Indies and Federal Minister of Trade and Industry* (Kingston: 1959) p. 9.

2. *Ibid.,* p. 14.

3. H. Zinder and Associates, *The Future of Tourism in the Eastern Caribbean* (Washington: 1969).

4. Kari Levitt and Iqbal Gulati, "Income Effect of Tourist Spending: Mystification Multiplied: A Critical Comment on the Zinder Report," *Social and Economic Studies,* September 1970, pp. 326–343.

5. Issa, *op. cit.,* pp. 23–24.

6. Louis A. Perez, Jr., Forms of Cultural Dependency: Tourism in the West Indies," *Journal of Communication,* Spring 1975.

7. *Ibid.*

8. The study was later released by the OAS as *Attitudes toward Latin American and Caribbean Travel: A Survey of United States Travel Agents* (Washington: 1975).

9. Barbados Board of Tourism, *Visitor Statistics 1973 — Barbados,* table II; Commonwealth of the Bahamas, *1973 Annual Report of Tourism,* table no. 13; Jamaica Tourist Board, *Travel Statistics — Jamaica,* 1973, p. 15; and Antigua Tourist Board, *Statistical Report for 1973.*

10. See John Fraser, "Ugly Canadian in the Caribbean," Toronto *Globe and Mail,* April 3, 1976, p. 40.

11. Norman Solomon, "Who Buys From Japan What They Sell in

Miami?" Nassau *Guardian,* March 19, 1975.

12. *Ibid.*

13. Suntours Limited, *Sunflight Guaranteed Holidays,* Fall, Winter, 1974–75, p. 5.

Chapter 11

1. Canada, Food Prices Review Board, *Sugar Prices and Policies* (Ottawa: July 1974) appendix 6, table B, p. 42.

2. Lewis Seale, "Pledge to Jamaica: Canada Plans Review over Sugar Purchases," Toronto *Globe and Mail,* August 3, 1967.

3. Geoffrey Stevens, "Canada Must Pay More for Sugar, Jamaican Leader Says in Ottawa," Toronto *Globe and Mail,* September 7, 1968.

4. See Marilyn Dawson, "Bittersweet Search for the Right Price," Toronto *Globe and Mail,* May 17, 1975.

5. See for example Robert MacDonald, "Lomé Convention Brings Small Powers to the World Stage," Nassau *Guardian,* February 19, 1975.

6. See Drummond Burgess and Last Post Staff, "The 'Judges' Affair: A Storm over the Wrong Issues," *Last Post,* June 1976, pp. 10–11.

7. Canada, Food Prices Review Board, *Sugar Prices II: The Canadian Refining Industry* (Ottawa: August, 1975), table 13, p. 22.

8. Canada, Senate, Standing Committee on Foreign Affairs, *Report on Canada-Caribbean Relations* (Ottawa: Information Canada, 1970), pp. 14–15.

9. See for example Robert Turnbull, "Canadian Financial Aid Big Factor in Caribbean," Toronto *Globe and Mail,* January 24, 1975, a sympathetic article in an otherwise generally critical series on Canada–West Indies relations.

10. The study was published as Lester B. Pearson et al., *Partners in Development: Report of the Commission on International Development* (New York: Praeger, 1969).

11. Teresa Hayter, *Aid as Imperialism* (Harmondsworth, England: Penguin Books, 1971); Denis Goulet and Michael Hudson, *The Myth of Aid: The Hidden Agenda of the Development Reports (New York: IDOC/Orbis Books, 1971); Steve Weissman et al., The Tro-*

jan Horse: A Radical Look at Foreign Aid (Palo Alto, California: Ramparts Press, 1975); Tibor Mende, *From Aid to Re-colonization: Lessons of a Failure* (New York: Pantheon Books, 1973).

12. Michael Hudson, "The Political Economy of Foreign Aid," in Goulet and Hudson, *op. cit.,* p. 74.

13. See for example International Bank for Reconstruction and Development, Washington, "Address to the Board of Governors by Robert S. McNamara, President, World Bank Group, Nairobi, Kenya, September 24, 1973," pp. 10–12.

14. Quoted in A. Palacios Hardy, Litvinoff Martinez et al., *Canadian Aid: Whose Priorities?* (Toronto: Latin American Working Group, 1973) p. 4.

15. See Kari Levitt and Alister McIntyre, *Canada-West Indies Economic Relations* (Montreal: Canadian Trade Committee, Private Planning Association of Canada/Centre for Developing-Area Studies, McGill University, 1967) pp. 107–123, for an account of early Canadian aid to the West Indies.

16. International Bank for Reconstruction and Development, *op. cit.,* p. 31.

17. Hardy, Martinez et al., *op. cit.,* p. 6.

18. Quoted in "See You in Bongo Bongo: Trade versus Aid", *Last Post,* September 1973, p. 50.

19. Export Development Corporation, *Annual Report,* 1974, pp. 14–15.

20. Export Development Corporation, *The Foreign Investment Insurance Programme: "The Facts Behind It"* (Ottawa: 1975), p. i.

21. Export Development Corporation, *Annual Report,* 1974, pp. 18–19; Overseas Private Investment Corporation, *Annual Report,* 1974, pp. 7-12.

22. Export Development Corporation, *The Foreign Investment Insurance Programme: "The Facts Behind It",* op. cit., p. i.

23. *Ibid.,* p. 2.

24. Levitt and McIntyre, *op. cit.,* pp. 116–117.

25. Pearson et al., *op. cit.,* p. 172.

26. Edwin M. Martin, Chairman of the Development Assistance Committee, *1973 Review: Development Co-operation: Efforts and Policies of the Members of the Development Assistance Committee*

(Paris: Organization for Economic Co-operation and Development, 1973) pp. 61–65.
27. Canadian International Development Agency, *Canada: Strategy for International Development Co-operation: 1975–1980* (Ottawa: Information Canada, 1975), p. 32.
28. *Ibid.*, p. 32.
29. Sheldon E. Gordon, "Cida Cuts Some Strings Attached to Foreign Aid," *Financial Post,* September 13, 1975.
30. Caribbean Development Bank, *Annual Report,* 1970, p. 14; *Annual Report,* 1973, pp. 39, 41.
31. Caribbean Development Bank, *Annual Report,* 1973, p. 24.
32. Inter-American Development Bank, *Canada and the Inter-American Development Bank* (Washington: 1974), pp. 7-8.
33. Inter-American Development Bank, *Fifteen Years of Activities: 1960-74* (Washington: 1975), pp. 36, 58, 72.
34. Figures from *World Military Expenditures and Arms Trade 1963-1973* (Washington: U.S. Arms Control and Disarmament Agency, 1975) table II.
35. "Grenada Gets a Modern Fish Plant," Trinidad *Guardian,* December 17, 1974.
36. See for example Caribbean Development Bank, Bridgetown, Barbados, "Statement by the President, Sir Arthur Lewis, at the Third Annual Meeting of the Board of Governors, in Jamaica, April 26, 1973."
37. University of Western Ontario, School of Business Administration, *The Undergraduate Program in Business Administration 1975-76,* pp. 30–31.
38. See Kenneth E. Schnelle, *Case Analysis and Business Problem Solving* (New York: McGraw Hill, 1967), for a description of the case method.
39. University of Western Ontario, School of Business Administration, *op. cit.,* p. 32.
40. Sagan Nanansingh, "Career Patterns of Graduates of the Management Studies Programme University of the West Indies St. Augustine 1965-1971" (St. Augustine: 1972), table II, p. 30.
41. *Ibid.,* table VII, p. 34.

42. University of Western Ontario, School of Business Administration, *MBA Program at Western 1975-1976,* p. 5.

Chapter 12
1. *Scarboro Missions,* June 1975, p. 3.
2. "Diamond Jubilee: Naparima College Looks Back with Pride over the Last 75 Years: Message from the Principal," Trinidad *Express,* February 23, 1975, p. 27.
3. Charles Alexander Dunn, "The Canadian Mission in British Guiana: The Pioneer Years, 1885-1927," Master of Arts thesis, Department of History, Queen's University, 1971, pp. 55-56.
4. *The Maritime Presbyterian,* September 1888, p. 267. Quoted in Dunn, *op. cit.,* p. 31.
5. The Morton Papers, Morton's Address to the General Assembly of the Presbyterian Church in Canada, 1900. Quoted in Dunn, *op. cit.,* p. 68.
6. Rudolph W. Grant, "The Contribution of the Presbyterian Church in Canada to the Education of East Indians in Guyana: 1894-1964," Master of Arts in Education thesis, University of Toronto, 1967, pp. 147-148.
7. See Dunn, *op. cit.,* for accounts of the work of Cropper, Fisher and Scrimgeour. Brief personal sketches of them appear on pp. 107-110.
8. Rev. J. D. Mackay, "Under the Southern Cross: A Story of East Indian Indenture in British Guiana: IV. The New World," *Presbyterian Witness,* October 1, 1904, p. 322.
9. Rev. J. D. Mackay, "Under the Southern Cross: A Story of East Indian Indenture in British Guiana: VI. The Cane Fields," *Presbyterian Witness* October 15, 1904, p. 338.
10. Harold Sonny Ladoo, *Yesterdays* (Toronto: Anansi, 1974), p. 106.
11. See Peter Such, "The Short Life and Sudden Death of Harold Ladoo," *Saturday Night,* May 1974, pp. 35-38.

Chapter 13
1. Claudio Lewis, "Racial Melee in Etobicoke: Stabbed Black

Youth in Critical Condition," *Contrast*, August 15, 1975. p. 1.

2. "A Night of Terror," *Contrast*, March 21, 1975, p. 1.

3. Arnold Auguste, "Black Grandmother Mauled: Toronto Thugs Strike Again," *Contrast*, April 11, 1975, p. 1.

4. Arnold Auguste, "Jamaican Accuses Police," *Contrast*, June 28, 1974, p. 1.

5. Marq de Villiers, "Face of Fear: Racism in Canada," *Weekend*, June 28, 1975, p. 14.

6. Statistics from Canada, Manpower and Immigration, *Canadian Immigration and Population Study: Immigration and Population Statistics* (Ottawa: Information Canada, 1974), table 3.2, pp. 32-37.

7. Toronto *Sun*, May 8, 1975.

8. Nancy Cooper, "In Toronto, and Your Skin is Black," Toronto *Globe and Mail*, April 10, 1975, p. 43.

9. Quoted in Errol Townshend, "Chaos Reigns: Green Paper Circus Comes to Town," *Contrast*, June 13, 1975.

10. Canada, Manpower and Immigration, *A Report of the Canadian Immigration and Population Study: 1. Immigration Policy Perspectives* (Ottawa: Information Canada, 1974), p. 12.

11. See for example Toronto *Globe and Mail*, April 24, 1975.

12. Canada, Senate and House of Commons, Special Joint Committee on Immigration Policy, *Report to Parliament* (Ottawa: Information Canada, 1975).

13. Quoted in William Johnson, " 'We are Getting So Terribly Crowded': Ottawa's Mail on Immigration Has One Strong Theme: Stop It," Toronto *Globe and Mail*, September 19, 1975, p. 8.

14. "Jamaica's High Commissioner Speaks Out Against Racist Murder," *Contrast*, May 16, 1975, p. 1.

15. Quoted in Ewart Walters, "Envoy Alleges Racist Police Beat Up Jamaicans in Toronto," Toronto *Star*, September 24, 1975.

16. "Racism," Toronto *Sun*, May 12, 1975, p. 10.

17. "Rum Jamaican," Toronto *Sun*, May 15, 1975, p. 10.

18. Quoted in Kushwant Singh, *A History of the Sikhs: Vol. 2: 1839-1964* (Princeton, N.J.: Princeton University Press, 1966), p. 169.

19. See Canada, Manpower and Immigration, *A Report of the Canadian Immigration and Population Study: 2. The Immigration Pro-*

gram (Ottawa: Information Canada, 1974) pp. 3–34, for an account of the twists and shifts in the discriminatory provisions of Canadian immigration law.

20. See Kari Levitt and Alister McIntyre, *Canada–West Indies Economic Relations* (Montreal: Canadian Trade Committee, Private Planning Association of Canada/Centre for Developing-Area Studies, McGill University, 1967), table 31, p. 93.

21. *Ibid.*, p. 92.

22. See Freda Hawkins, *Canadian Immigration and Population Study: Immigration Policy and Management in Selected Countries* (Ottawa: Information Canada, 1974) pp. 3–8, for an account of changes in U.S. immigration policy.

23. G.W. Roberts, "A Note on Recent Migration from the West Indies to Canada," in *West Indies–Canada Economic Relations: Selected Papers Prepared by the University of the West Indies in Connection with the Canada-Commonwealth Caribbean Conference, July 1966* (Mona, Jamaica: Institute of Social and Economic Research, 1967), table 1, p. 66.

24. *Ibid.*, table 4, p. 70.

25. Levitt and McIntyre, *op. cit.*, table 32, p. 94.

26. Canada, Manpower and Immigration, "Countries Covered by Posts with Area Responsibilities"; "Foreign Service — January 31, 1975"; "Immigration '74: Quarterly Statistics — Fourth Quarter", table 1, pp. 2–5; and "Immigrant Applications Received, by Post, January-December 1973–1974", table 1, pp. 2,3, and table 2, pp. 5,6.

27. Canada, *Report of the Commission of Inquiry Relating to the Department of Manpower and Immigration in Montreal*, Claire L'Heureux-Dubé, Judge of the Superior Court of Quebec, Commissioner (Ottawa; Information Canada, 1975), pp. 114–115.

28. "Canada's Integrity is Being Violated," Toronto *Star*, October 24, 1972, p. 6.

29. Eric Dowd, "Import 1,500 Workers," Toronto *Sun*, September 26, 1972, p. 1.

30. "Immigration Flow Shows Sharp Drop," Montreal *Gazette*, September 4, 1976.

31. Levitt and McIntyre, *op. cit.*, p. 88.

32. Ramesh Deosaran, "Canada Plans to Curb Entry of W. Indian Doctors," Trinidad *Express*, February 9, 1975.
33. "Emigration, Lethal Yellowing and Crime Have Paralysed Economy," Jamaica *Star*, March 15, 1975, p. 10.
34. "Why I Left Trinidad — by Vernon Charles," Trinidad *Express*, December 30, 1974, pp. 10–11.
35. Rupert Pennant-Rea, *Workless of the World* (London: World Development Movement, 1974).
36. Christie Blatchford, "Fruits of Their Labour: The System Works, Doesn't It?," *Weekend*, November 15, 1975, p. 7.
37. Darryl Dean, "Our Migrants," Toronto *Globe and Mail*, September 24, 1975.

Index

Leeward Islands 20,31,50-51,53,234; tourism in: 29,175; banking in: 116; aid to: 197
Leeward Islands Air Transport (LIAT) 37,169
Levitt, Kari 9,174,194,230
Lewis, Gordon K. 27,47
Life of Jamaica 127
Little, Jane 106
Localization of banks: 110-111,119-127; of insurance: 126-128
Ludwig, Daniel K. 95,98
Lyford Cay Co. 93-95

MLW-Worthington Ltd. 88,192
Macaulay, T.B. 67,69-70
MacEachen, Allan 79,195,225
McIntyre, Allister 32,194,230,237-238
Mackasey, Bryce 229
Mackay, Rev. J.D. 207,214-217
McKinley, William 33
McLaughlin, Earle 94,237
McNamara Robert 189
Maguire, Liam 15-17
Manley, Michael 22,38-39,43-45,119-120,146,148-150
Manley, Norman 30,44
Manufacturers Life Insurance Co. 127
Manus, Allen 99-101
Manus, Cecil 99
Marigot Investments 70,72,160-161
Maritime Life Assurance Company 121,127-129
Maritime Life (Caribbean) Ltd. 127-129,231
Maritime Life Hatters 128
Martinique 51,53,72,84
Mark, Ainsley 201,203
Marley, Bob 22,58
Maroons (Jamaica) 65,226
Marti, José 32-33, 144
Martin, Paul 144
Matalon family 44-45
Mathis, Johnny 21
Mauritius 92; sugar industry in: 185
Menard, Yves 167-168
Merchants' Bank of Halifax 64
Mexico 38,88,114,131,178,234

Military assistance program 81-82
Missionaries 65-66,207,210-217
Moko group (Trinidad) 46
Montreal Trust Company 100,126
Montserrat 20
Morgan, C. Powell 100
Morgan, Peter 178
Morton, Rev. John 65-66,212-213
Multinational corporations 33,56,60, 77-78,86,87,90,106,115, 123-124,126,131,138-141, 148-149,186,189,192-194,239; Canadian: 66-67,69,77-78,82-84, 123-124,151-152,192-194,238-239; in Guyana: 41-42,131-132,140-141,143; in Jamaica: 149-150; in Trinidad and Tobago: 54

Naipaul, V.S. 21-22,25,41,55
Naparima College (Trinidad) 26,212
National Commercial Bank 118
National Hockey League 155
National Joint Action Committee (Trinidad) 74
Nationalization 87,131,138-139; in Guyana: 41-42,131-132,137-145,211; in Cuba: 84; in Jamaica: 150; of banks: 84,117-118,119-120; of bauxite: 41,131-132,137-145, 150,211
New Jewel Movement (Grenada) 50
New Providence Development Co. 95
New World movement 46
Niagara Grape and Wine Festival 209
Nimrod Caper exercise 81-82
Nixon, Richard 45,87
North American Life Assurance Company 127
Northern Aluminum Co. 133,135
Nunes, Fred 200-204

Oakes, Sir Harry 91-93,101
Obeah 45,47,59
Oil Industry 85-87,106,146-148,189, in Trinidad: 28,34,46 in Venezuela: 37
Oldroyd, M. 153-154
Omega Navigation System 34
Ontario Teachers' Federation 204